THE AFORESAID CHILD

THE AFORESAID
CHILD

A Wartime Childhood

CLARE SULLIVAN

GUILD PUBLISHING LONDON

This edition published 1988 by
Guild Publishing
by arrangement with William Collins Ltd

First Reprint, 1988

© Clare Sullivan 1986

Printed in Great Britain by
Richard Clay Ltd, Bungay, Suffolk

For S.

I would like to thank Bernard Crick, Eleanor Scott, Prue Seymour and Mark Hamilton for their encouragement and help; Philip Evans for being such a caring and sensitive editor; and my husband for his constant support, without which this book might not have been written.

FOREWORD

This book tells the story of the life and world of a child who has lost one parent, lost or mislaid the other, and is homeless. It is set in England during the Second World War, when it was easy to become homeless – with two hundred thousand homes demolished by bombs and a further quarter of a million rendered unusable. Losing or mislaying one's parents was a different matter. When Ernest, in Oscar Wilde's *The Importance of Being Ernest*, confessed to having been found in a handbag in a railway lost property office, Lady Bracknell merely thought him socially inept. 'To lose one parent, Mr Worthing, may be regarded as a misfortune; to lose both looks like carelessness.' If you were also destitute, such carelessness could have quite other consequences. As the child in the story discovered, you got taken into care, and that – in the 1940s – was not always the safest place to be.

There were a hundred and twenty-five thousand children growing up in care in the 1940s. Of these, about eighty thousand had been taken in solely as a result of some family tragedy, through homelessness due to the war, or through the poverty caused by the unemployment of the 1930s. Few people at the time had any idea of the conditions these children were forced to accept. Some, like Meg, were living with people who were themselves impoverished and who consequently exploited them. Some were living in workhouses or in century-old 'Barrack Homes' which, in appearance and regime, were little better than prisons. In the wake of the war there were major social changes going on in Britain, but the plight of such children might have continued unnoticed without the vigilance of one compassionate woman, Marjory Allen. Her campaign to expose how many of these children really lived has been recorded in *Memoirs of An Uneducated Lady* (Marjory Allen and Mary Nicholson, Thames and Hudson, 1975). Although attempts were made to discredit her work, the government of the day was forced to set up a Commission of Enquiry. Its findings (*Report of the Care of Children*, Cmnd 6922, HMSO, 1946), were so damning that legislation was eventually introduced to give protection to all children who, for whatever reason, find themselves 'deprived of normal home life'.

It took some years for the worst abuses to be dealt with. The shipping of unwanted children to the colonies was stopped. No child would now be boarded out with someone like Sarah Dawkins. Boys from institutions are no longer automatically steered into the army and girls into domestic service. Some of the larger and more oppressive institutions have been closed down. But St Anne's is still there. It seems a friendlier place than it was, with boys and girls living together in the same cottage, no longer on opposite sides of the street. The gates have gone, together with the night watchman. The children come and go and no one gets punished for acknowledging a brother or sister. Nobody now stays long at St Anne's. Just for a few weeks at a time. The Miss Braddocks have gone. They probably meant well, even if they seemed to have little understanding of what they were about. Perhaps, these days, children find it easier to talk to professional social workers. Perhaps social workers talk more to children.

Today there are still a hundred thousand children in care and, as happened in the 1930s, many of them are being brought in as a direct consequence of unemployment – and of the poverty and family stresses and strains which follow in its wake. In some cases, children are coming into 'provisional care' only to find it turning into 'permanent care'. Clearly, there are circumstances in which the State must step in to protect children from grievous harm; these circumstances may result in a child being taken away from its family for good. But when a child is taken into care it loses its sense of belonging and can experience great loneliness. Is it not then in danger of losing one of the most precious ingredients of childhood itself: the chance to be free?

The story is based on fact, though the names of people, places and institutions have all been changed and I have taken some liberties with the characters and the order of events.   C.S.

CONTENTS

BOOK 1

—◆◆◆—

September–December 1943

'. . . I am not yet born; O fill me with strength against all those who would freeze my humanity . . . and against all those who would dissipate my entirety, would blow me like thistledown hither and thither or hither and thither like water held in the hands would spill me.

Let them not make me a stone and let them not spill me. Otherwise kill me.'

Louis MacNeice, 1944

PART 1

Journey From St Anne's

The fit – if it was a fit – stopped, as suddenly as it had started. Bundling both children into a compartment, Miss Braddock pulled the carriage door firmly shut.

'Naughty, naughty girl! How dare you behave so disgracefully! What on earth did you think you were doing?'

The child turned her head and pressed her face against the window. The train was already moving. Her companion, with a quick look in her friend's direction, leant forward to address Miss Braddock. 'Please, Miss,' Kathy began timidly. Miss Braddock stared at her frostily. 'I think she was frightened. Weren't you, Meg?'

'Frightened?' Miss Braddock echoed. 'Of what?'

'The train, Miss. *I've* been on a train before. My granny took me,' Kathy informed her with a knowledgeable air.

Miss Braddock continued to stare, and then frowned. Was it possible that she, a Visitor employed by the London County Council, was escorting a child who had never seen a train? How old was she – seven? So she had been in the orphanage three years. She would have gone in as a four-year-old in 1940. Did they *never* go out?

Kathy, her confidence growing, again leant forward. 'P'rhaps she didn't know it was a train . . . p'rhaps she thought it was a dragon,' she suggested hopefully, adding by way of afterthought, 'that was coming to eat her up!' Clapping her hands together enthusiastically, Kathy beamed at Miss Braddock. 'Ooh, Miss, is it a dragon?' And without waiting for an answer, she slid along the seat to her now smiling friend.

Dragons indeed! Miss Braddock shrugged impatiently. Why couldn't they teach these children the difference between fact and fantasy? It wasn't that St Anne's was a bad place – unlike some she knew – even if it was a Poor Law establishment, and why everyone persisted in referring to it as 'the orphanage' always puzzled her, since it must be at least ten years since the LCC had taken it over and changed its title to 'residential school'. The Council had introduced some changes, but old habits die hard.

The St Anne's Management Committee was made up mostly of the former members of the old Board of Guardians, which had run the place for decades – no, generations. Old Philpot had to be getting on for ninety. He was probably around when they built St Anne's in the 1880s. Of course many of the children who had passed through the place since then would always have been orphans; though strictly speaking, as a 'Cottage Home', St Anne's was established to house destitute children, irrespective of whether their parents were living. The main trouble was its size. It looked less like a Home than a village, with its two rows of buildings and cottages on either side of a broad street. The boys lived in six cottages on one side, the girls in the same number on the other, and no contact was allowed between the two – not even between brothers and sisters. With the nursery cottage for toddlers and children of both sexes up to the age of five, there were thirteen cottages with thirty or more children in each. The boys' cottages had names such as Drake, Nelson, Wellington. Less heroic ones for the girls' – Appletree, Cherrytree, Buttercup and Daisy. They were not exactly what you would call 'cottages', however, but more akin to Victorian rectories, with their red brick façades and gabled roofs. With no gardens to speak of; instead, just the strips of earth behind the air-raid shelters, which the children were supposed to cultivate as part of the 'Dig for Victory' campaign, but which always resembled those dirt yards chickens scratched in for grit . . .

What were the other buildings? A school, a chapel, a drill hall and staff recreation room, a storeroom-cum-office, the Superintendent's house (he being the principal of the establishment, with matron as his deputy), and the reception centre. A chill place, the reception centre, where children entering St

Anne's were taken – like laundry – to be numbered, stripped, washed and then dressed in orphanage clothes. Opposite the nursery cottage was the infirmary. Sensible, that. With so many children around, infectious diseases could spread like wildfire.

Further along the road was the bakery, which produced all the bread for the establishment, and a variety of 'industrial shops' – a cobbler's, a tailor's, a carpenter's, a needlework room and engineering and paint-spraying units. When the Board of Guardians ruled the place, twelve-year-olds were put to work in these shops. Now they were only used for vocational training. At one end, the establishment was enclosed by a fence, beyond which lay the pastures and playing fields St Anne's had once owned, but which were requisitioned at the outbreak of war for use as allotments and grazing land. At the other end stood the iron entrance gates, next to a porter's lodge, where visitors presented their permits before they could enter. A watchman patrolled the gates and fences at night, both to stop children from breaking out and to prevent relatives, who wanted their children back, from breaking in.

St Anne's wasn't a bad place. If it had drawbacks, these were due to its location: close to one of Fighter Command's aerodromes. As a Spitfire base, the airfield could be a magnet for enemy attacks. Bombs probably intended for it would occasionally land on the orphanage buildings. St Anne's was also on the outskirts of London, uncomfortably near the East End. Most of the children of the neighbourhood had been evacuated, but where could you place four hundred such as these – destitute and homeless? Precautions had been taken, of course. Shelters were built and the children practised fire drill; and in the aftermath of the blitz civil defence had agreed to give them full code fire protection.

'Is your journey really necessary?' The poster facing Miss Braddock across the compartment merely served to fuel her mounting indignation. To depart at five past nine in the morning on a journey which should have taken three hours and to be still miles from her destination at a quarter to four was unforgivable. The train was filthy and, for the second time since lunch, had ground to a halt on an isolated stretch of track; this time for the best part of an hour. Worse, the windows in the compartment wouldn't open properly and with the weather unexpectedly hot the atmosphere in the train was stifling. A stickler for order, Miss Braddock felt that summer should have ended on 31 August – not dragged on to late September. At least her green serge suit and matching hat demonstrated that she knew what was correct for the time of year and for such an occasion.

'I shall lodge a complaint,' she announced. But she knew what the answer would be: 'Don't you know there's a war on?' The fact that it had been 'on' for four years was no consolation to anyone, particularly not to Miss Braddock in her present mood.

Across the compartment the two small girls sat motionless and silent. Miss Braddock was thankful that by her standards they, too, were sensibly clad. They were also fortunate, considering their circumstances, to be so well turned out. Both wore knee-length socks below woollen jumpers and skirts, with coats that buttoned at the throat. The only pity, she decided, as she surveyed them, were the velour hats. Broad-brimmed and rather large, they came low on the girls' brows, almost concealing their eyes as well as most of their ears. All one could hope, Miss Braddock concluded, was that in time their heads would grow; and in an effort to be kind she told the children to take the velours off. Neither child responded. She leant forward to address them more sharply, but one of them motioned her to be quiet. The other child was sleeping. Miss Braddock drew back, annoyed.

She looked at her – this Margaret Chandler. Something about her didn't seem right . . . something about her being unnaturally small . . . something about the eyes. Against the olive skin and bright, if ragged, brown hair (cropped short after a recent bout of ringworm) the grey eyes were too pale, too steady. An elf, Miss Braddock thought uncomfortably; she doesn't look human. And why doesn't she ever speak? The other girl, Kathleen Woods, chattered whenever she could

14

but this one seemed lost in thought. She wasn't 'clever' was she? Miss Braddock liked people to be 'normal'. In any case, Miss Braddock's experience of children from institutions was that they tended to be a bit limited, as well as immature for their age. Not that it was their fault. Once inside an institution the children usually stayed until it was time for them to leave school, when boys – for the most part – were encouraged to join the army or emigrate, girls to enter domestic service. There was limited provision for boarding out, but with there being so many evacuees the number of foster homes available was small. The LCC's policy was to allocate them to some of the more adaptable and intelligent of younger children, since it was thought that their school work might benefit from what was officially termed 'a more friendly setting'.

Miss Braddock consulted her notes. Yes, all this would appear to fit Margaret Chandler. Nevertheless, cleverness in children was dangerous; it only made them sly and difficult. It was her job to supervise this girl's future welfare and report on her behaviour to the LCC; but how, except by learning docility, could a child such as Margaret Chandler hope to be accepted by the society she was about to enter, a society that would expect the girl to repay with dutiful respect the time and money it was prepared to spend on her? It wasn't as if Miss Braddock was old-fashioned. She was always embarrassed by her mother's unfailing habit of enquiring each evening: 'And how were the little paupers today?' In any case, it had been noted that the children themselves were given to over-reacting to such name-calling. There was the recent incident at St Anne's when two girls absconded and were missing all night, simply because their housemother had called them 'work-house brats'. Such terms were therefore best avoided. Miss Braddock always tried to address her charges by name, for she subscribed to the view that they should be encouraged to develop some sense of their own identity, provided this did not go too far. She knew some of her LCC colleagues did not share her views, nor agree with her methods of assessment. 'How can you tell, simply by looking at them, what they are like?' one had asked. 'Look at them long enough,' Miss Braddock explained, 'and they can't help but give themselves away.' But Miss Braddock did not spend much time in London, since she was attached to the Witheringham Boarding-Out Committee. It was to Witheringham she was taking the children – if only the train would move! Fixing her eyes firmly on the Chandler child Miss Braddock began to stare. This – since her eyes were slightly protuberant – she had always found by far the best method of bringing any recalcitrant child to heel.

Unfortunately for Miss Braddock, what she was doing had been done to Meg before, and, though the child never understood the precise purpose of this kind of scrutiny, she knew it spelt danger. Almost before the first waves of concentrated attention flashed across the carriage seats, a general alarm sounded – calling for that special state of vigilance most children know is required to protect them from grown-ups who are behaving suspiciously. First Meg imperceptibly slowed her breathing. This enabled the muscles in her face to freeze, so that they appeared relaxed. Once she knew that her face would not betray her, the rest was easy. All she had to do was become invisible. This would happen when she started to count . . . one, two, buckle my shoe; three, four, knock at the door; five, six, pick up sticks; seven, eight, lay them straight. As it dawned on Miss Braddock that her stratagem might not be working, she tried staring harder. But the child sat, apparently unmoved by the quelling power of Miss Braddock's eyes. For this child, clearly, she, Evelyn Maud Braddock, did not exist!

'Margaret Chandler, what are you thinking?' The child did not stir. 'Margaret, I am speaking to you.' Again no response. 'Do you hear me?' The woman spoke so sharply that Kathy, asleep in the corner, woke up and began to whimper.

The child turned her head slowly towards Miss Braddock and lowered her eyes. 'Yes, Miss,' she murmured.

'Well, I'm waiting!'

'Nothing, Miss.' The child spoke dully.

'What do you mean, nothing?' Miss Braddock retorted. 'And don't call me Miss, when I speak to you. You will address me as Miss Braddock.'

'Yes, Miss Braddock.'

'Very well. But next time I ask you a question, answer me properly. Is that understood?'

There was a pause before the child replied. 'Yes, Miss.'

The train began to move.

Meg sat with Kathy, her face pressed against the train window, her doll Dodo tucked safely in the crook of her arm. She was silently incanting, aware from Kathy's smile that she, too, heard the song: 'Here we come, here we go, Kathy, Dodo and Meg . . .'

Over and over she repeated the phrase, matching its beat exactly to the train's onward thrusting wheels. As the world outside flashed by she offered up a prayer: that this movement would continue for ever. Absorbed, she gazed at what lay beyond the carriage window – a world of strange, almost unknown forms: meadows full of ragged grass; criss-cross patterns of stubble-burnt fields; strips of raw, newly ploughed earth; pastures dotted here and there with queer-shaped bushes; vast stretches of woodland; trees dipping and swaying, heavy with leaves glinting gold and scarlet in the afternoon sun.

From a garden someone waved. Both children drew back, uncertain what to do; then, with a quick glance in Miss Braddock's direction to establish that she was still asleep, Kathy tried it first. Lifting her fingers up, she pressed their tips against the palm of her hand. Next she waggled her wrist and, finding that it worked (by this time Meg had joined in), they flapped cautiously at the next house or tree they saw. Delighted with the effect, both now waved happily in celebration of anything and everything – grass, trees, birds, clouds, sun, sky. Then it was over. With a shrill whistle the train shot them into sudden darkness. 'We're in a tunnel,' Miss Braddock said, the first time it happened. 'It's just a hole we'll come out of soon. There's no need to feel afraid.' But Meg was afraid. She didn't know this word 'tunnel'; nor, before now, before meeting Miss Braddock, had she known what it was to be plunged into total darkness. Why should she believe this grown-up, when nothing made sense any longer? It was as if day – and with it everything that was real – had been taken over by night; and nights, with their screaming sirens, could be terrifying as well as long. What had happened to the sun? Why did it keep coming and going, almost as if it was going out? Was it in some kind of danger?

She began to recite her multiplication tables. If only there were someone she might ask. Kathy, she sensed, didn't really understand and, anyway, it was difficult to explain. If she asked Kathy, mightn't it worry her? That left Miss Braddock, who was a grown-up, and you never asked a grown-up anything – not even about your number. She fumbled at her throat, searching for the disc. It was still there where they'd put it when she arrived at St Anne's; still hanging round her neck on its leather thong. Now she was on a 'train'. But she lived at St Anne's. That's what her number meant – she was the twothousandsevenhundredandthirtysixth person to have lived at St Anne's. Someone told her that the number was there to stop you from getting lost or mislaid. But grown-ups said things that weren't true. Only once had she asked Miss Doubleday, her housemother in Cherrytree Cottage, a question. It was when she had a blister that stung badly, on the tip of her tongue. Miss Doubleday said it meant she'd been telling lies – and she hadn't!

The other problem was that Miss Braddock was hostile – something Meg was unused to from an adult; from another child, perhaps, but not from a grown-up. Grown-ups could be angry, though most of the time they were busy with other things. 'There was an old woman who lived in a shoe, she had so many children she didn't know what to do.' Meg didn't mind because at St Anne's it was safer to keep out of the way of all grown-ups. If you said anything to them, you might be called a sneak or snitch.

Her prayer had failed; the counting hadn't worked. The darkness hadn't gone away, nor her fears about being cut off, about further separation. She felt the dry constricted pain in her throat, the stickiness of her hands, the dampness at the back of her neck, the taste of salt in her mouth, the jumpiness of her limbs. She was finding it difficult to concentrate. Was it last night when, for the first time in memory, she and Kathy had neither slept in adjoining beds, nor in the dormitory itself? It must have been. She was sure she hadn't slept since.

Meg was so abstracted she scarcely noticed that the train had returned them to the light once more. She caught Kathy's anxious look of enquiry and, in an effort to dispel their mutual bewilderment, she pointed again to the world reeling past outside. The two children re-entered that silent communication that was theirs, and theirs alone. Only Meg's topsy-turvy reflections left her with the idea that it was not they who were moving, but the world itself, and soon they were both giggling at the very idea of trees walking and houses flying; remembering – just in time – to control themselves in case they disturbed Miss Braddock, who was dozing in the corner.

But Meg's foreboding remained. She knew something wasn't right with her world. She looked at Kathy. Kathy and she had always existed at St Anne's as a pair, rather than as separate beings. But suppose Kathy wasn't there? As she felt the first flickerings, she began to tremble. She pushed the feeling down . . . not yet . . . not yet.

Think! she commanded. How many days since they had left St Anne's? What other evidence was there? Food! Relief flooded through her. Of course it must be the same day, for Miss Braddock had only once produced some fishpaste sandwiches and an apple. Momentarily her unease abated. Then she felt sick. She had made a mistake. It wasn't true that she and Kathy had always been together until last night. She would have done anything, given anything, not to have to think about this, but something about what was happening now made it imperative. For hours she and Kathy had been travelling on trains – this was the third that day – and neither of them knew where they were going. None of the places they stopped at had names. Someone had painted the names out. How could she be sure she was still on earth? For all the sense it made to her, she and Kathy might have been travelling to the moon. She was tired, but it was no good being tired. She must concentrate, must get at the truth. What about the time she was in hospital – the first time? Hadn't she been somewhere else, before she arrived at St Anne's – before she arrived, in an ambulance, at St Anne's . . .?

She remembered she lay in a twilight, sometimes grey, sometimes an eerie green. A heavily-shaded lamp hung down from the middle of the ceiling. The blinds were always drawn. At times it was so dim the ladies in the white caps would stumble against the end of the beds. There was no day or night then. Outside was that constant and horrible wailing sound. Children were crying. She was crying. The ladies in the white caps went: 'Ssh! Ssh!' The ladies in the white caps were singing. What were they singing?

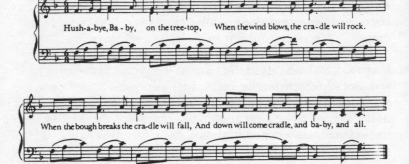

Where was she? What was the matter with her? Where had she come from? Why was she so frightened? What was going on outside? It was something terrible – even she knew that; and it went on every night.

Opposite her was a little girl who kept sitting up. Why did she keep doing that, when everyone was supposed to lie down? You weren't supposed to sit up, not even to eat or drink. You were fed from a teapot with a long spout. She distinctly remembered being told something terrible would happen to anyone who disobeyed. Would something terrible happen to them all?

She became fearful, because no one explained what this terrible thing was; and since she knew that sometimes everyone got scolded for something just one person had done, she did so wish this other child would stop being silly. Then she woke one morning to find the other child gone. At first, she took little notice – not, that is, until she remembered the noises in the night. They weren't the same as those she heard outside; these had come from inside the room. People had been moving round the bed opposite, the one that was now empty . . . moving round it in the middle of the night.

With a sudden, horrifying certainty, Meg convinced herself that the child was dead. She was filled with a sense of dread – a dread which finally confirmed what she had long suspected: that the world was a dangerous place, and she was going to have to be alert at all times. And with the dread went the desolation – echoed in the ruins of the city outside.

Across the gangway a slight movement alerted the child to the fact that Miss Braddock was awake. She found that by shifting her body very slightly and by looking out of the corners of her eyes, she could observe Miss Braddock unnoticed. The woman stood up, straightening her skirt, and twisted round to see if her stocking seams were as straight as they should be. A thumb run round inside the waistband of her skirt pressed her blouse into place. Next she did something the child had never seen before, turning what had started as an idle game of observation into a more serious scrutiny. Re-seating herself, Miss Braddock raised her arms to her head, removed her hat and extracted an enormously long needle which, to the child's astonishment, she placed in her mouth. Goodness! Meg exclaimed inwardly. Suppose she swallows it.

Spinning the hat round, Miss Braddock teased at the fluff

surrounding a tiny coloured feather tucked jauntily in the hat's band. Next she turned her attention to her handbag. This was shaped like an envelope and had seams over-thonged with leather. From the way Miss Braddock was holding the bag open, Meg guessed she was studying her face in a looking glass. She was staring in the same fixed way as the big girls did – except they only had broken pieces of mirror to peer into, pieces that were kept hidden because they weren't supposed to have them. Like the big girls, Miss Braddock also rubbed obsessively at invisible marks on her face, before going on to enact the same pantomime which had always intrigued the child: pursing lips, baring teeth, narrowing eyes, twisting nose and jerking head from side to side – as if she were making sure they all still worked. After recomposing her face into its by now familiar pugnacious expression, Miss Braddock picked up her hat. Raising her hands a second time she placed the hat firmly on her head, tilting it forward over one eyebrow. Then she removed the needle from her mouth and with a quick stab and a twist deftly skewered the hat, anchoring it so securely that little short of a hurricane was likely to knock it off.

All the work which had gone into Miss Braddock's facial and hat exercises had quite undone her earlier efforts at tucking in her blouse. These had now to be repeated. That's silly, the child told herself. She's got her order wrong! Miss Braddock's attention switched to her jacket. This garment, which was already a perfect model of neatness, was straightened out and pulled into place. Pockets that were perfectly flat, were patted into further flatness. Now she looked down to inspect her jacket lapels. To do this she had to squint and her chin disappeared. Before Meg could discover why this was necessary, Miss Braddock bent down, apparently to see if her feet – in their shiny brown shoes – were still there, side by side on the floor. Miss Braddock seemed satisfied. Sitting upright, she closed her bag, uncrossed her eyes, and thrust out her chin.

The train was edging slowly along a narrow track of rail. Flanking it on either side were jagged outcrops of stone. From her seat Meg caught glimpses of scorched earth, of sun-bleached grass, and spikes of bramble, broom and gorse that tumbled down the steep slopes. Then they were engulfed in gloom as the cutting partially eclipsed the afternoon sun. It was this moment that Miss Braddock reached up to fumble for the children's luggage: two small cardboard boxes, neatly labelled and tied with string. Unable to contain their nervousness, the children began to giggle, until Miss Braddock ordered them to stand up, straighten their socks and keep silent, while she checked them for neatness. Were their collars flat, their coats buttoned up, their gas-masks lying exactly across the middle of their stomachs? They were then ordered to sit down, sit up, sit straight and under no circumstances whatsoever to move.

The train steamed out of the cutting and came to a halt in a deserted railway station. Miss Braddock moved forward to open the door which was solid at the bottom and had a window set in the upper half. The window, when it was pulled down with the help of a leather strap, was supposed to slide into the bottom half of the door. Then all you had to do was lean out of the upper half, grasp the handle which lay on the outside, give it a firm twist – and the door would swing open. This window, however, appeared to be jammed. Miss Braddock was quickly reduced to despair. Dutifully she pulled again but, apart from the few inches that had been open all the time, the window refused to budge. She pulled harder. Nothing happened.

The children watched her gravely without feeling any call for alarm – not, that is, until Miss Braddock started banging on the window and kicking the door. As Kathy crept closer to Meg, both children cautiously inched their way down the seat in the direction of the place farthest from the door. Certainly they thought that Miss Braddock was odd; neither, until now, had suspected that she might also be deranged!

'Hallo there!' Miss Braddock shouted, waggling her fingers through the crack at the top of the window. 'Is there anyone there? I want to speak to the stationmaster.' Her voice rose to an unnatural squeak. 'Can you hear me? I want to get off this train . . .'

No answer.

Miss Braddock renewed her onslaught on the door, while Meg put her arm round Kathy, who had started to cry.

'This is ridiculous!' Miss Braddock panted and grasping the strap with both hands, she pulled with all the force she could muster. The result was startling. Down fell the window, but with such a crash that the compartment shuddered from the impact. Taken unawares, Miss Braddock, who had been resting her not inconsiderable weight on her heels, hurtled backwards, and encountered the children's legs which were sticking out. This swept them to the floor. Sensing that she was about to join them, Miss Braddock made a valiant effort to regain her balance by forcing herself off her heels and on to her toes. In this she was successful and instead of staggering backwards she shot forward – like a cannon ball. At which point the door swung open.

Had Miss Braddock fallen off the train, it would not have been so bad. What she did was to catapult out of it – into the arms of the stationmaster, whom she mistook for a porter. He eyed her with a mixture of disbelief and suspicion.

'I do believe he thought I was drunk, because he had the impertinence to sniff me!' Miss Braddock was later to tell her mother.

Struggling to extricate himself from Miss Braddock's embrace, the stationmaster stared at her bright red face, at the blouse which was falling out of her skirt, at the hat which sat on the back of her head at a drunken angle.

'Now then,' he growled, pushing her hands away, 'what's all this then?'

'The stationmaster,' Miss Braddock whispered. 'Kindly go and fetch him. I wish to make a complaint.'

'Oh do you now?' The man, hearing a child crying, moved forward to peer into the compartment. 'What you got in there?' His voice sounded ominous, and before Miss Braddock could stop him, he was climbing in.

It was Kathy who was weeping while Meg was trembling from head to toe because she was being carried off the train by a man; she knew nothing about men. In addition this one had hair all over his chin and under his nose! For once Meg wished Miss Braddock would do something. But the latter with her dishevelled appearance simply looked dazed – as well as peculiar. Fortunately, she soon reasserted herself. When she finally examined the children she betrayed nothing of what she saw. In place of the two neat little girls she so recently had inspected stood a pair of the filthiest creatures she had ever laid eyes on.

'You can't imagine what it was like to touch them,' she told her mother later. 'Even the labels round their necks were covered with soot.'

'Get the stationmaster,' Miss Braddock ordered icily, without looking at the man. 'And after that you can fetch the children's luggage.' She turned her back on him and rummaged in her bag for a handkerchief. The man did not move. 'Didn't you hear what I said,' she barked, 'or are you deaf as well as insolent?'

'I'll be danged,' the stationmaster exploded. 'Now you just listen to me . . .'

But before either of them could speak again they were interrupted by the sound of running feet. It was a young-looking woman. Everyone waited till she drew level with them on the platform.

Meg was freezing. She groped for Kathy's hand and concentrated on its feel. She was so tired. If only she might walk away and keep on walking until she dropped. Why didn't she tell these people what it was they were about to destroy? But she knew she wouldn't; that even if she could, she wouldn't. They didn't understand. At least, she thought, glancing quickly at the breathless woman standing before them, she will be kind to Kathy – because she had, of course, come for Kathy, even though no one had said anything. She just knew. It was like that sometimes – she just . . . knew. And Kathy needed love. Kathy wouldn't survive without being loved. That was why Kathy was so lovable.

'Oh dear, I must sit down,' said the lady, as she led them to a seat further down the platform. 'Now.' She beamed. 'Which of you be Kathleen, then?' She looked hopefully at the golden-haired child. Meg gave a wintry smile.

'That's me,' Kathy responded eagerly.

'Then you must be Margaret.' The woman nodded, rather than looked at Meg, when she spoke.

Miss Braddock butted in hurriedly. 'They are great friends, Mrs Turner, so we hope they will be able to see each other occasionally.'

Kathy looked bewildered, turning from her new-found friend who had just bestowed a kiss on her, to look at Meg. Miss Braddock drew the woman aside to join the stationmaster. From where she sat, Meg could catch snatches of their conversation. Kathy put a hand out to Meg, but Meg shook her head. It's started already, Meg thought. She and Kathy could no longer communicate, when all she wanted was to tell Kathy it was all right; she didn't blame her, and liked the look of Mrs Turner.

'She does look nice, doesn't she?' Kathy said. And suddenly Meg felt better, even though she knew it was the end. Her apprehension had been justified.

'I really don't think I can wait any longer, Miss Braddock.' Meg heard the doubt in Mrs Turner's voice. 'You see, we was waitin' such a time, I 'ad to go back. Mr Jarvis, the stationmaster, said the train was ever so late, an' the mite looks that worn out an' all.'

Meg couldn't catch what Miss Braddock was saying, but Mr Jarvis sounded angry. 'You're never telling me you're sending her to Ma Dawkins – a tiny creature like that, and you being that Lady Visitor Mrs Turner's been going on about all day!'

Meg shivered. What did Mr Jarvis mean? And why was Mrs Turner arguing with him?

'Now, Mr Jarvis,' Mrs Turner was saying, 'all yer got to do is send one o' your lads to tell 'er the mite's arrived. Prickler's 'Ill ain't far off. While she's comin', Miss Braddock 'ere can git back on the train an' be 'ome fer 'er tea. 'T'ain't 'er fault the mites 'ave come to live in Clayhurst parts. It's three miles to Witheringham. Yer can't expect 'er to walk it, now can yer?'

'All right. All right. But I don't like it, and that's a fact.'

*

26

Miss Braddock sank thankfully back into her seat and closed her eyes. In ten minutes from now, she told herself, she would be safely indoors, in the house she shared with her mother, a few minutes' walk from Witheringham Central Station. Annoyed as she was with the wretched man Jarvis, he *was* the stationmaster and it wasn't as if she had left the girl unattended – even if, when she last looked at her, she was sitting alone on the platform seat. Clayhurst was a quiet community; no possible harm could come to the girl, who was probably already with Mrs Dawkins. She would see her, when she cycled over after tea. But what a stupid idea it had been to stop at Clayhurst station in the first place. The stationmaster at Witheringham would never have behaved so disgracefully. No. Clayhurst wasn't a place she much liked. Where Witheringham was elegant and civilized, Clayhurst – one of the town's two industrial suburbs – was rough and ugly, with its mean brick houses, narrow streets, and the gasworks . . .

'You all right, lass?'

It was Mr Jarvis again. It was the second time he had come out of his office to look at her, and each time he had shaken his head and gone back, as if he understood that she wanted to be alone. She was trying to concentrate, trying to listen to a secret voice – one she disliked, but trusted. 'Don't you dare cry,' it was saying. 'What d'you think you are – a baby? Listen and do as I say. First, you are to breathe properly . . . listen, I said!' The child was panicking. Something else was struggling to get control of her; something which was fighting with the voice. 'Meg,' the voice commanded. 'Listen to me.' The child obeyed. 'Start,' it told her, 'with your easiest table.' The child began mechanically: two ones are two, two twos are four, two threes are six, two fours are eight.

Gradually the child eased back into herself. Within the framework of ceaselessly recited multiplication tables she was concentrating on something else. Kathy had gone. Miss Braddock had gone. Miss Braddock said she was 'a good girl'. She didn't make a fuss when Mrs Turner walked away hand-in-hand with Kathy. She wasn't making a fuss as she sat, all by herself, on the railway platform. She had listened in silence when Miss Braddock told her Mrs Dawkins was 'coming for her'. Mrs Dawkins was the lady she was going to live with. Mr Jarvis was 'keeping an eye on her'.

The child imagined Miss Braddock's face and saw her mouthing words. But she herself was floating somewhere else.

'I do not know you Miss Braddock.'
'I do not know who or what you are.'
'I am seven years old.'
'My father is dead.'
'I do not know where my mother is.'
'Is she dead?'
'I do not know where my brother is.'
'I do not know where my sister is.'
'Are they dead?'
'I do not know if I have a granny.'
'I do not know if I have a grandad.'
'Do I have an aunt?'
'Do I have an uncle?'
'Do I have a cousin?'
'Where have they taken Kathy?'
'Tell me – will she die?'
'I do not know Mrs Dawkins.'
'The world is killing everyone.'
'I think it's going to kill me.'
'Who are they all out there?'
'What are they all out there?'
'And God – where are you?'
'Can you tell me where I am?'
'Can you tell me where I live?'
'Can you tell me who I am?'
'Stop it!' the voice commanded coldly. 'I know who you are.'

As the child fought to keep her nerve, Mr Jarvis sat in his office. They must be out of their minds, he thought. Everyone in Clayhurst knew what Ma Dawkins was like – the last person you would hand a child to. He knew she took children, but never as small as this one. God only knew what she would do to it. He could hear his wife's voice: 'I can't understand what you've got against Mrs Dawkins. She's such a respectable woman, and a widow – poor thing. Her daughter's ever so lady-like.'

'You don't know Sarah Dawkins,' he told her.

'Oh, and I suppose you do! I've heard old Wagstaff talking. If it weren't for the eggs and the bit of bacon he brings, why, I wouldn't have him near the place. He's nothing but a common gypsy. He's always had it in for the Dawkins family, you know that. And as for the stories he tells, some of them aren't fit for decent folk's ears.'

The stationmaster grinned when he thought of the old man's tales, but where Sarah Dawkins was concerned he believed Will. You had only to look into her face to see what she was. Wagstaff might do a bit of trading on the side, but he wasn't malicious.

'What if Will's folks were gypsies once? Clayhurst is gypsy land – unless you've forgotten? There were gypsies here before the railway.'

'*Was* gypsy land,' his wife retorted. 'You'll be telling me next that Witheringham belongs to the dinosaurs, just because they used to live there.'

'Who's to say they still don't? Nothing would surprise me about Witheringham – and those what live there. No, your trouble is that you're taken in by smooth words and by what folks have got on their backs. You never look to see what's really there – what's inside.'

'Well, what I always say,' his wife would declare, 'is that if you mind your business, others'll mind theirs. Otherwise, you'll have nothing but trouble.'

And the awful thing was, he thought gloomily, she was right. Still . . . what harm would there be in having a quiet word with old Will? Perhaps if the Wagstaffs kept an eye on the child.

*

Back and forth the battle raged as Meg struggled to contain her agitation. The atmosphere was charged with danger. In a daze she lifted her head and saw an old woman approaching, walking slowly, one hand resting on the shoulder of a girl, while the other grasped a big stick. Run, Meg whispered to herself. Run now! But she couldn't move. She began to whimper, rocking herself on the seat. Abjectly afraid, she now knew what had happened. She had been abandoned – to this. Please, she pleaded, please make it go away . . . 'Concentrate!' It was the voice, calling her urgently, compelling her to listen while there was still time. Seconds before the old woman reached her, fixed her with her eyes, the child's terror was transformed into something which till that moment – the moment she first saw Sarah Dawkins – she didn't know existed: hate. Her being was flooded with hate – a hate that filled her with cold calmness, a new-found energy. She was still afraid, but the fear was manageable. She knew exactly what was standing before her: a person who, even before the child was born, had been destined to be her implacable enemy. This was a human being who had only one goal in life – to break the will of others.

> There was a little man, and he had a little gun,
> And his bullets were made of lead, lead, lead;
> He went to the brook, and he shot a little duck,
> Right through the middle of the head, head, head.

But, vowed the child, it will never be me.

The walk to Sarah Dawkins' house was lost in the child's memory. Meg did remember entering the house, where some of her fear temporarily receded, only to be replaced by confusion. She found herself faced – for the first time in memory – with the interior of a private home. The most immediate impression was one of colour. The house itself she did not understand at all. It was smaller than Cherrytree Cottage, and its layout was entirely different. For all the sense it made at the time, Meg might have come straight from living in a grass hut, or an igloo, or a tree-top.

After undressing the child, Sarah tried to get her into a tin bath, half full of water. 'That's not right,' Meg told her. In an effort to placate this terrifying woman, Meg had abandoned her usual taciturnity. 'I only have a bath upstairs. It's in a room with white shiny things on the walls.'

'Is that so?' remarked Sarah. 'Well, while you're in my house, you'll have your bath where I say.'

The same thing happened when she was taken to the lavatory. 'Why do you call it "the dyke"?' the child enquired. 'It's real name is lavatory. I can spell it for you if you like. And I don't do Big Job and Little Job. What I'm doing now is called Number One, and when I pooh, it's Number Two.'

All of which the old woman and the girl (who was tall like the big girls at St Anne's and called Dot) seemed to find very funny. Meg was relieved, even though she knew they were laughing at her. It became a kind of game, a frightening one – one she much preferred not to play. But they insisted. They wanted her to name everything in the house, aware that in doing this they were making her look very foolish. Not that this worried Meg. She knew names such as: door, floor, window, stairs, bed, wooden chair, bench (which they did not have), table, pillow, mattress, sink, lavatory, wash-basin (also missing), knife, spoon, fork, mug, plate. And that was about it. But Sarah Dawkins' house had things she had never seen before: armchairs, sofa, piano, carpet, rugs, sideboard, pictures, photographs, radio, clock, cabinet, chest of drawers, wardrobes, vases, tablecloths, chamber pots, bolsters, eiderdowns, counterpanes; as well as a host of smaller objects such as saucepans, bottles of cough medicine, newspapers – about which the child scarcely knew a thing. Eventually, too tired to eat any tea, she was put to bed, where she immediately fell into an exhausted slumber.

A much revived Miss Braddock was wheeling her bicycle up Prickler's Hill. Puffing and panting, she was thinking what a funny old thing Mrs Dawkins was. Dreadfully genteel, of course, but very respectable and quite marvellously clean. Miss Braddock knew of no other house that shone and sparkled from so much freshly applied polish and soap. Only one thing puzzled her: why Mrs Dawkins looked so old. It must have been 1938 when Sarah Dawkins first applied to take children. Miss Braddock was sure she had given her age as fifty-five. That would now make Sarah Dawkins about sixty years old. Yet she would have placed the old lady's age closer to seventy. But the Witheringham Boarding-Out Committee was more than satisfied with Mrs Dawkins' performance with the Randall girls and anyway, mature age was an advantage – in Witheringham, if nowhere else. The Chandler child could consider herself fortunate.

Propping her bicycle against the wall in front of the Dawkins' house, Miss Braddock pushed open the gate and made her way down the brick passage leading to the front door, noticing, as she passed the parlour window, the lace curtains twitch. At the door she waited a moment – to give the household time to compose itself – and then raised the heavy brass knocker.

Sarah ordered the older girl upstairs before sending her daughter, Cissie, to open the door. Miss Braddock entered the kitchen where Sarah Dawkins sat on one side of the table, her friend Amelia Truscott on the other. As Miss Braddock returned Amelia's nod, she found herself wondering why it was that she had never heard Amelia or Cissie speak, whenever she visited the house. As for Sarah – she was eyeing the Visitor sternly.

'Perhaps before I sit down, I ought to . . .' Miss Braddock's voice was trailing slightly.

'See if she's arrived?' Sarah finished for her. 'Cissie will take you up. She's fast asleep, so mind you don't wake her up. She looked as if she'd spent the day travelling down a coal mine.'

'I can explain that,' Miss Braddock murmured hastily.

Upstairs, the child lay curled in a ball, her fingers caught in a tangled lock of hair.

'A bit small for seven, wouldn't you say?' Sarah said as Miss Braddock sat down.

'She has a problem gaining weight.' Miss Braddock looked at her notes. 'There have been the usual childhood illnesses:

measles, scarlet fever, chickenpox and, of course, impetigo. A bout of rickets at five, and diphtheria in 1940.'

'That usually polishes them off – diphtheria.' Sarah reached for the teapot. 'What about the others? What happened to them?'

'Others?'

'Who caught diphtheria – in the orphanage?'

Miss Braddock leafed through her notes. 'She didn't catch it there. Now, there are a couple of points . . .'

'Where, then? Where'd she catch it?'

Miss Braddock shifted uneasily. 'The workhouse,' she said, glancing quickly at Cissie. Cissie avoided her eye. Amelia gave a slight cough. Sarah, she noticed, had put the teapot down. What a pity! Miss Braddock had been hoping Mrs Dawkins would offer her tea.

'Workhouse!' Sarah folded her arms. 'You never said anything to me about her being in the workhouse. I don't hold with people who've been there. I thought you knew that, Miss Braddock.'

'It was temporary, Mrs Dawkins. Only temporary. The blitz, you understand. 1940. They had nowhere else to go.'

'They?'

'The child and her mother. We got the child out when she fell ill. That's why she's been living at St Anne's all this time. The mother's a widow.'

Sarah lifted the lid of the teapot and peered inside. 'Seen a workhouse, have you?'

'I beg your pardon?'

'I asked if you'd seen one – the inside.'

'Well, yes. As a matter of fact, I have. But I don't think that need concern . . .'

'Big, was it?'

'Too big.'

'How many d'you reckon it could hold?'

'People? Oh, I don't know. Hundreds I suppose. Perhaps a thousand. It was for just a few weeks, Mrs Dawkins. I'm sure the child doesn't remember. It's nothing to worry about, I do assure you.'

Sarah poured the tea.

Miss Braddock, her eyes on the teacups, said: 'It was dreadful. Quite dreadful. Just like a prison, I thought. All those buildings, you know – infirmary, asylum, mortuary and common baths. Workshops, too.' She smiled when Sarah picked up a cup, passed it to Cissie, who handed it to the guest. 'Thank you,' she murmured, 'most kind.'

'And all mixed up, I dare say.' Sarah sipped her tea. 'Old, young, the sick and the loonies. Not that I know anything about it. You'd not catch me in the workhouse. I'd kill myself first.' She drained her tea and banged her cup and saucer down on the table. Cissie leaned forward to pat her arm.

'Not many left now, Mrs Dawkins,' Miss Braddock hastened to reassure her.

'Criminal, I call it,' Sarah declared grimly. 'You work hard all your life and where d'you end up? In the workhouse. On the scrap heap.'

'Come, now!' Miss Braddock was laughing. 'Those were the bad old days. There's nothing like that going on today. No, you've nothing to worry about – not where the girl is concerned. She is more what we call a "disposal".' She stopped. 'Oh dear, I really didn't mean to use that word.' The women round the table were staring at her. 'Actually, it's a word we reserve for a child who is being returned to its own family – not one that's just been boarded out.'

'Family!' Sarah exclaimed, 'but I don't hold with family. I've told you that before. I don't like them bothering me and unsettling the girls. Are you saying I'm going to have trouble? Because if you are, you'd best take her back.'

'No, no, Mrs Dawkins. None of that, I promise. The mother doesn't know we've moved her daughter. She won't find that out until she next visits St Anne's.'

'Suppose she complains?'

'Then she'll find our complaint procedure both thorough and lengthy. I doubt very much she'll be able to re-establish contact.'

'What about the staff there, won't they tell her where the girl is?'

'They can't. We never divulge destinations.'

'Did she visit much?'

'Hardly at all. The reports say she did at first, but tended to turn up on the wrong day and without a permit, which meant she couldn't have access. Not that the woman understood, apparently. Complained that she couldn't always afford the fare or get time off from her work in a munitions factory. It's been almost a year since she last saw her daughter.'

'Perhaps she's dead,' Sarah suggested.

Miss Braddock frowned. 'I hadn't thought of that. I had better ask someone to look into it. There are two other children, it seems. Both evacuees. They're older, of course; they were evacuated from London in 1939 under the government scheme for evacuating parties of school children. Margaret was too young.'

'Why didn't the mother take the girl and clear off herself?'

'I don't really know. Not everyone wanted to leave in 1939. Some only got evacuated in 1940. Others left it too late and got caught by the blitz.'

'At least you've not sent me an evacuee.' Sarah pursed her lips. 'You know my views on *them*. Riff-raff, that's what they are, if the ones round here are anything to go by. You wouldn't credit the tricks they get up to. Take that flock of sheep. They say the farmer had a heart attack next day. Sheep are silly at the best of times, but to see them wearing gas-masks! And what about the goldfish?'

'Goldfish?'

'Don't tell me you've not heard – the pair of evacuees who raided a goldfish bowl and fried the fish for their tea!'

Miss Braddock smiled faintly and then glanced at the clock. 'Perhaps,' she suggested, 'I might raise a couple of points.' She cleared her throat. 'This particular girl came into care under the old Poor Law regulations, which means she is chargeable for maintenance to the borough in which she was born.'

'Does that mean I'll have trouble getting paid?'

'No. Control of the child was given to the LCC. The borough concerned will pay us, and we pass it on to you.'

'What happens if they don't cough up? One of those London boroughs got themselves locked up for not paying the rates. You're telling me she's *on* the rates?'

'Yes and no. And what you're referring to happened a long time ago, Mrs Dawkins. We'll include the girl's payment with that which we send you for Dorothy Randall. It's for us to deal with the borough council concerned . . .' She stopped suddenly.

'Yes?'

Miss Braddock sighed. 'It's just that I have a feeling no one at the LCC has remembered to tell the borough people of Margaret's transfer to Witheringham. I hope they don't make a fuss when they find out. Borough councils can be very touchy about their children disappearing. In this case they should be grateful. The girl is fortunate to have been placed in a home as good as yours, Mrs Dawkins.'

'Have another cup, Miss Braddock,' Sarah responded graciously, 'and then tell me how you've been keeping, and your mother.'

Miss Braddock would have preferred to leave, having almost finished her work, but she knew the old lady liked to observe all the courtesies. As she relaxed she found herself describing some of the horrors of the journey. 'Of course,' she said, 'despite Margaret's behaviour earlier in the day, her conduct at St Anne's was regarded as very good, and she has no dirty or naughty habits. You do understand, Mrs Dawkins, that she is still a very young child, but perhaps I should warn you that she can be difficult at times.'

'Don't you worry on that score, Miss Braddock,' Sarah assured her. 'We'll soon have her sorted out. She's not too young to stand correction. Why, in a few weeks' time, you'll hardly recognize her as the same girl!'

How straightforward, how firm Mrs Dawkins was! People like her were the salt of the earth. Miss Braddock delved into her bag to extract some documents. The first was brief and to the point: a duplicated slip of paper resembling a receipt.

Boarding-out of a child under the provisions of
the Children and Young Persons Act, 1933,
the Education Act, 1921, or the Poor Law Act, 1930.

I, *Sarah Dawkins (Mrs)*

of *33 Pricklers Hill Witheringham*

hereby acknowledge that I have this day received *Margaret*
Chandler aged *7* years, from the London County Council on the
terms and conditions contained in the annexed undertaking; and that I have
also received for the use of the child aforesaid the articles of clothing
set out in the list appended hereto.

Dated this *20th* day of *September* 1943
(N.B. - Exact date that the child is received into the home.

(Signed) *Sarah Dawkins (Mrs)*
(Address) *33 Pricklers Hill Witheringham*
(Witness) *Amelia Truscott*
(Address of Witness) *Mon Repos, Prospect Close, Witheringham*

List of Clothing

(Here set out the articles in detail)

2 Liberty bodice	2 vests	1 woollen jumper
2 knickers	1 pinafore	1 coat
2 prs socks	1 hat	2 pr shoes
1 pr stockings	2 nightdresses	1 pr sandals
1 pr gloves	3 handkerchiefs	1 slipper

The second document, a more grandly laid out, printed affair,
was a model of legal propriety, notwithstanding the fact that
it managed to record the child's date of birth incorrectly, no
one having bothered to check her birth certificate. But this
was a trifle compared with some of the major shortcomings
of the documents. If it contained faults, they lay more in the
fact that it offered Sarah Dawkins no guidance on how to
bring up a small child. More seriously still, it offered the child
no protection from how Sarah Dawkins chose to interpret

certain of its tenets – for example: 'to train the child in habits of . . . obedience'.

I *Sarah Dawkins (Mrs)*

of *33 Pricklers Hill, Witheringham*

do hereby engage with the London County Council, in consideration of

my receiving the sum of *12/- plus 3/- clothing* each week, to

bring up *Margaret Chandler* aged 7 years

on the *31st* day of *May* last, as one of my own children, and to provide the child with proper food, lodging and washing; to endeavour to train the child in habits of truthfulness, honesty, obedience, personal cleanliness and industry; to see that the child receives religious instruction in accordance with the tenets of the religious denomination to which the child is stated to belong; to take care that the child shall duly attend school according to the provisions of the law for the time being; to make such provision as may be necessary for the escort of the child to and from school; to provide for the proper repair of the child's clothing, and, if the child becomes ill, to report such illness to the above-named Boarding-out Committee; to inform the Education Officer immediately by telegraph or telephone, should the child at any time be lost or removed from my custody without authority; to permit the child to be visited, and the house to be inspected, at any time by any member of the Boarding-out Committee, or by any person specially appointed for the purpose by the Secretary of State for the Home Department, the Minister of Health or by the London County Council. I do also hereby engage, upon demand of the London County Council in writing, to give up possession of the child.

Dated this *20th* day of *Sept.* 19 *43*

| *Sarah Dawkins* | Signature (in full) of Foster-parent | *Amelia Truscott* | Witness to the Signature of Foster-parent |
| *33 Pricklers Hill, Witheringham* | Address of Foster-parent | *Mon Repos, Prospect Close, Witheringham* | Address of Witness |

PART 2

Prickler's Hill

What's death like? the child wondered idly, only to shelve the question when she remembered it was Sunday. She often thought about death on Sundays after she came to live in Sarah Dawkins' house.

She was sitting in the kitchen waiting for her tea. The only sounds in the room were the hiss of the iron kettle – black with age – which simmered on the range and the ticking of a toffee-coloured clock, shaped like Napoleon's hat, which stood in the middle of the mantelpiece together with a shell-covered souvenir from Scarborough and two brass candle-sticks. Behind the clock hung a mirror without a frame that tilted forward as if longing to crash; and to its side, a sepia-tinted print depicting the story of the lighthouse keeper's daughter, Grace Darling. Cresting a wave she sat, hair stream-ing to the wind, frenziedly rowing her boat to the rescue of the fifty-odd sailors struggling to keep afloat, or still clinging to the rails of their once good ship the *Forfarshire*. Meg shivered in sympathy.

The kitchen was small and dark, its black-out curtains hanging limply on either side of the window. This was covered with adhesive paper, glued criss-cross fashion to create a series of diamond shapes which still further reduced the light filtering into the room. Meg had grown up to accept unquestioningly that most windows were covered like this, without realizing the paper was there to stop the glass from shattering if a bomb were to fall nearby.

Sarah was sitting at a corner of the table close to the stove, her feet resting on a faded mat made of rags and backed with sacking. Lined up before her were four tea-cups into which she was pouring a stewed and topped-up brew made a couple of hours earlier. Being wartime, tea was scarce and Sarah – who was an addict – rarely emptied the teapot until she found the brew undrinkable. At another corner sat Cissie (short for Cicely), Sarah's middle-aged daughter. Like her mother, Cissie smelt of mothballs and violets and was dressed in her Sunday best. Around her waist she wore a gingham apron with a deep pocket, which kept her knitting clean; she knitted all the time, her needles going clickety-click in tune with the ticking of the clock. Throughout the long afternoon Meg watched Cissie's hands move ceaselessly to and fro; hands that were never allowed to be soiled by 'rough' work. They had to be kept white and 'lady-like', since that was the role which Sarah had cast her daughter in from birth. What intrigued the child more were Cissie's adornments: a strand of crystal beads around her neck; a gold watch, given to Cissie on her twenty-first birthday, which she was allowed to wear only on Sundays; an opal ring, which she wore on the fourth finger of her left hand. The ring was bought by her parents when she was eighteen, to consolidate in perpetuity Cissie's engagement to themselves – the first intimations of which were heralded in the quotation from Ellen Sturgis Hooper that Sarah wrote in her daughter's autograph album when Cissie was ten years old:

> I slept and dreamed that life was Beauty;
> I woke and found that life was Duty.

To Meg, Cissie, with her pale moon-shaped face and round anxious blue eyes, seemed a shadowy sort of person who was, perhaps for that reason, in no way threatening, despite the handful of black hairs that sprouted from her chin.

Behind Sarah's chair – a padded affair with wooden arms, which only Sarah might use – was a cupboard. This, like the rest of the woodwork in the room, was painted dark brown. The upper half of the cupboard housed the heavily-crazed everyday plates and cups the household used, which Sarah had no intention of replacing – not simply because she had been told that crockery was almost unobtainable. In Sarah's gloomy view there was little point, since they were all going to be blown to pieces anyway. Food was also stored in the cupboard, and its contents revealed a great deal about Sarah herself, particularly how she reacted to the coming of the Second World War.

Sarah was fond of saying how, on principle, she did not (and never would) vote in a general or local election. Likewise she forbade Cissie to use her vote. Such things were not for women, especially gentlewomen. This did not prevent Sarah from holding pronounced political views, which stretched in a long and always conservative line from Benjamin Disraeli (who died in 1881, when Sarah was five) to Neville Chamberlain; both she admired for being not 'upstarts' but 'real gentlemen'. It was therefore with regret that she had felt compelled to transfer her loyalty from Mr Chamberlain to Mr Churchill (whom she thought it disgraceful to refer to as 'Winnie' despite her familiar references to 'Dizzy' of long ago). Though others did the same in 1940, Sarah's switch came two years earlier when, she said, she first learnt that her hero was sitting down to talks with that 'goose-stepping clown', whose name she refused to have spoken aloud in her house. When Mr Chamberlain returned from Munich waving his piece of paper, and talking of 'nettles', 'danger' and 'peace in our time', Sarah had shaken her head, sad that such a good man should be so foolish. She, for her part, examined her savings and remembering her experiences during the First World War, quietly set about preparing for the Second – like Noah confronted with the impending flood.

First she bought as much dried food as she could afford, as well as a supply of fleecy-lined bloomers. Second, she started to shop at the same grocer and butcher each week in a part of Witheringham far enough from the house to deter neighbours from prying. What she hoped was that, as a 'regular customer', she would be served first when food supplies became short. Third she tipped, and then continued tipping, an astonished coal-man. This was to ensure, in the case of fuel shortages, that he would not be late delivering to her. More challenging for Sarah was how to keep the government's hands off her daughter. She had already proved adept at stopping them from taking her husband in the First

World War. Then she had argued that since her family had 'done their bit' in sacrificing one of her brothers in the Boer War, it was now the turn of other families 'to do theirs'. Mr Churchill, she thought, would be understanding on this score when it came to Cissie, but not that 'dreadful man Ernie Bevin'. He, it seemed, committed the unpardonable crime of trying to conscript grandmothers.

'It will be your turn next,' Sarah told Meg darkly. 'Then you'll find out what life's about, once they get *you* making bombs.'

Cissie, Sarah decided, was not 'eligible' for war work. Her duty was to support her mother. Under no circumstances was she going to allow her daughter to go gallivanting off and mixing with those dreadful women who painted their faces and did other 'unmentionable things'. Her special hate was the Women's Land Army, whose members she described as 'fast' and 'loose', as well as smelly from all the muck-raking they did. Sarah's next move was to block what she thought were attempts to draft her daughter into munitions work. In this she was successful, except for one concession: once a fortnight Cissie, in order to demonstrate her patriotism, would have to do fire-watching duty for her employer, a firm of retail chemists. Reluctantly Sarah accepted the proposal. But since, as a matter of policy, Sarah rarely admitted defeat, she made a point of registering her feelings by entering into a sulk after every night Cissie spent on the roof of her employer's shop. As Sarah saw it, she was an aged widow and Cissie's dependant. She also had a 'dicky heart' with a medical certificate to prove it, as well as a bottle of brandy bought for medicinal purposes on her doctor's advice. To be on the safe side, however, she decided it would be just as well if she were to acquire some dependants of her own.

In 1938, in the wake of Mr Chamberlain's capitulation, she opened her house to children no one quite knew what to do with. This proved useful on two counts. First, since a payment was made for their board and lodging, it swelled the household income. Second, after war broke out and food was rationed, they brought their ration books with them; and if the children themselves would never taste the meagre butter ration or the occasional egg, Sarah had ways of ensuring no one outside the house knew this.

By 1943, her hoard of tea and sugar had gone and she had to rely on the monthly rations. But the food cupboard was still well stocked with condensed milk, Oxo cubes, Foster Clark soup powders, pearl barley and black treacle. It also contained vast quantities of dried split peas which Sarah was for ever turning into pease pudding. Meg had never eaten anything quite as horrible – not even the tapioca she had been served every day for the previous three years which, because it reminded her of runny noses, she always ate with her eyes shut. Pease pudding was appallingly indigestible. She did her very best to eat it, but within minutes of its descending into her stomach, it ascended – back on to her plate. So cross did Sarah become at this, she scooped it up and forced it back down the child's throat, whereupon Meg was violently sick. This went on day after day, till Sarah eventually recognized that it was not the child's obstinacy, but its stomach that was refusing the wretched stuff.

The lower half of the food cupboard was more mysterious. All Meg knew about its contents was that it housed Sarah's ancient Singer sewing machine. She had no means of discovering what else lay within, as Sarah controlled everything Meg did. The child was not allowed to open a door or drawer, stand up or sit down, leave the room, have a drink of water, blow her nose, go to the lavatory, speak or move, unless Sarah ordered or approved.

Like Sarah, Cissie too had her own chair. Although it was wooden like the others round the table, it differed by having a lower back and a seat covered with an embroidered cushion. In an alcove behind Cissie's chair was an armchair Meg never saw anyone sit in. This stood next to a latch door which led into a cupboard under the stairs. It was here that Meg hung her hat and coat – next to brooms, brushes, bottled plums, jars of chutney and pickled onions, rhubarb and ginger jam, the gas and electricity meters, castor oil, gas-masks and cough medicine. There was no light in this cupboard – not that electric light was used much anywhere in Sarah's house, except in the kitchen where only Sarah might switch the supply on or off and where candles were used more frequently than electricity. Cissie carried a torch to light her way upstairs and Dot – after she left school – was allowed a candle in her room. Meg had to learn to move in the dark. But with double summertime in operation it was rarely completely dark when the child went to bed at half-past six in the evening. The darkness affected Meg at night. When the sirens wailed an alert she would crouch in the stair cupboard and shake with terror. She much preferred it when Sarah herded them all under the kitchen table.

Sarah herself would never take refuge in the cupboard, nor would she stoop to the indignity of crawling under the table. Instead, she sat in her chair literally armed for battle, a steel poker in one hand and a carving knife in the other. As the bombers droned overhead, she would scream 'Cowards!' at the top of her voice or sing patriotic songs such as "Rule Britannia" and "There'll Always be an England". If the raid continued, the household had a choice of "She'll be Coming Round the Mountains When She Comes" or the National Anthem. If the black-out curtains were open, the room might be lit by intersecting searchlights sweeping across the sky in their hunt to pin-point an enemy intruder. Spotlighted thus, Sarah's appearance resembled that of an ancient, embattled Britannia. So unnerving a picture did she present that Meg was more afraid of her than of the 'Boche', about whose identity she had not the remotest idea. She had also heard Sarah refer to 'jerries' but, after her introduction to them as chamber pots (one lived under her bed, though she was forbidden ever to use it), she became hopelessly confused. Now, faced with the warrior Sarah, she shut her eyes tightly, praying with all the fervour she could muster that whoever this 'Boche' was, he or it would not be so foolish as to try to enter Sarah's house, so convinced was she that Sarah would butcher him on the spot.

Certainly the table was solid; it even had an extra 'leaf' that could be pulled out for the guests who never came. Sturdy and square, it stood in the middle of the room on a piece of linoleum as brown as the varnished boards surrounding it. At meal times Meg sat on the side of the table closest to Cissie, in front of a many-mirrored sideboard. From here she could just see through the lace curtains draped across the papered windowpanes. To see the world through such a complex screen of fractured patterns both startled and reassured her. She learnt to play endless games, piecing the fragments together as if she were handling a constantly shifting jig-saw puzzle. At other times, she altered her vision so as to ignore the patterns, focusing instead on what lay outside: the top of the wooden fence separating Sarah's brick yard from that of her neighbour Mrs Shipley along with the dark outline of the trees which stretched through Nokes Wood at the back of the house away to the sky beyond.

Opposite the kitchen range stood a cabinet. Sarah said it was made of oak and was hand-carved – or so her grandfather, who had been a cabinet maker, had claimed. This same grandfather never used a plate or cutlery: he cut his food with a knife he carried in his pocket, used a wooden bowl and spoon, in addition to a pewter mug which Sarah displayed on the sideboard. On top of the cabinet stood a wireless. This was large and made of Bakelite. Sarah would switch it on and off very gingerly, since – like Thurber's aunt – she was convinced electricity 'leaked'. Were she to fiddle, the wireless might blow up in her face. So, while everyone held their breath, it was left to Cissie to twiddle its big fat knobs when it crackled.

The high-backed chair standing next to the cabinet Meg came to dislike intensely. She often had to sit on it (sometimes as long as two hours at a stretch) without moving or speaking, her back straight, her hands folded in her lap. This was to ensure that, as a child who might be seen but not heard, she would not be tempted into any of the mischievous tricks Sarah believed all children got up to. Meg taught herself many ways of relieving her boredom. If she were not gazing through the window playing pattern-games, she watched the raindrops sliding down the panes, racing even faster as they merged, or studied the wallpaper with great intensity. The background was dark beige (circa 1890 in conception but probably stuck to these particular walls in the 1920s) and covered with either marigolds, dahlias, or chrysanthemums. These were orange in colour. Tied in stiff bunches, the flowers had trailing blue ribbons and bows, with sprigs of forget-me-nots and what might have been ostrich feathers dotted in between.

At other times she studied the frieze – a narrow band of zig-zagging black and green with gold – below a picture rail from which two massive portraits were slung on chains, just above the wireless. One depicted an improbably young Cissie dressed in layers of frilly frock and petticoat, her long hair tied back with a floppy bow. The other showed a poker-faced man with a drooping moustache, whose stiff high collar looked as if it were choking him. This was Sarah's late husband, Henry Dawkins. He, it seemed, had called Sarah 'Mother' (a term it took Meg a long time to sort out). Sarah, for her part, usually addressed her husband's memory and his portrait as 'Mr Dawkins', which impressed Meg enormously. But though Sarah spoke of Mr Dawkins' sudden departure from this world respectfully – a ruptured spleen had 'carried him off' seven years earlier (the child longed to ask where he had gone, but never dared) – she was nonetheless very cross with him for having vanished so precipitately. Sarah was also annoyed with her father who, in his case, had 'passed on', but so long ago (at least fifty years) that Meg decided he must have gone to what she had heard described as 'the Colonies'. Just what Mr Dawkins and Mr Dobbs (Sarah's name for her father) had actually done to make Sarah so angry when she spoke of them Meg found difficult to grasp. All she knew was that it had something to do with Sarah having to live 'in reduced circumstances'. This, apparently, was dangerous, because if you were not careful you 'ended up in the workhouse' or 'joined the scum'; and although the child did not know the meaning of either phrase, she did not like them, nor the venomous manner in which Sarah looked at her when she spoke them.

Sitting in front of the portraits, but seemingly oblivious to them, was the fourth member of the household: Dorothy – alias Dot or Dotty (a name the child had already decided she would not like for herself, since she knew it was like 'Loony Lou'). At thirteen, Dot was six years older than herself. Between the two girls there had quickly developed something akin to a state of undeclared war. Dot was a pretty girl, proud of her glossy black hair which she tossed from her brow in practised imitation of the film star Veronica Lake, and even prouder of her perfect white teeth. These she was for ever baring in a dazzling, studied smile, trying to copy the current glamour of Rita Hayworth. Meg knew instinctively that Dot experienced acute disappointment when she first saw the newcomer. But Dot was not without sympathy and had, on this sole occasion, made an effort to conceal it; though she had not been able to suppress her laughter – a laughter Sarah encouraged with: 'Lord, what a scarecrow! They'll never make a swan of this one. She don't look no bigger than a four-un!'

It was this last remark which had given Dot an idea: how she might take advantage of the child, might exploit her with her friends. Meg was not only small, she was so thin and light she could be carried quite easily, rather as one might carry a large doll. For two days Dot tried carrying her around and introducing Meg as her 'little sister'. But Meg was an old hand at this game and knew exactly how to make her body stiff and unbabylike. As for being quiet and well-behaved – no one wants a 'baby' that can kick, spit and bite. Meg's status in Dot's life rapidly changed from 'little sister' to 'Ugh, you ugly brat!', which the child accepted equably, having had plenty of experience of other girls like Dot. Two things however brought them together. The first was that they were both lodgers in the house of Sarah Dawkins. The second was the united front they showed to the worst insult either of them knew: the catcall 'Yah! You ole orphan Annie!'

In such circumstances it came as small surprise that Meg frequently dreamed. When, exactly, had she met her friend Kathy? Kathy whose hair was like fine-spun gold and who had eyes of the most beautiful deep, deep blue.

She must have been four. They had been sitting next to each other in the nursery cottage, one tea-time, trying to solve the problem – or rather Meg was – of how to get more food. Tea consisted of bread thinly spread with jam, folded into a sandwich. The children were given one each, handed to them or placed on their plates by one of the big girls who patrolled the room, carrying the sandwiches on wicker trays. When you finished your first one, you waved your hand for another – even shouted, if you had to. If you ate slowly, then you might not get any more. Some children solved the problem by seizing food from another's plate and wolfing it down before they were reported. Others would hide their sandwich in their knickers and show an empty plate to prove they merited a second helping. But these children were usually caught and punished with a smacking. Clearly, the faster you ate, the more you got. So Meg introduced Kathy to an experiment. They tried nibbling like rats to reduce the bread to crumbs that would slip more quickly down the gullet. This was very trying on the jaws. The second idea was to gobble the bread down, taking the largest bites possible and swallowing them whole. This proved more successful. But as one or other of them would vomit up the undigested bread an hour or so later the experiment soon came to an end. Yet it had one positive outcome. She and Kathy discovered one another.

Kathy had charm and sweetness of disposition whereas Meg had a nose for danger, which she used to extricate them both from all sorts of trouble. This beset the unwary on all sides, so absolute was the rule administered – not by the staff but by the older girls. If you wanted to survive peacefully, you needed to know something of how it worked. Meg had enough of an idea to be able to steer the pair of them through some of the hazards: where, for example, to hide when the big girls were scrumping apples from the superintendent's orchard.

Real control, as all the younger children knew, lay in the hands of the older girls. If you were little you were looked after by one of them; in Meg's case it was Miriam, aged twelve. Yet the community as organized by these older girls had certain rules. While Miriam might occasionally slap Meg (though technically this wasn't allowed), she would defend the child if anyone else tried to, because Meg was 'hers'. On the other hand, if someone played a dirty trick on a child, the victim was expected to find her own means of punishing the perpetrator without involving the older group. Once this happened to Meg. She had allowed her attention to wander and in a flash her breakfast slice of bread vanished. There was little point in showing that she had noticed. The thief would only have dropped it as soon as a search was organized. So Meg sat and sipped her tea as if nothing had happened. A few days later she and Kathy, together with some other little ones, waited until the culprit was washing sheets in the cottage wash-house. As the older girl emerged with her basket of wet laundry, the group moved forward, apparently to chase a ball, and knocked into the girl, tipping her basket to the ground. Then, in 'helping' to retrieve the contents, they muddied the washing so that the girl had to do it all again.

Only once did Meg threaten to break a rule, and it was the most important one of all – that which forbade you to 'sneak'. There were two things which, for her, became deeply intertwined: the air-raid shelters and a game called 'mothers and fathers'. The shelters were bad enough at night, with their chill smell of mildew and damp earth. But something went on in them during the day as well, although the children were forbidden to enter them unless the siren went. What it was Meg didn't know – not for a long time. All she knew was when it was happening, and at such times she had to rack her brains to think of somewhere Kathy and she might hide until the danger passed.

'Can't we play here?' Kathy asked peevishly, when Meg tried to pull her away from the back of the cottage.

'No,' Meg insisted, giving a brief, nervous shake of her head. 'And if I tell you to run, you must. Run as fast as you can to the front and stay there.'

'But why?'

'You've got to promise, that's all. Promise to run, if I tell you to.'

'All right. I promise,' Kathy said, seeing Meg's expression.

Only then did Meg relax. Sometimes, when the hunt for the little ones was on, she whisked the pair of them to the safety of another cottage, hiding in the lavatories or the laundry room. But one day they were both trapped and forcibly carried into the shelters. There they saw several older girls stripped to the waist and two small girls being forced to suckle at their nipples. Meg's reaction was to freeze, while Kathy shrank back. Suddenly Meg acted. Stamping her foot on the ground she probably did the bravest thing of her life up till then.

'No!' she declared, holding on to Kathy's hand. 'Don't you dare touch us!' She stamped her foot again, her eyes flashing furiously. 'If you do, if you even come near us – then I will tell. If you let us out now, then I won't. But I mean – now!'

They did, though Kathy and Meg were followed to see what they would do. For safety, the two children retreated to the day room in Cherrytree Cottage, where they sat trembling in a corner, their arms around each other, their faces turned to the window and the empty path beyond.

Kathy, with her more trusting nature, was less good at sensing trouble. If Meg's role was that of protector, Kathy's was that of comforter. It may even have been Kathy's ability to comfort which first cemented their friendship, as Meg was essentially a loner. After each occasion Meg spent in hospital she became more frail, more withdrawn. One time she returned to St Anne's thin and bandy-legged. Although her legs straightened, there were times when it seemed she could not walk and she had nightmares of being trapped by a bomb in fallen masonry. Her legs would go numb. She would slide to the ground and crawl. Sometimes this partial paralysis lasted several days. She also developed a stammer and at times would neither walk nor talk; it was then Kathy would sit with her, her arms around Meg's neck. The need to crawl eventually disappeared, but the stammer remained. That was why, at seven, Meg rarely spoke; though this had annoyed Miss Braddock, it never seemed to bother anyone at St Anne's. Perhaps this was because it wasn't as if Meg couldn't talk – at times both fluently and rapidly – but usually she had to be excited or angry for the stammer to vanish.

What had happened the night before she left St Anne's? It was when they started to curl her fringe with strips of damp rag that Meg knew something was afoot; but seeing the same being done to Kathy, she didn't worry unduly – though she knew this was the signal that they were about to disappear.

Everyone in Cherrytree Cottage knew that. If Meg felt anything at the time, it was irritation: she did not want her fringe curled. She only objected, even struggled, when she discovered she was to sleep in Miss Doubleday's strange room – strange because she had never seen a room with just one bed in it before. Clutching the bedclothes, her heart thumping wildly, Meg opened her eyes to find a weird creature standing at the side of the bed. Worse, it was climbing into the bed and – the child let out a piercing wail for help.

'But I am Miss Doubleday,' the creature kept saying, while Meg yelled louder for the housemother to come. For now the creature was hugging her, was trying to stop her struggling.

Certainly it sounded like Miss Doubleday, but it didn't look like Miss Doubleday – not at all like the Miss Doubleday Meg knew. The familiar one wore a cross-over pinafore and had short hair set in crisp waves and curls. Miss Doubleday covered her hair during the daytime with a golden hairnet and at nights, in the air-raid shelter, with a pink or blue turban. What had climbed into the bed, and sent Meg scrambling for its edge, wore a white gown reaching to the ankles and, in place of blonde waves, brandished a head covered with a formidable array of silver-coloured objects which resembled rows of metal teeth. Wriggling to escape the creature's embrace, Meg toppled out of bed, crawled under it, and refused to come out till fully reassured it really was Miss Doubleday up aloft. Though what eventually brought her out was the promise that she would see Kathy in the morning.

How silly, the child reflected, to have forgotten what everyone in Cherrytree knew: that you never spent your last night there sleeping in the dormitory. Yet it never occurred to Meg that she and Kathy would vanish, because it seemed that they had always lived at St Anne's. Was that why she had felt so uneasy? Or had the unease been merely an echo of what all the children felt the morning after one of them disappeared? At least she could console herself that Miss Doubleday didn't eat you up. Miss Doubleday was a jolly-looking woman, not at all the kind of person you would imagine went round eating people. Meg had so few dealings with her. It was Miriam who saw that she washed herself properly, snapping at her when she was slow. It was the same with her hair; Miriam it was who always snatched the comb from her, yanking it through the child's hair in an effort to get her ready faster. The result was that Meg let her do it, spending the time thinking about all the things that really interested her. Sometimes Meg's dreaming got her into trouble. She found it terribly difficult trying to remember which were her clothes, even though each of her garments had her number sewn on it. Worse, she was forever losing them and then Miriam got cross.

She imagined lying in bed, just 'feeling' Cherrytree Cottage, travelling down its corridor to the bathroom where she washed, down the iron staircase with its slippery wooden treads. When it was her turn to polish them, she relieved her boredom by peeping through the gaps to the hall below. There she would see another girl wiping the tiles stuck to the lower half of the walls – tiles that were chipped and cracked and dirty white; that were sticky with fingerprints from grubby hands that trailed over them on their journey from the day room to the refectory. In her travels Meg saw no flowers, no pictures, no mirrors, no lockers, no cupboards – except one in the day room, and that was bare. She saw no books. How she longed for a book, longed to possess one. Except for a toy, no one owned anything, unless you counted your toothbrush.

Apart from the shelters (and to some extent chapel) the other place she really disliked was the day room. It was a sad room – less on account of its lack of toys, even of furniture, than because no one seemed to speak or play in it. All they did was to sit and stare into space, as if every child had sunk into a lonely reverie which took it back, in a fractured, painful way, to a time and place where it had once belonged. There, sometimes, Meg too caught the memory of a laugh – a warm, tinkling, merry laugh, as well as snatches of song. Or when she looked at Kathy's hair, in place of gold she saw a gleam of bronze, a woman's hair, shimmering and flashing as red as the last rays of the setting sun. But the ache this brought she always pushed away.

It was here that relatives of the children were brought. The matter of visitors was upsetting both for those who had them and for those who hadn't. Sometimes the atmosphere in the day room got so bad, Meg would try to slip away in an effort to find somewhere to 'breathe'. The room was charged with distress, anger, apathy, loneliness and envy. No one who had a visitor dared boast of the fact, or the others might turn on it. Some children dealt with the situation by 'sharing' their visitors with friends or the group generally. Kathy's granny was a great favourite. She knew the children's names and always brought some jelly babies to be shared around. But it was a strain on Kathy. Meg would see her clutching the sleeve of her granny's coat, or leaning heavily against the motherly figure as if to draw from the contact something which belonged specially to her; and Meg would move away in an effort to give Kathy the privacy she needed.

It was better in summer when it was warm and everyone was outside. Then it was easier to play – for visitors as much as children. What was the game she had liked so much? The one where a visitor lifted her up and, with her legs wound round the person's waist, dangled her head downwards, while the rest sang:

> Under the water, under the sea,
> Catching fishes for my tea.
> Twist – Turn – or Roundabout?

But confined to the day room, Meg was always glad when it was time for tea and she could join in the scramble to get to the long table with its wooden benches in the room next door. Seizing Kathy's hand, she would push and pummel the way to get to their places, with Dodo, her beloved doll, clamped tightly under her arm. She carried Dodo with her everywhere. The doll was the first Christmas present Meg was given when she came to St Anne's, and she would allow no one, apart from Kathy, to touch it. If they did, she attacked them. Small though Meg was, and much as she disliked fighting, she could fight – and win – often against someone much bigger. Thinking of this, she grinned to herself as she lay awake in the dormitory.

She liked being awake at night when everyone else was asleep. Swivelling round, she gripped the iron rail at the top of her bed and leaned forward to peer out of the window. It was silent outside, everything still. She could see the outlines of the cottages opposite, but not the bakery with its tall chimney, standing further down the great dark path. Her ears strained for the sound of planes, but there was nothing, and she relaxed, content to absorb the quietness which lay around her. She was looking at the world through a curtain of gauze. In this strange half light she was, she realized, between day and night. No, she corrected herself: she was between night and day. Satisfied with her discovery she drifted off to sleep.

If at the time Meg lacked the means to know she was looking at a less familiar form of twilight (that which precedes daybreak) she did at least know the name of the other one: dusk. She loved it, loved its gentleness, the way it slowly stretched and arched its way from light to dark. When she was surrounded by bustle and noise, when tea was being prepared, when Miriam was scolding her, she would become oblivious to everything except what was happening to the sky. She had a secret, a very special one; she kept it from Kathy, even from Dodo – though she thought Dodo guessed what it was. Her secret was that she knew how to listen to the sky. If she was cut off from it, was shut indoors where she couldn't see it, it didn't matter. Inside herself she could see it – could listen and feel what was happening; could join in the great unstretching, enfolding movement going on outside. It was a secret she must never reveal – for fear others would spoil it. Gazing at the sky's hugeness, its magnificence, the way it reached down in great streaking fingers of interwoven colour to touch the very ground itself, so flat was the terrain beneath, was the most precious thing she knew. Compared with this – this utter beauty, a beauty that left her awestruck – everything else was irrelevant. Occasionally in winter she caught glimpses of the sun setting, with great banks of cloud shifting, lightening, intensifying, changing colour even as she gazed at them, forming and re-forming themselves endlessly into the landscapes she had seen in picture books . . . into worlds she wanted to explore. If only she could fly – up – up – up. So great was her longing, tears would sometimes stream down her cheeks – tears of sheer frustration.

Once, on a hot summer morning – so hot, everyone had been up since dawn – she and Kathy were practising handstands against the wash-house wall. There, as she stood resting her body on her head, she studied the sky as well as the ground; studied it with great concentration. Kathy, resting in the same position, decided after a while to somersault down.

'You coming, Meg? They've got the long rope out down at Buttercup. Let's go and skip.'

Meg grunted but did not move. Kathy, seated, back slumped against the wall, bent her head and peered at her friend quizzically. 'What d'you see when you look like that?' she asked.

Meg wanted to tell her, but couldn't. How could anyone understand the vision which lay before her: of a world upside down – a world that felt so right it must be how it really was; for some odd reason she was inhabiting the world the wrong way up. She never forgot what she saw, nor how she felt – above all, that she wanted the world to stop, for time to stand still . . .

The dreaming ceased. The child's efforts to persuade herself she was having a nightmare, one from which she would soon wake up, stopped. It was a nightmare: a living one. The question was, how had she got herself into it and, having got into it, how was she ever going to get out? In this frame of mind, the child sat at Sarah Dawkins' tea table that Sunday afternoon – an unhappy and desperate little girl who was on the whole quiet, even docile, in spite of her independence of spirit; and one who was not easily goaded into violence and aggression.

The firelight was glinting on the gold-rimmed crockery, Sarah's best tea service. The 'sight' of Sunday tea enthralled Meg at first. In the middle of the table, which was covered with a starched, lace-edged cloth, stood a large bowl of jelly, and next to it a cakestand – a glass plate on a silver pedestal. Yesterday, she had been taught how to polish the pedestal. She was glad when Sarah gave her something to do; and from now on one of her jobs each Saturday was to clean all 'the silver' – not just the cakestand but the cutlery too, and the cruet frame that was shaped like a bird cage. Dot had shown her what to do. But what frightened Meg was that if Dot dropped anything, Sarah hit the girl across the face or punched her savagely in the back.

The cakestand was covered with a paper doily, which reminded Meg of some snowflake patterns she had once seen in a book. Resting on the doily was a pile of yellow buns, next to a plate of thinly-sliced bread and butter. Most of the food, Meg already knew, was only for show. She and Dot were allowed just one slice of bread with, perhaps, a bun – or half a bun – for their tea. The leftover bread was saved for breakfast or used to make bread pudding, and the buns would appear the next day, and the day after that. She was getting very hungry; she wasn't yet used to having her tea as late as six o'clock. She was tired of the waiting. There was something about the waiting which was convincing her she was trapped, that escape was impossible. As this fact sank in, all her initial revulsion concerning Sarah returned.

There was something in this woman. She dimly felt it was related to the power she saw Sarah exercising over the other two: Cissie and Dot. Meg also felt that Sarah Dawkins was only just managing to hold back from her. Soon, very soon, the 'thing' would break out. The tension in the child mounted. From her chair across the table, she listened to it seething, hissing, waiting to explode. She tried desperately to think of ways to prevent what was going to happen. But she could contain the tension no longer: she was compelled to look at Sarah Dawkins and felt sick with fear.

Sarah Dawkins was sixty-seven but looked at least a hundred. Or so it seemed to a seven-year-old child. She was a large, cruel-looking woman who wore her hair screwed in a knot on the top of her head. Her eyes were small black beads; they were expressionless too, like a doll's. Even on the odd occasion Sarah Dawkins enjoyed herself, Meg never saw in these eyes any flicker of kindness, sympathy or love. Rather, they glinted, sometimes with triumph, more often with venom. They were rheumy eyes from which tears never fell, though she frequently dabbed at them with a lace handkerchief. Her nose was long and thin, longer-seeming because it was set between two hollow flaps of cheek. With its wide-flaring nostrils and trailing hairs, it filled the child with a dread that the woman could breathe fire. Her skin was yellow and wrinkled, marked with two warts the size of fleshy white peas – one in the middle of her forehead, the other on the side of her nose. Her mouth was a thin blood-drained line, turned down at both ends to conceal what the hollow cheeks and sunken jaws could not: she was nearly toothless. All she had left were four elongated stumps of browning, yellowing bone: two up and two down, on which she gnawed her food, watched by a horrified Meg. In every way Sarah Dawkins both looked and behaved like the incarnation of the wicked witch in the only film the child had seen: *Snow White and the Seven Dwarfs*.

The child had been instructed to call this terrifying woman 'Mother'. When Meg first learnt what was expected of her, she had wanted to laugh; then had stared in disbelief. It wasn't even a question of sentiment, of clinging to some long-cherished memory that the word rightfully belonged, for her, to someone else. It had simply made her feel outraged that grown-ups could be so stupid. Her knowledge of the world might have been limited, especially concerning adults, but there was no possible way Meg could call Sarah by this name. For one thing Sarah was too old. Every day attempts were made to get Meg to accept Sarah as 'Mother'. Every day the child responded by sticking firmly to the term of address she was accustomed to at St Anne's and in school: 'Miss'. As Meg's desperation grew, an impulse welled up inside her to make it clear she could not accept this woman. The child's hands closed over the edge of the tablecloth, bunching it tightly together. She started to pull – first gently, then harder, till all her strength went into tugging the cloth off. As if she were watching something in slow motion she saw the milk jug topple over and the plates and knives go slithering to the floor. Sarah's mouth dropped open and she was pouring tea all over the bread and butter. Cissie had leapt up, knocking her chair over. Dot was sitting transfixed. Only the jelly, wobbling violently in its bowl, was standing firm against the tornado she had just unleashed.

There was a curious silence in the room. On Sarah's face the amazement was temporarily frozen. So absolute had been her rule, so well established, it was as if all her reactions – normally as swift as lightning – were momentarily suspended. Who, she seemed to be asking herself, has done this? Who, in doing this, has challenged me? Who, in doing this, has *dared* to challenge me? She looked about her.

'No!' Dot was shouting. 'It wasn't me. You know it wasn't me! You know I would never do such a thing. It was *her*!' Her voice raised to a scream as Dot pointed at Meg.

The child sat glued to her chair. In the silence she felt Sarah's eyes on her, but she dared not meet that gaze.

'So,' Sarah said, in a quiet, deadly voice. 'It seems we have a devil in the house – a fiend, a savage. A savage who hasn't been taught how to behave. Well, my little lady, we'll soon put that right, because I am going to show you what happens to fiends and savages – what in this house we do to them.'

Meg stopped breathing.

'Dorothy,' she heard Sarah say, 'go upstairs and get the doll, and fetch me the stick from the cupboard.'

That she had been naughty – really naughty – the child knew. She was appalled at what she had done. She knew she had never created such chaos before – had never done anything remotely like this before. She knew she should be smacked – would even say she was sorry, for she felt sorry. It had all looked so pretty and she didn't like spoiling pretty things. She would probably be smacked quite hard, perhaps on the hand, or on the inside of the forearm, where it stung, perhaps across the back of the legs – that smarted, too – or even, as had once happened at St Anne's, on her bottom. But this was the limit of what the child knew about physical punishment. When it happened at St Anne's, which was rare, it used to sting a bit afterwards, but it never hurt much. But now she wasn't at St Anne's and was worried by those words of Sarah's which had sent Dot racing upstairs. What was going to happen? She couldn't imagine. As she sat there, it did not enter her head that Sarah would punish Dodo, her only friend, her only possession, all that was left of the world she had come from that she might call her own. She saw the doll in Sarah's hands – a soft, knitted toy, grimy from constant handling and caressing.

'No!' she was screaming as she lurched off her chair. Pushing Cissie away she struggled past her to reach Dodo, to rescue her as Sarah, with a large pair of scissors, began to dismember the doll before the child's wild and disbelieving eyes, tearing and cutting at its limbs, its head – throwing the pieces one by one into the fire. Somehow she reached Sarah, was clawing at the woman's body, kicking, scratching, biting, spitting.

Sarah, her task completed, seized the child by its hair and, holding its neck in a grip from which escape was impossible, took up the stick, raised it aloft, and brought it crashing down – across the child's buttocks, back, shoulders, arms, legs. As the blows thudded down, swiftly, viciously, it was as though someone was dropping rocks on her. At each blow the child lurched in sick, unbearable pain, her stomach heaving in rhythm to the thudding stick. Her lungs wouldn't work properly. Between the intervals from when the stick left her body to when it came crashing back, she struggled to breathe. On, on it went – not once, not twice, not three times or four, but on, and on … She was slipping away from her own screams, her own pleadings, her own cries for help. She wasn't screaming any longer – all that came out of her was a broken, croaking sound.

She did not know it was Cissie who finally pulled Sarah off, before the woman could beat her senseless. From the great distance to which she had fled, the child knew that she had dirtied herself, that she was vomiting – over herself, over Sarah, over Cissie. None of it mattered. Nothing would ever matter again – now that she had reached the end of the world. As Cissie carried the child into the scullery, Sarah was screaming: 'Scum! Nothing but scum!' There was only one place for scum – at the bottom of the pile where they belonged.

Cissie laid the child on the floor and searched for some newspaper to place under the child's head. It was still retching violently, though in place of vomit there was now only a thin trickle of bile. As Cissie prepared to wash the child, she called Dot to fetch the child's nightgown. The weeping girl wanted to help, but Cissie advised her to stay in her room, where Dot had fled when the beating began. The child remembered little more, except the pain she felt when Cissie wiped her clean with a flannel. Upstairs, Cissie placed her face down on the bed. After drawing the curtains, she lit a candle and examined the child's body, ordering Dot to fetch some witch hazel. As Cissie dabbed the lotion on her back, the child wept soundlessly into her pillow. Only when Cissie pulled her nightgown down did the child give one last scream, so painful was the cotton against her skin. After that she lay in a stupor, incapable of taking in what had happened to her. She could hear Cissie's voice telling Dot to take the candle and to sleep in the little room which led off the girls' bedroom, but to leave the door open. Sitting on the bed, Cissie turned the child's head to stop her from suffocating.

'Meg.' The child heard her name. 'Try to get some sleep now. You'd best stay in bed tomorrow. Mother won't come near you, so don't worry. I'll come and see you in the morning and again at dinner-time . . .' Cissie's voice trailed away, and she awkwardly put out a hand to smooth the child's hair. 'It's no use crying, you know. What's done is done. But there's something you have to promise me — never, do you understand, never make her angry like that again. For your own sake don't. It's too dangerous. She can't help it, you see. You do understand, don't you?'

The child did not move.

PART 3

Gypsy Land

Sarah Dawkins' house stood on Prickler's Hill which, according to the local paper, the *Witheringham and District Gazette*, lay 'somewhere in Southern England'. Those who lived on the hill were more precise: they knew they were to be found on the boundary between Witheringham town and the brick works at Clayhurst.

'Dinosaurs,' Miss Harper was saying, 'are of course extinct. While once upon a time they lived in Witheringham, they do so no longer. Now who can tell me what a dinosaur looks like?' She stopped. The door had opened and Miss Wilkinson, the headmistress, was beckoning the class forward. The Vicar had arrived.

As a Manager of the school Meg attended, St Swithin's Church Elementary School for Girls in Clayhurst, the Vicar often appeared in the classroom to teach the children their catechism and question them on their knowledge of the Scriptures. On other occasions he regaled them with stories about the Empire.

School was a single-storey red-brick building with sloping roofs and soot-covered chimneys. Built at the turn of the century, its pointed windows (too high for a child to peep through) were faced with stone; windows that could only be opened with a long pole, or by operating a pulley made of tough cord. Dangling from the cords were varnished beads looking – in size and shape – like ripe acorns. In front of the school's entrance lay an asphalt yard surrounded by horizontal bars on which the children practised acrobatics of great daring – swinging over, doubling through till they could hang by their toes, and then repeating the act in reverse and vaulting free.

About eighty girls attended St Swithin's, their ages ranging from five to fourteen years. Miss Butterworth took the Infants' Group where Meg, still seven, was placed on her first morning. When, at dinner-time, Sarah discovered this, she took up her stick and marched the girls back to school, ordering them to wait on the pavement outside – as if to warn everyone that if her demands were not met, neither girl would cross the school's threshold again. What took place between Sarah and the head-mistress the girls never knew, but Meg was at once transferred to Miss Harper's group of eight to eleven-year-olds.

It was not that Sarah had the child's welfare at heart, since the fact that Meg could read and write fluently appeared to anger Sarah deeply. Nor, at first, did Miss Harper approve. Unused to a child who seemed to know much of what the teacher had to offer, Miss Harper was cross that Meg could not write script. Meg wrote like an adult, using an old-fashioned form of handwriting that was full of loops with each word written without removing pen from paper. Where and when she learnt to write like this, Meg did not know. To make matters worse, she not only knew her alphabet but could recite it backwards as well. Under Miss Harper, Meg was obliged to learn script, and wait a year before being re-introduced to handwriting. Sarah was interested in none of this. She wanted the child under Dot's surveillance; the Infants' class, with its separate entrance and strip of play-ground, was cut off from the main school.

The girls were taught in what was really one large room, divided by a thin partition of wood and glass. Miss Harper's group was housed in the smaller section. The headmistress, who taught the older girls, used the larger part; this housed the piano and Miss Wilkinson's imposing desk. The latter, its top inset with green linoleum, stood on a slightly raised platform, which enabled the headmistress to keep a look-out on the playground and the latrines at the back, as well as the grass-covered bank separating the school from Shoebury Lane and Grunter's Wood. At five minutes to nine a heavy brass handbell summoned the children into neat lines in the front playground, where no one might move until complete silence reigned. After a short blast on a whistle, the girls filed off briskly, shoulders squared and heads held high, to the cloak-room. After a quick scuffle, they shed their hats and coats before entering their respective classrooms to sit with hands on heads, fists in armpits, or arms folded uncomfortably behind their backs – according to their teacher's temper that day. Next the Register was called: with a red tick for 'present, Miss Harper', a black tick for absence, and a 'stand in the corner face to the wall' for late. After Register came Assembly. For this the partition was folded back and the two classes proceeded to lusty hymn singing accompanied by Miss Harper, her pince-nez swinging violently from a ribbon fastened to her bosom by a gold safety-pin. She attacked the piano keys with such vigour that it sent her bottom bouncing and squirming on the stool. The older girls rolled their eyes heavenward in an effort to contain their mirth. The younger ones dared not even look – especially at each other.

After Assembly the partition was again closed and the children's desks pushed back into position. These had iron frames, wooden benches and open shelves. When a lesson required writing, monitors (chosen for their responsible de-meanour) handed out paper, together with rulers, pens and blotting paper. Except for sums and practising handwriting, however, most lessons consisted of little more than endlessly reciting what the teacher said, or having to learn by heart what she wrote on the blackboard. If the supply of paper was meagre – due to wartime shortages – textbooks were non-existent; and reading books, battered with age, had to be shared between two or more girls. Weather permitting, there was drill daily in the playground. There, with the aid of piercing blasts from a whistle, the teachers got the girls moving in regimented formations to cries of 'One and two and three and four and swing your right foot up and drop and now your left foot up and down and push your fingers to your toes and one and two and three and four now straighten up and drop your arms and Marjorie Perkins stop that noise and keep your bottom in . . . and STOP!'

Under Miss Wilkinson, the senior group spent much of their time sewing, singing and reciting multiplication tables. In place of housewifery (for which there were no practical facilities or materials), the girls were given talks on hygiene (don't clean your ears out with a knitting needle) and nutrition (eat nothing but carrots); and practised selected arts and crafts which had been introduced into the curriculum by Miss Wilkinson. One occasion which made a lasting impression on Meg was the day the big girls were asked to bring old gramophone records to school. There, Harry Lauder ('Ha! Ha! Ha! Hee! Hee! Hee! Little Brown Jug how I love thee'), John McCormack ("When Irish Eyes are smiling"), Alexander's Ragtime Band, and even the great Melba herself trilling 'I dreamt that I dwelt in marble halls' – were transformed into 'ornamental pots'. To Meg the process appeared to be magical, though apparently it was all done with the help of the big black stove in Miss Wilkinson's room. The head-mistress was not to know that the big girls had other ideas. After school that day Meg saw them cavorting in the street, fingers in their mouths as they ululated like Red Indians, the 'ornamental pots' set precariously on top of their heads.

When the two classes were in session the noise was often deafening, as if two rival flocks of birds were trying to outbid each other in defence of their territorial rights. The older girls would launch into a gusty rendering of 'Bobby Shaftoe's gone to sea, silver buckles at his knee'; Miss Harper's group would be chanting tables. As the contest gathered momentum, the volume of sound rose to such a pitch that most children only found it possible to concentrate on what it was they were supposed to be doing by placing their hands over their ears and closing their eyes. To add to the bedlam, an air-raid siren might wail out its quavering warning, sending everyone slithering under their desks. Daytime alerts could be exciting, if it meant that school was closed early. Not that all the children went home. Some played in the deserted streets where, once out of sight and earshot, they cheered themselves hoarse, before wandering off to the woods and quarries where no one would find them.

Dot's way of surviving was to tell Sarah everything – at least, everything Meg did, as well as any gossip she picked up about

Sarah's neighbours. As Sarah's spy, Dot was able to satisfy Sarah's needs, less for information as such, than for the power which stems from it. Meg was not afraid of Dot. Separated from her family since before the war, Dot also suffered cruelly at Sarah's hands. But Meg disliked Dot's habit of telling tales, as well as the way Dot tormented her. The two girls shared a bed, something Meg had not experienced before, although she was used to sleeping in a dormitory. Now Meg had just an hour – until half-past seven, when Dot came to bed – to be alone. When Dot discovered Meg knew stories, she poked and pinched and pulled the child's hair, to get Meg to tell her one. These were stories Meg had heard or read for herself at school (for neither of the girls possessed a book of her own – not even a Bible). One story Meg loved from the moment she first read it: Hans Christian Andersen's *The Little Mermaid*. It was long, so it didn't matter if Dot fell asleep in the middle; it was best related in episodes, anyway. At first Meg wondered what Dot would do when she reached the story's end. But Dot simply asked to hear it again till, eventually, it was reduced to just its beginning – with small, uninteresting bits left out.

Far out in the wide sea, where the water is blue as the loveliest corn-flower, and clear as the purest crystal, where it is so deep that very many church-towers must be heaped one upon the other in order to reach the lowest depth to the surface above, dwell the Mer-people. Trees and plants of wondrous beauty grow there, whose stems and leaves are so light, that they are waved to and fro by the slightest motion of the water, almost as if they were living beings. Fishes, great and small, glide in and out among the branches, just as birds fly about among our trees. Where the water is deepest stands the palace of the Mer-king ... In this palace lived the Mer-king with his six little Princesses, all of whom were beautiful, but the youngest was the most lovely of them all. Her skin was as soft and delicate as a rose-leaf, her eyes were of as deep a blue as the sea itself, but like all other mermaids, she had no feet. Her body ended in a tail like that of a fish ... Each Princess had her own garden where she might plant and grow what she liked ... the youngest made hers as round as the sun ... In the centre of her garden she placed a marble statue of a boy she had found and planted a weeping willow by its side ...

If Meg did not understand Dot's passion for this passage, it was because, unlike Dot, she was not yet caught up in fantasies of wishing she were a princess rather than a changeling. What she did know, and understand, was that Dot was equally as afraid of Sarah, though her fear and unhappiness took a different form. Some nights Meg woke to find the older girl tossing around in bed, throwing the bedclothes from her. Her nightmares were very distressing and not helped when Sarah came charging into the room to shake her awake. Then Dot, who was confused as well as frightened, got hysterical and broke into heart-rending sobs. Meg, who had spent years listening to similar, though less noisy, scenes in her dormitory at St Anne's, had learnt not to be too disturbed by them. There, she had also been awakened, but for a different reason. At St Anne's the children were taught to sleep always on their right sides. When the housemother did her nightly round, any child found in a different position was turned to the correct one, with the result that Meg, by way of protest, was never again able to sleep on her right side.

If Dot was one of Sarah's sources of information, it did not explain all Sarah knew or found out, and for a long time Meg believed Sarah was in some way all-knowing, as well as all-powerful. The only areas Sarah's omniscience did not encompass were the woods and fields, to which the child retreated to be alone with her thoughts. But she feared that, even where her thoughts were concerned, she was in danger of being invaded unless she took special care.

The anxiety Sarah's constant surveillance gave rise to merely deepened the child's mistrust of all adults – a mistrust first nurtured in the orphanage. Never tell a grown-up anything, especially anything personal. Once, shortly after another bad beating, there was a medical examination at school. The nurse who examined Meg found bruises across the child's back and, dissatisfied with the child's explanation that she had been practising somersaults in bed and had fallen off, called in the school doctor. Yet Meg was simply too afraid to tell the doctor more; she believed Sarah to be more powerful than him, and that if she talked it would only result in further punishment from Sarah. But it was not only her fear which stopped her from telling him; it was also her pride. She was prepared to lie rather than admit publicly the humiliations that she was subjected to. In addition to the daily round of punches, slaps and blows across the back of the head, which were turning her into a highly-strung little girl who flinched from any sudden movement, there was the insult of Sarah never addressing her by her own name. Instead, the child was forced to answer to Judy, Polly, Lady Muck, Guttersnipe, Clara Butt, Moaning Minnie, Doleful Dilly, Eliza Jane, Dirty Moggy, Hoity-toity, Mary Ann, and 'Where's that Skivvy?'

Some days the child would arrive at school, lay her head on the desk, and weep or sleep her way through the morning or afternoon, refusing to speak or respond to anyone. When it first happened, Dot, who appeared to understand it no better than anyone else, was questioned by Miss Wilkinson, and even Miss Harper, who had begun by treating the child coldly, now wanted to help. Fortunately, Meg's spells of melancholy were rare. As her class-mates grew used to her, they also minded less when Miss Wilkinson sent for her to teach her more advanced arithmetic. Miss Wilkinson also let her read a lot, though Meg still had to do spelling lessons. With hands on heads, or fists in armpits, the children chanted their spelling sing-song fashion in the form of jingles: Missis D. Missis I. Missis FFI. Missis C. Missis U. Missis LTY – DIFFICULTY! As for the treatment Meg received from the headmistress, this was always kind but formal. Whatever made the child remote at times, Miss Wilkinson never enquired directly as to the cause. Instead, she brought books to school for the child to read – story and history books as well as books of poems. Before long, school was a place of refuge for Meg.

Within weeks Dot grew bored with her role of custodian. Once out of sight of Sarah's watchful eye, when they turned the corner at the top of Prickler's Hill, Dot dropped Meg's hand (to their mutual relief), telling the child to 'get lost' and warning her that if she were so stupid as to be late for school she would 'thump her one'. Off like a young colt Dot would gallop along North Street to where the boys' school was. Here, with her friends, she spent her time yelling, strutting back and forth, tossing her hair, and hurling insults at the boys who lounged outside the school gates, looking at the girls with studied indifference, running combs through carefully sleeked-down hair.

Soon 'dinner time' became one of the child's happiest hours. With morning school finishing at noon, the two girls ran as fast as possible so that they could be indoors by a quarter past twelve. Wolfing down their dinner, they washed and dried their plates and, if not sent on some errand, were out of the house again – as ordered by Sarah – before Cissie returned from work. Since afternoon school did not begin until two o'clock, this left Meg a blissful spell of time to spend by herself.

The weather, for late October, was warm and drowsy. This new life – despite its backcloth of loneliness and harshness – dazzled Meg with the opportunities it offered for discovery. Every minute the child could win for herself she spent wandering along the paths which skirted the quarries and meadows near school. Around her the alders rustled in the breeze. She stood quite still, her fingers moving lightly over the bark of a tree, following the tracery of its ribbed lines as if it were a maze, watching the sparrows as they attacked the crimson berries on the hawthorn trees. Some of the hawthorns were huge, their boughs cascading in all directions. Dipping to within a few feet of the ground, they shook under the sparrows' greedy onslaught. Twisting upwards round anything that would give them support were the climbers: smooth, green-leaved ivy, wild sprawling hop, yellow and red-berried bittersweet and the white-flowering woodbine; while thrusting their prickle hooks through any space that would lift them to the light were blackberries. These Meg picked, storing them in a cornet twist made from a dock leaf – to eat at leisure later on.

Sometimes she collected leaves; she was fascinated by the variety of leaves, by their structure and shape as much as their texture and colour. Starting with the spine, she noted how the leaf was composed of a network of threads; the rest was only a covering. She found it puzzling that some were thick and tough to her touch, others were more delicate and bruised easily. But she wanted to touch them in a different way – against her cheek, her mouth, over her eyes. She did the same with stones – feeling, licking, stroking, in an effort to know them better.

When it came to flowers, her real favourites were always the most delicate she could find: the diminutive star-faced chickweed, white with pale stems; and the brilliantly coloured speedwell – so vividly blue, brighter than the sky above. Faced with these tiny, exquisitely-wrought plants, Meg was filled with wonder at such intricacy in something so small, and felt towards them a special tenderness. They seemed so fragile and transient she wondered how they survived; that they had, gave her hope. Occasionally, a butterfly came fluttering by, opening and shutting its gaily striped wings, as it alighted first on one leaf, then on another. Thankful to be alone, Meg lifted her face to the sun and closed her eyes, waiting for the warmth to permeate her being. As she unwound, as the tension dissolved, the child entered a different world – one where she was no longer a solitary being. Here, everything seemed to pulse effortlessly. Here, the tangle of nerves which served as her antennae, reached out and adjusted – naturally and instinctively – to changes of light, temperature, humidity and sound.

On Saturday afternoons Dot and Meg were sent to pick blackberries, or to gather rose-hips and nuts. Sometimes they looked for apples – windfalls scrumped from a nearby orchard – and would run like hares if the farmer appeared, brandishing his stick in the air. When the girls brought crab apples back, Sarah made jelly. The crab apples were small, and with pear, plum and quince grew wild on the waste land above Nokes Wood. With great daring, Dot would take a mighty leap, grab one of the crabtree's boughs and swing herself hand-over-fist till she reached the crook of the tree. From this commanding position she sat, or stood, to shake first one branch and then another. On sampling a crab apple, Meg found it sour, but it did not produce the grimace she made when she tried to eat a quince. This was so hard and bitter it dried up all her saliva and, hopping frantically about, she all but choked.

Less of a wood than a copse (compared with Grunter's Wood behind St Swithin's School, which was full of great beeches), Nokes Wood was mostly furze and scrub, with a few old and gnarled oak trees. The wood backed on to that part of Prickler's Hill where Sarah's house stood; and the quickest way into it was through Sarah's back garden. The snag was that a brook ran parallel to the fence, making entry difficult. Occasionally the girls went in this way, carefully skirting Sarah's currant and gooseberry bushes, the compost heap and rhubarb patch, slipping through gaps in the old wicket fence. But as the fruit bushes were Sarah's pride and joy, she rarely let them take this route for fear of the damage they might do.

Normally the girls entered Nokes Wood by descending Prickler's Hill until they came to Back Lane – an ancient cart track lined with willows. Halfway up the lane, and opposite the wood, the land dipped down into a dell. Interspersed with hawthorn, dog-rose and sweet briar, the dell was covered with allotments and attendant bee-hives, dung heaps, scarecrows and lean-to sheds, as well as rabbit hutches, pigsties and chicken runs. In the distance the land swept upwards again to where, cresting the hill, the parish church of St Dunstan stood. The church had a steeple, a bell tower and a clock – with four golden faces – that could be seen for miles around. Meg knew the sound of the clock as it struck each quarter hour; but she had never heard the bells. (At the outbreak of war all the church bells in the country had been stilled, so when she eventually heard them in May 1945, they startled her, but that was all, since the significance of their pealing was not made clear to her.) As the girls made their way along Back Lane, avoiding the muddy ruts for fear of twisting their ankles, they regularly met Will Wagstaff. Perched high on his cart, he wore a red-spotted kerchief at his throat and, when the weather was colder, a sack slung across his shoulders. A grizzled, muscular-looking man he looked as if he spent his nights as well as his days out of doors. Passing them, he always removed his pipe, nodded his head and grinned broadly. The first time this happened, Meg smiled shyly back – only to be cuffed sharply by Dot and called 'a little fool'. They were not, Dot told her, even supposed to look at 'Ole Wagstaff', let alone return his greeting.

The problem of who she might, or might not, greet was beginning to give Meg headaches. If Sarah were on friendly terms with someone, then the child was expected to say 'Good Morning' followed by the person's name. But if, as was always happening, Sarah had rowed with someone, then not only must Meg ignore the person (despite their friendly address), but also was ordered to cross the road so as to make the snub more pointed. How Sarah managed to conduct her many feuds was difficult to fathom. She rarely (or so it seemed to Meg) left the house; not even on Cissie's half-day on Wednesdays. The grocer delivered the household's rations, while Sarah's daily shopping was done for her by the children. But Sarah did spend time studying her neighbours' movements from behind the lace curtains in the parlour. She was always ready to step outside to greet one of her currently 'acceptable' neighbours at the front gate. There she would pick up any gossip that was going, and embroider it thoroughly, before passing it on to the next comer. When, as sometimes happened, an aggrieved neighbour appeared 'to have it out with her', Sarah usually managed to persuade the victim that it was not she who had wronged them since, as they knew all too well, she had 'always been one who kept herself to herself'.

Sarah's greatest feud was with the Wagstaffs. This went back to 1901 when the Dawkins family had originally left London to settle in Witheringham. Mr Dawkins was setting up a mineral-water manufacturing business and sought premises in a locality where there were also houses to rent. The most suitable neighbourhood was Prickler's Hill, where the Dawkinses decided to live. Off Netherfield Road, at the foot of the hill, was Netherfield Lane. This linked with Lonsdale Road – a prosperous thoroughfare full of large houses, where Sarah's husband hoped to sell his bottled cordials and siphons of soda water. Netherfield Lane had some outhouses vacant. These were an outbuilding with a loft, where Mr Dawkins set up his machinery – a syrupper and filter; a workshop to house his carbonic acid appliances and bottle-washing and labelling equipment; a store-house; a stable for his horse and cart; and a brick-paved yard for unloading crates. There was only one drawback. The premises backed on to six cottages inhabited by the Wagstaff family. Henry Dawkins, a farmer's son, had the relaxed tolerance of the born countryman, but for Sarah it was a different matter. As the daughter of a tradesman – a London fishmonger – and now the wife of one, she felt duty-bound to show nothing but contempt for what she termed 'the labouring classes'; and this included the Wagstaffs, whom she called liars, cheats, thieves, sluts, slatterns, bastards, vagabonds and drunks.

The Wagstaffs were an easy-going family, numbering – if one included the sons who were soldiers in the war – about fifty members. Much of the time, even when the wind blew cold and the ground crunched underfoot with hoar frost, the doors of their cottages stood wide open so that anyone passing could see through the passage ways to the Dawkins' former premises. Some of the family would be sitting or working outside in what was a communal yard for all six cottages. This expanse of well-beaten earth, frequently awash with muck, compared very unfavourably with the neat front gardens cultivated elsewhere in the neighbourhood. Nor did the cottages resemble the uniform terraces of sombre brick houses surrounding them. With their grimed timber and plaster walls, the cottages had a tumble-down appearance, which perhaps justified Sarah's caustic description of 'slum'. The older Wagstaff women dressed in layers of ankle-length skirts and shawls – a costume which, with the gold rings dangling from their ears, betrayed their gypsy origin. And they sat, their stubby clay pipes clamped in their mouths, weaving baskets of pliant young willows and hazel twigs, which they sold in the town and villages; baskets that, in springtime, were full of pale primroses and daffodils set in the delicate ferns they gathered in the wild. As the younger women lounged against the cottage walls, bouncing their babies on their hips, the girls – Old Wagstaff's many daughters – were stirring the pigswill for the animals their father kept in the dell; while at their feet a clutch of toddlers, chickens, ducks and geese scratched, squawked, waddled and flapped in happy – if chaotic – abandon. Such were Sarah's feelings about this family that, if she so much as caught sight of one of its members, her face turned puce. They, for their part, ignored or laughed at her; all, that is, but old Wagstaff himself. Whenever he passed her in the street, he flicked his whip, leant out of his cart, and spat (something Meg never saw him do to anyone else), leaving Sarah impotent with fury and shaking her fist at his fast-retreating back.

Dot and Meg were blackberrying in Back Lane. Now that the older girl was satisfied Meg could be relied upon to do as she was told (on this occasion to pick enough fruit for them both), Dot set off for a clandestine meeting with friends. Meg set about her task quickly. Once she had filled both baskets, she pushed aside a willow bush, stepping past its stems to enter Nokes Wood. Penetrating deeper and deeper she found a spot she thought was safe: one where no one would disturb her. The light in the wood was eerie and dim where the oaks stood tall and were still covered with leaves. The quietness relaxed her. She let her mind wander, to day-dream, to become part of a world where time, for a while, might yet be suspended. Meg slowly sat up, looked about her, and began to play with acorn cups strewn on the ground. She would have a tea-party.

None of her guests were ever real people. She invited only those that she met in books. These were now her friends. The principal guest was usually the little mermaid accompanied by her sisters (but not the prince, whom Meg felt had treated the mermaid badly). Then there was Topsy from *Uncle Tom's Cabin*; Elise and her eleven brothers (who had been turned into wild swans by their wicked stepmother); Little Gluck from *The King of the Golden River*; and sometimes Mercury, whose winged hat and shoes made him such a wonderful messenger for the Greek gods. She invited Demeter, also: the goddess who journeyed far and wide in search of her kidnapped daughter. She would like to have invited the daughter, but while she could spell Persephone's name, she did not yet know how to pronounce it. She also excluded animals, not because she disliked them – though her experience of them was very limited – but because she didn't like stories where they talked and behaved like human beings; for the literal reason that they were not human.

Engrossed in her tea-party, several seconds elapsed before she sensed she was being watched. Feeling herself freeze, she carried on a little longer, but began inching her body slowly back towards the tree trunk behind, and drawing her legs up in readiness for headlong flight. Only then did she look up to see, peering at her from behind some bushes, the dirt-streaked face of a girl, and one Meg recognized; she had seen her so often perched up on the cart beside her father, 'Ole Wagstaff'. It was Charity, generally known as Char'ty. The girl, who was about Dot's age, grinned cheerfully and Meg – relief flooding through her – timidly smiled back. Noiselessly, the girl emerged from the thicket and squatted on the ground several yards away. Neither girl spoke. Meg, who had become as tense as a tightly coiled spring, slowly relaxed, while Char'ty chewed quietly on a piece of grass.

'D'yer want to see an owl?'

Meg nodded and followed with her eyes the direction in which Char'ty jerked her head, towards a hollow tree standing further along in the copse. 'Doan yer git up. I'll show yer later.'

Char'ty fell silent. Now her eyes were fixed on the bough of a tree. Meg, following suit, caught a glimpse of a grey squirrel streaking along it. Her face lit up with delight. Char'ty rolled over on her stomach and gazed at the child with a frank, open expression, leaving Meg to study Char'ty's face in return.

Char'ty had huge, solemn brown eyes, fringed with lashes so long and thick they cast sweeping shadows across her cheeks. When she laughed her teeth flashed as brightly as the gold in her ears, while the throatiness of her laugh set her blue-black curls dancing and tumbling down her face to encircle her shoulders. Meg thought she was very beautiful and, in wistful admiration, compared Char'ty's magnificent mane with her own neatly shorn wisps of hair. The fact that Char'ty's clothes were ragged, that she wore a man's jacket and hob-nailed boots, made no impression on the child. Nothing could detract from the girl's natural beauty.

'You'rm young Meg,' Char'ty announced. 'Yer live wi' t'ole witch, Ma Dawkins.'

Meg jumped in alarm. While she suspected Sarah was a witch, to have it confirmed was terrible!

Char'ty laughed. 'Nah! She's jist an ole 'orrer. Doan yer fret.'

Meg was so pleased, so relieved someone else knew this, she found herself smiling at the girl.

Char'ty began to burrow for acorns for her father's pigs. At first, Meg watched; then she joined in, placing her acorns in neat piles for Char'ty to scoop up and store in her voluminous pockets. Char'ty produced an apple, munched half of it and handed the rest over to Meg who chewed it valiantly. When Meg handed back the core, Char'ty told her she might have it: a great honour, as both children knew.

Char'ty lay back, her arms folded under her head. 'Poor-un,' she murmured, looking away from the child. 'I'll tell yer summat me Ma sez to tell yer, an' me Pa, too.' She swung round abruptly, confronting the child. 'Doan yer touch whi'tun. Doan yer ever touch whi'tun in Clay'urst parts.'

Bewildered, Meg watched as Char'ty sprang to her feet and quickly gathered some twigs which she twisted into little bunches. Then she began to mime – showing Meg the imaginary basket resting on her hip, the rat-a-tat at the door, the greeting, the offering of the little bunch from the basket, the pinning of the bunch on the breast, the proffered palm for the money, the fingers closing over the coin, the depositing of the coin in the pocket of an underskirt. Twice Char'ty went through it till, suddenly, Meg clapped her hands together in order to tell Char'ty she understood. It was the white heather the gypsies sold at the door! Only last week she had seen Sarah buy some, saying it brought good luck. Now Char'ty seemed to be telling her the opposite.

Meg cocked her head in a gesture which asked 'Why?'

Char'ty sifted a handful of soft earth moodily through her

fingers. Finally, but without looking at Meg, she said: 'Be a secret.' Then she stopped and broke into such a peal of laughter, it sent tears scudding down her cheeks. When it subsided, she spoke again: 'Clay'urst is gypsy land. The whi'tun – 't'ain't wot it seems. Me Ma doan want yer to touch it. That way us'll know t'ole witch can't really 'arm yer.' Char'ty's arm moved in a great sweeping movement to embrace not only the wood but the child as well. ' 'T'ain't 'er'n yer see. An' you'rm not 'er'n neither.'

Meg stared at the girl wonderingly, a sweetness flooding her being. From the lane came the sound of Dot's whistle. Char'ty vanished, melting back into the thicket from which she had come, leaving the child to rub her eyes and ask herself if she had been dreaming. She hesitated a moment before stooping quickly to unearth a treasure she had buried earlier in the afternoon: a pale wood dove's feather. Shaking it free of earth, she carefully dusted and examined its slender, translucent spine. As she left the wood, her fingers smoothed and stroked the feather's fibres, till they felt as warm as silk against her cheek. Rubbing them briskly in the opposite direction, she pulled and separated the strands, moulding the feather into a shape resembling a prickly leaf. Emerging from the wood at a point where Dot would not see her, Meg planted her gift in a clump of thistles, knowing, instinctively, that Char'ty – and only Char'ty – would find it. Nor was Meg disappointed. The next time she saw Char'ty the feather stood proud and stiff in the girl's lapel. That night, overwhelmed with gratitude, the child slept peacefully, waking refreshed for the first time in a month.

If all life appeared full of mystery to Meg, it was the part that money played which was to prove the most baffling. It was a commodity she never thought about except in the abstract, when she was tackling one of Miss Wilkinson's arithmetical problems. When it came to everyday reality she was totally ignorant of its role. At St Anne's they never used it. Food appeared – already cooked – on the table. She never saw anyone buy it, or cook it for that matter. This, at Sarah

Dawkins' house, was her first surprise: to see Sarah hand Dot some money which Dot, in turn, handed to the greengrocer after he had filled their shopping bag with some potatoes and a cabbage. In personal terms, the only money Meg encountered was called 'pocket money'. This she thought a strange description, since the penny a week she was given (at St Anne's and at Sarah's) was never allowed to get anywhere near her pocket. Each Saturday morning at St Anne's she would stand in line with the other little ones, stretch out her hand, palm upwards, to receive her penny. Then, coin in hand, they solemnly crossed the road in front of Cherrytree Cottage to the boys' side (an awesome event in itself). After climbing the wooden staircase to the storeroom-cum-office above, Meg – her eyes just level with the top of a high table – would swing her arm up and hand her penny back, staying to watch as it dropped through the lid of a large metal box. If she stood on tiptoe, she could just see someone sticking a stamp in a book bearing her orphanage number. At Sarah's almost the same thing happened, except that now the penny was divided into two ha'pennies. One she 'posted' in a money-box Cissie produced. The other she learnt to tie in the corner of her handkerchief, carefully untying it and handing the ha'penny to Miss Harper when she reached school – after Assembly and before Scripture. This time the coin was exchanged for a stamp that was stuck in a small blue book with her name printed in ink on the front. Meg had become a member of the 'Piggy Bank' Savings Movement.

None of it bothered the child much, since whether she liked it or not she had always had to give up her penny; and, it seemed, she was making a contribution, however involuntarily, to the 'War Effort'. 'Lend, don't spend!' she read on one boarded-up shop. 'Lend to Defend the Right to be Free' (a sentiment she not only understood, but subscribed to wholeheartedly) was plastered on walls near the gas works. 'Every penny is a nail in Hitler's coffin' also made sense – once she knew who he was. The National Savings Movement was always thinking up ideas for how to persuade people to save more, with competitions between towns to raise money for particular projects – 'Wings for Victory Week'; 'Buy a Battleship'; 'Buy a Spitfire'. Witheringham went in for battleships, but Meg's favourite was the Spitfire. She had often watched these fighter planes taking off and landing at the aerodrome near St Anne's, and now she saw them circling overhead in Clayhurst.

While the lack of money made little difference to Meg, she quickly discovered that the children of St Swithin's dealt in a different currency: shrapnel. She had seen these odd-looking pieces of heavy metal before. Some were elongated like thick ribbed splinters; others were more lumpy and twisted. What mattered was that they were highly prized. Meg, already familiar with the principle of barter, was anxious not to be left out and here it was Char'ty who came to her aid. A quarry Meg visited regularly turned out to be a bomb crater. Although fenced off, there were several hollows where a small child could wriggle under the wire. Char'ty helped her to value what she found in the quarry and also passed on other pieces from places too far for the child to go without being detected. The only problem was Dot. Meg soon realized that her chances of entering the barter market without Dot finding out were slim. She decided to take Dot into her confidence, buying her silence with a share of the booty. Dot was delighted since her own attempts to enter this field had not proved successful; anything she now got from Meg she could exchange for the cheap cosmetics and film magazines she coveted (but which had to be hidden for her at a friend's house).

Meg supplied Dot with enough shrapnel to satisfy some of her needs while Dot, for her part, arranged to get Meg what she wanted more than anything in the world: pencil stubs and paper. These were carefully guarded by Miss Wilkinson because of wartime shortages and were difficult – though not impossible – to obtain, particularly as one of the monitors responsible for handing out writing materials was friendly with Dot. Once the exchange was made, Meg disappeared into the school lavatories where, while a friend stood guard outside, she removed her shoes and stockings, secreted the pencil stubs between her toes and the paper – folded neatly – under the arch of each foot. Her feet were her only safe hiding place, since Sarah searched both girls' pockets and clothing each time they returned from school. Now, in the hour she had before Dot came to bed, Meg spent many happy moments writing, hiding her store of paper under the linoleum and the pencil stubs in the hems of the bedroom curtains.

The urge to write first came after Miss Wilkinson asked Meg to compose a letter, telling her to begin by putting her address at the top right-hand corner of the page. Seeing the child hesitate, the headmistress added: 'your home address'.

'Do you mean Mrs Dawkins' house?' Meg asked. Miss Wilkinson nodded. The child hesitated again. 'That isn't my home address. It's only where I live.'

Miss Wilkinson looked at her. After a pause she said: 'Then put the address of where you live.'

Meg's next problem had been to decide to whom she would write. She chose an acquaintance, a girl at St Anne's whom she thought might enjoy receiving a letter, just as she herself, while living at the orphanage, had always hoped someone would write to her. She couldn't remember ever having received a letter – not even on her birthday, though since she didn't know when she had been born (only that she was seven years old), she couldn't expect anyone else to know either. Then she received a shock. At regular intervals Miss Harper had the habit of writing on the blackboard 'Happy Birthday' (followed by a girl's Christian name). On arriving at school, the girl in question stood at Miss Harper's side, while everyone sang 'Happy Birthday to You'. Meg's difficulty was that two other girls in the class were called Margaret. How would she know when the greeting was for her? And how could she possibly explain her ignorance to others? Even to think about it made her blush with shame. The anxiety tugged at her remorselessly till, one day, when she was handing Miss Harper her 'savings', she noticed the register open and there, to the side of each girl's name, was a date. Quickly scanning the page for her own name, she memorized the numbers 31/5/36. Since the 36 looked right – if she was seven she must have been born in 1936 – the 5 had to mean the month (May) and the 31 the day. Not till she was ten did anyone discover they had all got the day wrong; something the child, by that time, simply laughed off when her friends asked in a puzzled way, 'but didn't you know?' She had felt a freak but at least had had time to get used to being one.

Whether the letter Meg wrote reached its destination, she never knew. No reply came but then, even if one had, her chances of seeing it were nil. Sarah opened all the post to the house as a matter of course. But at least Meg's writings – her letters and scribblings – were safe from Sarah's prying eyes. The child discovered a very special posting-box. The brass bed she slept in was made up of rails and bars. At each corner the rails were topped by a large and fluted brass knob which unscrewed. Inside, the rails were hollow. Here, in little twisted tapers, or tiny screwed-up balls, she 'posted' all her secret notes, fully aware that once they had been dropped they could not be retrieved. This was just as well, since one of her regular missives read: 'I hate Mrs Dawkins. Cross my heart and hope to die.' Posting such messages always left Meg feeling cheerful.

PART 4

Dinosaurs and Shrimps

The history of Witheringham begins with its geography. In Purbeckian times the place is believed to have been the site of a huge lake of freshwater origin, in which lived aquatic reptiles such as the dinosaurian brontosaurus, together with turtles and crocodiles and a myriad of small creatures allied to the shrimp and water-flea of the present day. The flora comprised the simpler forms of trees and ferns, including a type of monkey-puzzle tree. Nothing of note occurred there until, in the seventeenth century, a young lord who was visiting the neighbourhood stopped to quench his thirst at a stream. A few days later he was astonished to find that a particularly tiresome ailment he suffered from had vanished. Convinced he owed his cure to some miraculous properties in the water he had drunk, he rushed back to London to tell his friends. Before long the place was beseiged by the cream of Stuart society, many of whom pitched camp on the hills above. The gypsies, who had roamed the area for years, found themselves deprived of their traditional sites and decamped further north to Clayhurst.

As time passed, Witheringham acquired a reputation as a fashionable health and holiday resort, the medicinal properties of its waters being especially famed for promoting virility, fecundity and longevity. While the waters were eulogized, the character of those who took them earned the town a less enviable reputation. One visitor described the place as 'a rustic rendez-vous for ... gamblers, cardsharpers, rogues, buffoons, praters, cuckolds, whores and hypochondriacs.'

The eighteenth century brought Witheringham an improvement in manners – if not in morals. Fine stone basins were laid over the springs. The adjoining ground was properly paved and a colonnade of shops and places of refreshment built on either side. Nearby, a model village, complete with church, was laid out. Market stalls flourished, and in the Colonnade itself there were luxury goods for sale to a clientele that was both rich and discerning. The prerequisite for admission to the Colonnade and its society was the drinking of the water. The minimum quantity to be consumed daily ranged from three to fifteen pints, preferably drunk at dawn. For those who needed resuscitation after this ordeal, there were coffee houses for the ladies and taverns for the gentlemen. As for entertainment, this was so extensive and varied that by the middle of the eighteenth century Witheringham had become one of England's most favoured spas. If this is what made the place so popular with the ladies, the attraction for the gentlemen was the town's main business – gambling.

Against a background of political unrest as the English fought the French, colonized the Irish, ignored the Welsh, slaughtered the Scots, conquered the Polynesians and lost the Americans, the Parliament of the day was divided on the issue of gaming. After war it was the nation's favourite pastime. Drink followed in third place; hunting, shooting, hanging, branding, flogging and penal servitude were equal fourth; allegorical writings and tea-drinking fifth; religion sixth; and social reform – not at all. Once the anti-gaming restrictions began to be applied, the gentlemen lost interest in Witheringham. They preferred to pursue their passion in the privacy of a friend's house or in Brighton, where the expansive presence of the Prince Regent (whose liking was for salt water anyway) afforded better protection from the law than the niggling Dissenters of Witheringham. The latter were the descendants of the Puritans who, a century earlier, had quietly entrenched themselves in the hills above the town, bequeathing to them names which exist to this day: Naboth's Walk, Gideon's Way, Zemaraim Place and Hosannah Crescent.

When the Georgians left, the 'season' left with them. In their heyday – fickle though their patronage was eventually to prove – the fashionable members of that society bestowed upon the town an elegance, a prosperity and above all a gaiety, the like of which Witheringham would not see again for another two hundred years. In its grief the town took to religion as a man might take to the bottle. When the retreat gathered momentum, the Dissenters entered into their own: they descended from the hills and set about building chapels. In their wake came John Wesley, whose impact on the town was immortalized in a hymn written by his brother Charles:

> O may Thy powerful word
> Inspire the feeble worm
> To rush into Thy Kingdom, Lord,
> And take it as by storm.

The shopkeepers, tired of pondering gloomily on their dwindling prospects, now switched to property speculation. A century later, their foresight was confirmed with the arrival of Charles Darwin – not so much in person, but rather his book: *The Origin of Species by Natural Selection, or the Preservation of Favoured Races in the Struggle for Life*. This, when published in 1849, precipitated one of the many crises to which the early Victorians were prone: the crisis of faith; the one that sent them fleeing for refuge, irrespective of denomination, to the nearest place of worship they could find. To visit a town so full of churches must at that time have been deeply reassuring. So much so that those who had once come to Witheringham in search of longevity, now took up residence to protect their souls.

The first wave of Victorian newcomers was mainly drawn from the middle classes: the wealthy (merchants, bankers and industrialists), the retired (army officers, colonial administrators and civil servants), together with a few men of letters and a large number of doctors (even religion cannot cure hypochondria) and – more ominously – their widows and their widows' spinster daughters. Soon the notoriety on which Witheringham's fortunes once depended gave way to a new sort of repute: for sobriety and irreproachability. Understandable, when the town's other peculiarities were taken into account: its elderly population and its superfluity of women, who from 1850 till 1950 were to outnumber the men of Witheringham by two to one. The main task these early Victorians undertook was the building of a new, much larger town, half a mile north of the Colonnade. As the copses were cleared, the land sprouted mansions and around them larches, cypresses and laburnum trees; with ornamental shrubbery and elaborate exotica – such as the ubiquitous *Araucaria Imbricata*, the monkey-puzzle tree, whose curving boughs and sharp-pointed leaves commemorated the downfall of the Darwinians as much as the dinosaurs.

The second batch of newcomers caused Witheringham's population to swell from 8000 in the 1840s to 34,000 by 1900. In the process, the town underwent a further change. The new arrivals – shopkeepers and clerks – brought with them a more radical brand of religious belief. Sex was sinful ... alcohol evil ... children were wicked ... so all must be washed in the Blood of the Lamb. Their zeal helped spread Witheringham's fame as a centre of Nonconformism, though only in the sectarian meaning of the word. When it looked as if the new Local Government Acts would abolish the Witheringham Commissioners (drawn from the town's autocracy of retired colonels and magistrates) and also as if neighbouring Toddington would swallow it up, twentieth-century Witheringham successfully petitioned for its civic independence. With no further change in its population until 1950, the town was free to pursue its destiny impervious to any outside interference.

Meg's introduction to Witheringham first came from Sarah's weekly rummaging through the local paper, the *Witheringham and District Gazette*. Sarah read aloud from it to the household every Friday evening, beginning with her favourite column – 'Fashionable and Personal'.

There was a time when this column was spread over a whole page of the *Gazette*, such was the importance the editor gave to the 'doings' of the town's residents and its visitors (the latter reported – for brevity's sake – as 'arrivals', 'dispersals' and 'removals'). With the outbreak of war the removals and dispersals led to such a thinning of the ranks that, to Sarah's annoyance, the town's social activities were much curtailed, and so was the space they occupied in the newspaper; it shrank to a mere half column. Out, too, went the flamboyant notices about Grand Balls, Fancy Dress and Garden Parties, and Illuminated

Water Fêtes. Other casualties included dispatches from far-flung parts headed 'Imperial Skirmishes', and Religious Controversies which gave blow-by-blow accounts of local doctrinal differences of opinion, amply illustrated with biblical quotation. With the war the themes became more topical and their approach hortatory. Now the reader was subjected to sermons about incipient degeneracy in young people and similar burning issues; there were articles extolling 'The Benefits of Bee-Keeping' and 'How Hips and Haws can Help You'. Even the occasional historical piece such as 'Local Government before the Normans' could be made to reflect more solid national virtues. For light relief the *Gazette* reported on Maurice Frolic and his Gypsy Bandoliers and how to get tickets for innumerable dances – in aid of the Navy League, the Red Cross, the Nannies Guild. There were also films to suit the occasion. The week of Meg's arrival in the town was marked by Errol Flynn's appearance in *Edge of Darkness* at the local cinema, while *Rocks Ahead* could be viewed at the Congregational Church – admission free.

Meg welcomed these readings from the *Gazette*; it helped break the monotony of life at Prickler's Hill. But as Sarah never explained anything (nor would she permit interruptions in the form of questions or comments), the experience, while entertaining, was frequently puzzling as well. Most puzzling of all were the sayings of 'Aunt Mathilda the Children's Friend', who contributed a weekly column as well as running something called the 'Twinky Boo Club', which any child might join for the sum of 3d. More important was how reassuring Meg found the scraps of news and information – and not simply because they linked her with events outside. If, after her first weeks in Sarah's house, she had doubted her sanity, what she now learnt was that it was the entire world that was crazy – an impression Sarah's patchwork presentation of the town's affairs only heightened.

In the second week of December Miss Braddock called on the first of her quarterly visits, armed with a form designed to provide the authorities with the kind of information they thought it essential to have concerning the welfare of the boarded-out children in their care. And, being short of paper, they kept it as brief as possible:

BOARDED-OUT CHILDREN
REPORT OF VISITOR

Name of child   Date of Birth

Boarded-out with   at

General condition of child

Sleeping accommodation

If also occupied by other person, state by whom

If of school age, Name of school

Cleanliness of child

Health of child

Whether attending Sunday School   Chapel

How many other children resident in the home at the present time

General condition of the home

Complaints made by or concerning the child

If nearing the end of School life, are steps being taken
    to obtain suitable employment

If child is working, state name of Employer
    weekly earnings
    date commenced work
    (if subsequent to last report)

General remarks:

Date   Signature of
                                          Visitor

After four years of war, the files of the General Purposes Consultative Sub-Committee of the Education Department of the London County Council contained memoranda and correspondence approaching several million words – of which only a few thousand were in any way related to children in care. Lost in the middle of such voluminous piles of paper, it mattered little whether Miss Braddock completed her form perfunctorily and made her returns only twice a year. Most questions Miss Braddock usually ignored, confining herself to what was obviously a favourite heading: 'General Remarks'. Under this – without even having seen the child properly since she left her on the station platform – Miss Braddock felt confident in writing in her first report: 'has settled down all right'. Thereafter, between 1943 and 1946 (after which Miss Braddock, whether retired or translated to higher things, disappeared from the child's life altogether), Meg did encounter her occasionally, although they actually spoke to each other only once. Meanwhile, Miss Braddock continued to send in her reports of which the most favourable read 'generally satisfactory', although the child, it seemed, was to be regarded as consistently 'difficult'.

'Has, for once, been a good girl,' read one. 'Is getting too big for her boots,' read another, followed by 'knows too much'; 'seems happy enough, but is not an easy child to manage'; 'is given to sulking when corrected' and 'is a very strong-willed child and can be very obstinate'.

Whenever, on returning from school, the child discovered Miss Braddock ensconced in Sarah's kitchen, she at once was sent to sit in the scullery, where she remained until Miss Braddock left – except on one occasion. That day Sarah decided it was time Miss Braddock personally gave Meg 'a good talking-to'. It was important to Sarah that Meg's character as a 'difficult' child should be firmly established in the eyes of the authorities, especially as the child's teachers could not be relied upon to back her up in the same way. Summoned to the kitchen, Meg stood before Miss Braddock, her arms behind her back, and waited.

'I am not,' Miss Braddock said, shuffling her papers, 'at all pleased with your behaviour. I understand you've been upsetting Mrs Dawkins. What have you to say for yourself?'

Meg looked blank.

'You see,' Sarah said, 'she's as obstinate as a mule.'

Miss Braddock stared at the child. 'Don't you think it's time you showed a little gratitude?' she asked. 'Mrs Dawkins has been very good to you, you know. You might at least try to repay her generosity instead of being such a constant bother.'

Here Sarah interrupted and, dabbing her eyes, said in a tone which simulated anxious encouragement: 'Of course, she does try sometimes.'

'You are much too kind with her, Mrs Dawkins.' Miss Braddock leant forward in Sarah's direction. 'I'm not at all sure that's sensible. It's time she understood that she did not come into this world to take advantage of other people's kindness.' She turned and looked at Meg sternly. 'Perhaps you are not aware that a great deal of public money is being spent on you. Money to which you have no right – no right whatever. Is that clear?' Her tone indicated that a response was required.

'Yes, Miss Braddock,' Meg offered her.

'Well, then! What are you going to do about it?'

Since the child had no idea what Miss Braddock was talking about, she was puzzled; she was also distracted – by Sarah, who was finding it difficult to suppress her laughter, not laughter directed against Meg, but at Miss Braddock. Sarah was playing games and, it seemed, hoped the child would too.

'Well?'

'I don't know,' the child answered truthfully.

Miss Braddock regarded her coldly. 'Tell me,' she enquired, 'just who is it you think you are?'

'Margaret Chandler.' Meg spoke her name clearly, causing Sarah, who was sipping tea, to choke and fish hurriedly down the front of her frock for her handkerchief.

'Don't be insolent,' Miss Braddock snapped, to Meg's surprise.

They lapsed into silence.

'Well, all I can say is that you are a most ungrateful girl! What are you?'

The bewildered child repeated parrot-fashion, 'I am a most ungrateful girl.'

'And what should you be?'

Meg frowned in concentration. 'A good girl?' she tried.

'A grateful girl!' Miss Braddock's voice was impatient. 'Don't you understand – I want some expression of gratitude!'

As Meg's face closed tight, Sarah laughed. 'Ah!' – she wagged her finger at Miss Braddock – 'now that you will never get her to say – not in a month of Sundays.'

And with a wave of the hand, Sarah dismissed the child to the scullery. But as Meg left the room there was a curious moment of empathy between herself and Sarah: a real flash of understanding. Whatever degradations the old woman dragged the child through, they nonetheless shared something – a sense of pride. It was one of the very few areas in which they understood one another. Sarah may have been a tyrant, but even tyrants can occasionally show understanding.

December was interesting for quite different reasons; the most important being Christmas. For several weeks before the end of term, the girls of St Swithin's spent much of their time singing, an activity Meg loved. She knew some of the songs, which she now discovered were called carols. They practised so often that she quickly learnt the verses of familiar ones, such as "Once in royal David's city" and "While shepherds watched their flocks by night", as well as alternative sets of words which sometimes confused her, particularly if her mind wandered as it often did when she sang. When Miss Harper caught her singing the time-honoured words: 'While shepherds wash their socks by night all seated round a tub, a bar of Sunlight soap fell down and they began to scrub', she sent her to Miss Wilkinson for punishment (roll up your sleeve, hold out your arm, and get several sharp slaps with the ruler). But even this could not spoil Meg's pleasure and excitement at what was going on.

With Miss Wilkinson the girls made paper-chains: strips of newspaper gaily painted in red, blue and green and stencilled with a piece of raw potato, which they were asked to bring from home. Meg was too proud to ask a schoolmate for a piece, when Sarah refused to give her any, and with much misgiving she decided to raid Mr Loveday's vegetable patch. Dot often did this, though it set Meg quivering with anxiety. She liked Mr Loveday and she was frightened of stealing. Sarah was always talking of places where 'bad' girls who lied, stole or 'got into trouble' were sent – places where they could lock you up for the rest of your life. Sarah even knew the name of one: Borstal. The very sound of this word filled Meg with dread. If Sarah knew the actual name of the place then it must exist; Sarah wasn't simply trying to terrify her. The thought of being locked away made Meg's head go funny. She felt a kind of pressure building up inside, a pressure that made her wonder if her head might burst. Like this, she became desperate when shut indoors, waiting, holding on for the moment when she could get out into the streets. Certainly as a deterrent, Sarah's threats were extremely effective, though the child hadn't been in any way delinquent when she arrived from St Anne's. Lying and stealing never appealed to her. It wasn't because she held any moral views on the matter. It was more likely that she disliked getting into trouble unnecessarily, finding it futile and senseless, unless it was for something she felt strongly about. Nor, at Sarah's, did she change in this respect, except to learn gradually to lie by omission. (For Sarah, the truth was no more acceptable than a falsehood.) Yet Char'ty, as well as Dot, found it odd that Meg disliked 'nicking' from one of the many vegetable plots around. The trouble was that when Meg was really hungry she couldn't resist; then even the taste of raw swede or turnip became delicious.

Meg found it difficult adjusting to chronic hunger. It often kept her awake at night. Without starving the child, Sarah kept her very short. Only on Sundays – a day which, in other respects, Meg disliked – did the child get enough to eat. Of the twelve shillings Sarah received weekly for Meg's board and lodging, she spent only a third of it on the child's food. A true product of the nineteenth century, Sarah was brought up on a doctrine of thrift, and it was more natural for her to be interested in accumulating money than in spending it. She was also very systematic. The house was full of envelopes and matchboxes each containing sums of money and neatly labelled: 'Chimney Sweep', 'Rent', 'Coal', 'Cissie's Birthday', 'Corsets', 'Shoe Repairs', 'Bedroom Curtains', 'Mine' (the biggest box of all). When it came down to it Sarah liked money; but even if the authorities had offered her guidance as to how much of the allowance Sarah was to spend on Meg's food, Sarah would never have accepted it. After all, the term 'board and lodging' suggested a business – and business meant profits, however small.

Meg's breakfast consisted of a sprinkling of cornflakes moistened to sogginess with a tablespoon or two of hot boiled milk, followed by half a slice of bread and dripping. The main meal – 'dinner' – was at midday. Meat appeared hot on Sundays, cold on Mondays. Otherwise it was scraps: a stew of meat bones swimming in a sea of gristle, fat and pearl barley; suet pudding dotted with bits of fat and bacon rind; toad-in-the-hole (batter pudding with a third of a sausage); hot Oxo with a dumpling. For five days of the week menus like these were served with one small piece of potato and a dessertspoonful of cabbage – boiled by Sarah in bicarbonate of soda to a brown, evil-smelling mush. After the main course came 'pudding'; if not suet, then rice or semolina, cooked in water and garnished with a teaspoonful of jam. To last from noon of one day to breakfast the next there was only her tea-time slice of bread and jam and, if Sarah thought she had behaved that day, half a rock bun. Meg suffered from lack of food more than Dot because the older girl's helpings were larger and she was given supper. As time passed Meg found it increasingly difficult to contain her hunger and, funds permitting, she took to buying a ha'pennyworth of unrationed dog biscuits from a back-street grocer whom Sarah never used and who therefore could not give her away inadvertently. These she devoured ravenously; at least, that is, till he enquired one day after her 'dog'. Taken aback, Meg could think of nothing to say. The next time she visited the shop she switched to ordinary broken biscuits, which he sold off very cheaply, though she found them less sustaining.

With hunger went thirst. Crates of milk arrived at school

each day to be distributed at a ha'penny for a third of a pint, if a family could afford it, or free if it could not. Although Meg was badly in need of the milk, Sarah would not produce the weekly twopence ha'penny required for its purchase, nor allow the child to be registered for free milk. One reason was that it represented the charity she always vowed would 'never darken her door'; another was that in her objection to milk, Sarah was a fundamentalist. Never while Meg lived at Prickler's Hill did she taste milk straight from a bottle; similarly, she was forbidden to drink water from the tap. This was because both were 'cold'. What influenced Sarah was not that she was mean (though she was) but that she had been born in 1876. Sarah was always telling Meg how Prince Albert, Queen Victoria's husband, caught the typhoid which killed him because he foolishly drank cold water. The remedy which she practised for most of her life was simply a continuation of what she had learnt as a child: boil, and boil hard – be it water, milk, cabbage or sheets.

Sarah had other equally strong views. On days when it rained hard some mothers kept their children at home; but most of the girls arrived, like Dot and Meg, literally soaked to the skin. If some caught colds, the rest seemed to become inured to the damp, and no one fell ill with anything serious such as pneumonia. The locals attributed immunity from such infection to the sulphurous smell emitted by the nearby gasworks and would wheel their babies past it on Sunday afternoons for a good sniff. But Sarah dismissed such beliefs as superstitious nonsense and placed her faith in underwear. Not only was it safe, practical and sensible; more important – it was decent. Under her outer garments, the child was clad in a woolly vest knitted in garter stitch by Cissie. She wore the vest day and night – irrespective of season – because if Meg had an accident and had to be carried off to hospital, it would be seen that she was decently dressed. In any case, Sarah went on, uncovered skin was an affront to morality. For the same reason, Meg wore navy blue knickers which stretched to within an inch of her knees; a flannelette petticoat trimmed with lace; cotton stockings held up with elastic garters, and a liberty bodice. The bodice was like a padded waistcoat, ribbed and fleecy-lined, fastening with what to the child – as she fumbled on a bitter winter's morning, her fingers swollen and cracked with chilblains – seemed to be endless linen-covered buttons.

The main value of this abundance of undergarments was that it afforded some much needed protection against the cold in a house where, in winter, the normal indoor temperature (except in the kitchen) was well below freezing – judging by the icicles which hung inside Meg's bedroom window. Bedroom windows in Sarah's house were never closed, even in a gale, because Sarah believed in the unqualified benefits of fresh air, however cold. But the clothes did nothing to keep out the rain, and Meg had no mackintosh. When she got wet, the rain seeped through to her vest and knickers and the stockings shrank on her feet. All she could do was grit her teeth, to stop them from chattering, and wait for her body heat to dry her off. Not till Meg was undressed for bed did she shed her damp clothes – always excepting the vest. If Sarah noticed it was damp she gave no sign. Vests, according to one of Sarah's many rules, were never removed till bath night; and that was, as it had always been throughout Sarah's long life, once a week, on Fridays. If Meg caught a feverish cold Sarah's standard remedy was to administer a strong dose of castor oil, followed by a dab of wintergreen ointment on the child's nose. If this did not work, and Meg looked particularly flushed, Sarah gave her a bowl of bread and milk laced with cough medicine. Only when the school sent a note, advising that she be kept at home, was Meg allowed to remain indoors but, even then, never to stay in bed. 'That,' Meg heard Sarah say to Mr Loveday, 'is how people die.'

Nathan Loveday was a tall, white-haired man who had twinkling blue eyes. He lived only a few doors up the hill from Sarah. He was so nice that even Sarah never quarrelled with him. Perhaps, thought Meg, as she explored his potato patch, if he does find out, he won't tell. In this she was right, for the day came when he literally caught her red-handed, nibbling a handful of his radishes. Scarlet with shame and hopping in discomfort from one foot to the other, she was too scared to run and too tongue-tied to speak. Looking down at her from his great height, Mr Loveday laughed and said, 'So you're the little rabbit!' and patted her on the head. 'It's all right, lass,' he went on, when he noticed her trembling, 'there's plenty there.'

'I'm sorry,' Meg blurted out. 'I won't do it again, I promise.' She looked up at him anxiously. 'You won't . . .' Her voice trailed away miserably.

'No. No,' he answered quietly. And nodding quickly she fled, leaving him to ponder – not for the first time – about Sarah Dawkins whom, like the Wagstaffs, he had known for forty years. But unlike the Wagstaffs, he felt no hatred, no deep-rooted dislike of Sarah; only pity.

Nathan Loveday remembered when Sarah was a handsome, vivid woman, and full of life. She was too lively, too impatient a person to settle in a place like Witheringham – but then young Cissie had been a sickly child. The girl owed her life to her mother – not that Sarah, by all accounts, let her forget the fact. But Sarah was like that: one of the strangest mixtures he'd ever come across. When it looked as if Cissie was going to die from pneumonia, Sarah threw the doctor out of the house, nursed the child day and night, and pulled her through by sheer will-power. No, Sarah Dawkins shouldn't have come here – not to this town. It was an inhospitable place, always had been. It didn't bother him, because he himself came from a village where people had never gone in for living in each other's pockets. Here, everyone cold-shouldered everyone else. He felt sorry for Sarah, remembering how she had tried to make friends. The trouble was she had set about it in the wrong way, always trying to show off. She didn't mean to, not really. At least – that was how he saw it. She just didn't fit in. The Witheringham folk would never take to her: they were too snobbish for that; and the Clayhurst ones, well, they didn't like to be rushed. Sarah was too quick, too volatile and always a shade too inquisitive for them. Then there was poor old Henry. What a dance she had led him! Nagged him from dawn to dusk, not caring if the whole world heard what she called him, and then spring-cleaning the house in the middle of the night to stop herself from smashing the place to pieces.

What a woman! (Or as his Clarrie once put it: 'It's a demon she's got in there; a demon that'll be there till she dies, if it doesn't come home to roost before.')

Yet Sarah Dawkins impressed Nathan Loveday in one important respect. She was amazingly gifted with plants; whatever she touched flourished. She did not pamper them, scorning his advice to protect anything delicate from an impending frost. 'There's nothing kind in nature,' she told him once. 'Protect a plant and it'll get used to it. Then one night you'll forget, and it'll die. So it's best to get it used to the idea of surviving on its own, right from the start. If it makes it, then it'll make it right through. If it doesn't, well – it'll die, and that's the end of it.' It was a way of thinking that was foreign to him. His thoughts returned to his radishes. No, he decided, people are what they are and that meant you could never really tell. There was nothing he could do. It would only make trouble, even if he did think the child was every bit as hungry as she looked. A queer little thing, but she knew how to use her eyes. He had several times seen her in Back Lane looking at the coppiced willows lining the hedge; and looking in a way he, as a countryman, understood. Once, out of interest, he stopped and watched with amusement to see the child so absorbed, her eyes travelling from the leaves to the sky and back again.

'Well, then,' he commented at last. 'What do you think it is?'

'I don't know,' she answered him, frowning. 'They're showing their backs. I thought that meant it was going to rain, because that's what leaves usually do when it rains. But it doesn't look rainy.'

'What about the wind?' he suggested.

'I hadn't thought of that,' she confessed, turning about to feel it.

'Where do you think it's coming from?'

'Over there.' She pointed in the direction of the wood.

'Where's that?'

'It's where the sun sets.'

'Yes, but which direction is it?'

She shook her head.

'It's west,' he told her. 'When the wind is blowing from the west, it's the rain wind. That's why the willows have turned. If it doesn't rain before nightfall then you can be sure it will rain during the night – unless, of course, the wind changes. But I don't think it will.'

The child looked up and gave him a smile of astonishing sweetness. Taken aback, he raised his hat to her.

'Well, I'll be getting along. But there's just one thing. If the sun sets in the west, where does it rise?'

The child thought for a moment. 'Opposite,' she began slowly. 'Why, it must be in the east!'

'That's the way!' He smiled as she scampered off, giving him a wave of her arm.

A few days before Christmas Day, Cissie suddenly produced the money-box into which Meg had been dropping a ha'penny a week since her arrival in Sarah's house. Handing her a tiny key, Cissie told the mystified child to unlock the box. A pile of coins tumbled out on to the table. As Meg sat and stared at them Cissie, with an encouraging smile, told her to count them.

'How much is there?'

'Fourteen ha'pennies,' came the prompt reply.

'Which is what?'

'Seven pence.' Meg studied the neat pile she had made with interest.

'There we are then,' Cissie announced. 'Now you'll be able to get your Christmas presents, won't you?'

'Is it mine?' Meg whisperered in awe, 'seven pence?'

'Of course it is,' Cissie laughed. 'Hasn't it come out of your money-box?'

'What do I do with it?' Meg blurted the question out before she could stop herself, regretting it immediately when both Dot and Sarah snorted with laughter.

'Daft as a box of lights with a head like a sieve!' Sarah made a sudden movement, which caused the child to flinch. But the old woman was only reaching for the kettle. 'Silly little fool,' Sarah added contemptuously. 'Why you bother is beyond me.'

Even Sarah's sour comments could not detract from the excitement Meg felt, excitement which mounted with every minute as she set off with Dot the following afternoon on her first excursion into Witheringham. Meg knew the lower end of Lonsdale Road, but she had never before walked its whole length, about three miles. It would take the two girls an hour to reach the town, with the child trotting to keep up with Dot's much longer stride. As they passed St Dunstan's vicarage, Meg saw through the hedge a great lawn with a net stretched across it; a net that sagged and was full of holes. Sometimes Dot would answer her many questions, other times she refused. The lawn, it seemed, was a 'tennis court'. Meg repeated the words to herself, wondering what they meant. Now they were passing the entrance to something Dot called the 'wreck'. There they stopped, with the older girl debating whether or not to take that route into Witheringham – through the 'wreck', past the coal yards and up Iron Mill Lane.

'What's there?' Meg enquired, less interested in the vegetable plots that lined the path into the 'wreck' – vegetable plots which replaced the ornamental shrubbery of pre-war days – than in a bridge she saw in the distance.

'Oh, swings and things,' Dot replied vaguely, 'but we can't go on them. They've all been locked up.'

They continued up Lonsdale Road. 'Isn't it Iron Mill Lane you go to after school on Thursdays?' the child wanted to know.

'Yes.'

'Why?'

'None of your business.' Dot, kicking a stone, passed it to Meg, who flipped it back with the toe of her shoe.

'You'll know soon enough, after I leave school.'

'You going to leave then?'

'Next March.'

'What'll you do?'

'Get a job.'

'Like Aunt Cissie?'

'Better than hers!' Dot boasted. 'I'll earn more than she does. You see.'

'What'll I have to do on Thursdays then?'

'Take the cheque to the grocer.'

Meg looked at Dot enquiringly. 'You don't know what a cheque is, do you?' Dot taunted her.

''Course I do! It's a pattern – squares, like the curtains in the scullery.'

'That's different. I'm talking about money.'

'Oh.'

They walked on for a bit without speaking. Dot looked thoughtful. At last, she said: 'The grocer cashes it.' Meg said nothing. 'I bring it to her.'

'What?'

'The money, of course.'

'But it's she who gives him money, not the other way round!' Meg protested.

'I know. But first she has to get some money, doesn't she, stupid?'

'I thought she had money.'

'All right. Where does it come from?'

'I don't know,' Meg admitted.

'You don't know anything,' Dot told her.

There was another silence.

'Look,' Dot tried again. 'She gets money from Aunt Cissie, who gets paid for working at Lacey's. Right?' Meg nodded, but still felt out of her depth. 'Then she gets money for us.'

This was news to the child, who stopped to regard Dot with interest. 'Who from?' she asked.

'The London County Council.'

'What's that?'

'The people we belong to.'

Meg looked uncertainly at Dot. They were touching on a subject which made her nervous. She didn't like this word 'belong', having already decided that she didn't propose to belong to anyone if she could help it – not inside, at least. 'Did they buy us?'

'Buy us? What are you talking about? People don't buy other people!'

The child looked relieved. 'They used to,' she remarked briefly.

Dot stared at her, incredulous. 'Is that what you've been thinking? Truly?'

Meg nodded, but went on to say: 'Except I thought it was *her*.'

'You must be joking! She just gets paid for looking after us, that's all.'

'Why do we live with her?' the child wanted to know.

'I don't know.' Dot's face became expressionless. Preoccupied they walked along in silence, as if each were trying to find the answer to a riddle. It was the child who spoke first.

'Are they rich?'

'The LCC? Oh, I expect so.'

'What about us – what are we?'

Dot laughed. 'Guess.'

Meg thought for a bit. 'We're poor, aren't we?'

'About as poor as church mice, I'd say,' came Dot's rueful comment. 'But one thing I know. She doesn't spend a half of what they send on us.'

Past Iron Mill Bridge, where Meg caught glimpses of the railway line, the houses in Lonsdale Road were even larger than those further down; they were several storeys high and, though built of brick, had stucco fronts which were peeling badly. Meg did not notice this so much as their size, however, and the fact that they had enormous ground-floor windows, covered awnings and above the doors pretty fanlights made of coloured glass which gleamed with flashes of light from the wintry, December sun. Many of the houses were set in large gardens which were overgrown and contained trees and shrubs of a kind the child had never seen before. One so caught her eye that she stood quite still to look at it. Dot, realizing that she had left the child behind, came storming back.

'What are you doing?' she demanded irritably.

'Dot, look!'

'What?'

'That,' Meg cried, pointing at a garden. Dot slapped her hand down.

'I've told you before, you're not to point. It's common!'

'But what is it?' the child insisted.

Dot glanced up. 'That old tree?'

'Yes.'

'That,' Dot informed her haughtily, 'is a monkey-puzzle tree. Now for goodness' sake – come on!'

She pushed the child ahead of her, driving her just as if she were taking her to market. When the pace slackened and they were once more walking side by side, Meg asked, 'Why is it called a monkey-puzzle tree?'

The older girl came to an abrupt halt and regarded Meg coldly. 'Shall I tell you something, Margaret Chandler? You drive me mad! Why this, why that, why the other. Why I have to get saddled with you I don't know. It's not fair!'

Meg, however, was determined. 'Please, Dot,' she pleaded. 'It's such a funny name for a tree.'

It was so tall it made her dizzy even to look up at it. Dark green in colour it had a scaly-looking bark and cruel, sickle-shaped boughs that turned downwards. It was the most menacing-looking tree she had ever come across.

'We-ell,' Dot began slowly, 'I could tell you, but you'd have to promise not to tell a soul.'

Meg, eager to know, gave her solemn oath.

'The fact is,' Dot went on, 'it's less to do with the trees themselves than who owns them. They're not exactly people, you see.' She looked at the child meaningfully.

Meg, seeing the look, stopped dead in her tracks and looked up at Dot with eyes as round as saucers. 'What are they?' she asked, trying to keep the quiver out of her voice. Dot walked on. Meg ran after her. 'Dot,' she wailed, 'what are you saying?'

Dot shook her head and sighed heavily.

Meg tried to think, but was unnerved by the images forming in her mind. Plucking up her courage, as she trotted by Dot's side, she asked: 'They're not . . . they're not monkeys, are they?'

Dot paused, as if to think for a moment. 'No,' she replied carefully, 'they're not monkeys.'

'But if they're not people and they're not monkeys . . . then what are they?' Meg was bewildered now, as well as fearful. The trunk of the tree reminded her of something she had seen in a book – a thing with scales all over its body . . . a long sinuous head . . . a jaw full of teeth – the dinosaur which made her shudder. Then she saw Dot's face convulsed with laughter.

With a great whoop and a bound the older girl raced ahead, spinning in wild circles, her thumb to her nose as she waggled her fingers at the windows of the houses on either side of them. 'Old fogies!' she yelled at the top of her voice, 'nothing but miserable old fogies!'

When Meg finally caught up with her, Dot was sitting on a wall, still laughing uproariously. The child was perplexed as well as reproachful. Seeing her expression, Dot wiped the tears from her eyes and gasped: 'You don't even know what they are, do you?' Meg didn't know what to say, and they walked on, but as they walked she saw Dot's mirth subside. Now the older girl's face was sullen. She was often like this, swinging from one mood to another.

'I hate this place,' she exploded.

'Is it because of her?' Meg enquired, after a long silence.

'No. It's not just her – it's all of them. They hate us. When I grow up I'm going to leave this horrible town. I'll go away like Bess. (This was Dot's elder sister, who was shortly to marry a soldier. Bess had also been in Sarah's charge and was returning to Witheringham for Christmas.) And I'll never come back!' As if to emphasize the vehemence of her words, Dot tore angrily at a privet hedge, snapping and breaking twigs and scattering leaves on the pavement.

The child said nothing.

'D'you know why they hate us?' Dot asked suddenly. Meg shook her head. 'Because we're young – that's all. Just because we're young!' She waved her arms at the great houses which now loomed remote and detached from both road and passers-by. 'In there, and right through this place, are nothing but old people. Old like her. This place belongs to them, you see. That's why they hate us.'

'Would they hit us?' Meg felt anxious.

'No . . . At least, I don't think so. That's just her. They show it differently. They think we're scum.'

'But what have we done?'

'Nothing. Nothing at all. We've done nothing to them, yet all they do is pick on us.'

'D'you mean you and me?'

'Not us in particular. Just anyone who's young, who wants to live. They're waiting to die, you see. Bess says they're jealous.'

'Does everyone die?' Meg wanted to know.

' 'Course they do, one day. But I shall live to be a hundred; and so will you, if you behave yourself and remember to get out of this God-awful place when the time comes.'

The top of Lonsdale Road was thronged with people waiting at a busy crossroads for buses to pass. As the two girls made their way through the crush, they were twice pushed off the curb. Surrounded by elderly women, with only a few fierce, white-haired men striding along with straight backs and swinging canes, Meg was dismayed by the balefulness of the faces she saw. Caught in the crowd, the girls found themselves pressed against two women, who pushed them back with the points of their umbrellas. One of them reminded Meg of Miss Braddock; she had bulging eyes, a red face and an equally pugnacious expression. The other was mottled and leathery-looking, her skin hanging in folds from her chin; round her neck lay a fox, its eyes glittering brightly, while its bushy tail and claws hung down the front of the woman's coat. The child recoiled in horror, her eyes fixed and staring. The women stared back with ill-concealed disdain.

'Really,' said one, 'this town is getting worse. If they continue to let more riff-raff in I shall complain.' Not once, while she spoke, did the woman take her eyes off the two girls.

'They're impertinent too, especially the children,' the leathery-faced one said. 'We really shall have to do something about it, and soon.'

Meg moved hurriedly on, fearful of what was to come, while Dot glared at the women with all the venom she could muster. They only pulled their skirts around themselves protectively, however, and lumbered off like the pair of prehistoric monsters they resembled.

Blazing with temper, Dot dragged the child across the road and round the corner. Pushing their way through the crowds they eventually came to – a palace. Or so Meg thought. Looking up she saw it was called WOOLWORTH. She had never seen anything so magnificent and, as it seemed to her, full of every sort of merchandise. Clearly, she had just entered Fairyland. Trailing after Dot, Meg stuck as close as possible to the older girl, even going so far as to clutch at Dot's coat. Irritated, Dot slapped the child's hand away. But Meg had a problem; one which had been gnawing at her ever since Cissie let her open the money-box. Although she was now the proud possessor of fourteen ha'pennies, she didn't know what to do with them; and with Dot still cross, she did not want – nor know how, without losing face – to ask Dot for help. She decided to wait. She would watch what Dot did with her money. Stopping at a counter, Dot purchased a wooden spoon. Meg promptly did the same. Dot, with hands on hips, surveyed the child.

'And what d'you think you're doing?' she enquired sarcastically.

'I don't know,' Meg replied.

'Oh God!' Dot groaned, snatching the spoon from Meg's hand. 'Miss!' she bellowed. 'I'm sorry, but will you exchange this for something?' Dot pointed at the child. 'She's a bit daft,' she said, tapping the side of her head and screwing her finger back and forth to indicate her meaning more clearly.

'Wot, soft in the 'ead?' A buck-toothed girl peered at Meg, gawping with interest.

'Yes,' Dot smirked.

'Ga'arn! 'Ood ha' thought it! Relation o' your'n?'

'Not likely,' Dot muttered.

'Them that's soft in the 'ead doan live long, d'ya know that?' She stared at the child, open-mouthed. Clearly she already had her shrouded and dispatched to the next world. Meg, beside herself, tried to speak – only to find herself stuttering, which immediately confirmed in the assistant's eyes the story Dot had fed her. 'Never mind, duck,' the girl crooned at her. ' 'Ere, give Lil' yer spoon, an' she'll see wot she can find yer.'

In this way, Meg found herself in possession of a dish-cloth. Inwardly seething, Meg realized that she had no option but to confess her dilemma to Dot. What to others might have seemed self-evident was not to the child. All her previous Christmases (or those she could remember) had been spent under wartime conditions at St Anne's. Until now, there had never been anything special about the festive season for Meg. Christmas morning at St Anne's had begun like any other: with breakfast, followed by chapel – which made the day feel like Sunday. Only when, boys and girls together, they congregated in the drill hall, did anything unusual happen. Sitting on the floor, they waited to hear their names called out. As each child raised its arm, someone handed it an unwrapped present. With no money to spend, and no example set, it never occurred to Meg that people gave Christmas presents to each other.

'How stupid can you be?' Dot asked, looking down at the mutinous child. 'At Christmas, you always buy presents for other people!'

'Who've I bought the dish-cloth for?' Meg wanted to know.

'Her.'

'What do I give Aunt Cissie?'

Dot examined the child's funds. 'Come on,' she said, still snorting with laughter, and led Meg to a counter where she purchased two bundles of grey, furry-looking sticks that bent at her touch.

'Whatever are they?' Meg queried, unaware that she had just bought two packets of pipe-cleaners – one for Cissie and one for Dot – or that pipe-cleaners during the war were being used as hair-curlers and, by Dot and her friends, as appliances for secretly darkening their eyelashes with boot polish.

'For heaven's sake!' Dot exclaimed. 'They're cheap and they're useful. Now will you just shut up!'

To Meg's regret, the spending spree was over. With plenty of time left before Sarah expected them back at the house, Dot took her down the High Street and into the old part of the town. Descending Naboth's Walk, they entered the Colonnade. Seated on a bench beneath a tree in the middle of a deserted courtyard, they were inside one of the strangest places the child had yet seen. Despite the fact that the Colonnade was open at both ends, it felt enclosed. The entrances to the courtyard were narrow and on each side stood buildings and shops – some with overhanging storeys – set back under covered ways, which were supported by columns and roofs.

'I like it here,' Dot confided. 'Even if it is very old.' Meg was surprised. 'You know,' Dot continued, 'Miss Wilkinson says that once upon a time people used to come here every night to dance. Can you imagine!'

The child tried, but could not. Everything was damp, chill and tired-looking – empty shops with planks of wood nailed across their fronts, their windows thick with dust; inside, nothing but bare counters, overturned crates, solitary-looking objects. What was Dot talking about? There was nothing here. All had been forgotten, lost or abandoned. Meg looked upwards, her eyes searching the boughs of the linden tree, fanning out in a circle above, a handful of leaves as thin and bright as sheets of beaten gold. 'How old did you say it was?' she asked.

'Oh, hundreds and hundreds of years, I think. They built it when people wore long dresses, like at weddings.'

'Yes,' the child said dreamily, 'I remember . . . The dresses were made of satin and silk and the shoes had pointed toes – not square like Aunt Cissie's. There were silver buckles and velvet bows and the ladies carried fans . . .' Now she could both see and feel it all. She turned eagerly to Dot. 'It was like that, wasn't it?'

Dot led her to a well. Peering down, they studied the cracked, brown-stained basin first placed there nearly two hundred years before. Dot leaned forward, reaching for a length of heavy, rust-covered chain. Attached to its end was a battered, shallow metal bowl. She dipped it into the water, scooping up a handful of brackish water. 'Here,' she suggested, 'try some.'

Meg took a sip. 'Ugh!' she exclaimed, spitting it out. 'It's horrible!'

Dot burst out laughing. 'That's what they all came here for in the first place – to drink that. It beats me. It's filthy.'

'Why did they want to drink it?'

'Oh, some story got around that it was supposed to be

good for you. That's why everyone round here lives so long – worse luck!'

'It's dirty!' the child announced in disgust, looking again at the discoloured granite basin covered in slime.

As the children left, as they stepped beyond the threshold of the Colonnade, a sudden gust of wind tore through a mound of withered leaves outside, scattering them and sending them soaring again, like a company of vengeful bats. The child looked back – looked back to the Colonnade. As if through a mist, she heard the echo of a merry laugh. Relieved, she made for the Graze – the heath that lay at the edge of the old town – running fleet-footedly to catch up with Dot. Scrambling higher and higher, they went leaping from one tussock of springy turf to another till, panting for breath, they came to rest against some trees in Zemaraim Place. As they waited to get their breath back, the child looked down on the scene that stretched below them: the heath rolling its way across to a horizon, beyond which lay a great forest. 'It's so beautiful,' she whispered, startling Dot with her expression. She saw Dot's look and recovered herself quickly. She had been foolish to reveal herself so nakedly.

'You're a queer one, d'you know that?' Dot's voice was suspicious, almost resentful.

'Nah!' Meg mimicked, in an effort to distract the girl. 'Nah!' she repeated. 'Ah'm jist a bit soft in the 'ead!'

And laughing, the two girls made their way back to Clayhurst.

When Dot's sister, Bess, came to visit for a few days, Meg was given the best gift she was ever to receive in Sarah Dawkins' house: a room of her own. Since Bess was to share the big brass bed with Dot, the child was transferred to the slip of a room that lay above the scullery; and once there, she was never moved back. Tiny though the room was, it had a large window directly overlooking Nokes Wood and the setting sun. The joy Meg felt she concealed – for fear Sarah would snatch the room from her; and though she wasn't allowed to close her door – only to pull it to – having privacy at last was an overwhelming relief. What she didn't realize at the time was that it was Bess who persuaded Sarah to let her sleep with Dot, ostensibly to keep a sisterly eye on her. But Bess had a quite different motive.

In her room next door, Meg could catch snatches of the sisters' whispered conversation in bed, and what she heard intrigued her. Dot, it seemed, had to 'escape' – just as Bess had; but unlike Bess she would not be able to join the Women's Land Army; nor could she escape for several years. When Dot reached a 'certain age' she would be 'free' to walk out of Sarah's house and no one would be able to stop her. She must 'never let on to a living soul' (least of all Sarah) that she knew this. If she did, Sarah might do things to prevent it. In addition Bess advised her: 'For God's sake don't get into any kind of trouble – no pinching, and be careful with boys.' Otherwise 'they'll get you'.

All this talk of 'escape' fascinated Meg. The only thing she could think of herself was running away. The snag was, she didn't know where to go. There was St Anne's, of course, but she didn't know where St Anne's was – only that it must be a very long way away. It had taken all day to get to Witheringham on the train with Miss Braddock and trains moved faster than people. Even if she found the orphanage, would they let her back in? Anyway, wasn't it the people there who had sent her to Sarah's in the first place? Suppose, if she got there, they sent her back? What would Sarah do to her then? She shuddered at the thought and hurriedly put the problem away in the back of her mind. Besides, she was too excited about Christmas and all her attention was really focused on how best to wrap the gifts she had bought – gifts of which she was very proud.

The first surprise, as Christmas morning dawned, was the Christmas stocking. Cissie had explained that if Meg was extra good, Father Christmas might call with something for her. The child had heard of this person, though she had only the vaguest notion of who or what he was. But she had done her best to behave as perfectly as possible in the hope that he might remember her. Waking while it was still dark, she fumbled around until she found a paper bag at the foot of her bed, and shivering with excitement, tiptoed over to the tin trunk standing – covered with a heavy quilt – in front of the window. Opening the bag in the moonlight she found an apple, two toffees, some kind of puzzle that rattled when she shook it, and a hooter. She blew the hooter, hesitantly, and was enchanted when a feather shot out.

There were more surprises at breakfast. By the side of each plate lay a pile of presents; but only when everyone had finished eating might they be opened. Meg was in such a state of fevered anticipation that she was hardly able to eat her food – a special dish of fried bread and streaky bacon with a bottled tomato on top. At last Sarah gave the signal and, watching what the others did – how they thanked each other for what they had received – she reached for her largest parcel. Holding her breath, and conscious of everyone's eyes upon her, she slowly untied the wool, folded back the wrapping paper and saw – a doll. A beautifully knitted doll . . .

As her hands fell away, the child was aware of nothing save a terrible exhaustion – an exhaustion so great that she now wanted nothing more from life than to crawl into a corner somewhere and sleep in the hope that she might never wake up. She seemed to be floating, to be looking down, as if from a great height, on the faces of the strangers beneath. Sarah's face was twisted, contorted with rage; Cissie looked embarrassed; Bess sat expressionless; Dot was staring at the tablecloth.

It was bitterly chill in her room. How long she had been sitting on the trunk by the window she neither knew nor cared. With her forehead pressed against the windowpane, she gently traced with her forefinger the feathery ferns of ice that lay, as if incised, on the glass. Through the ice lay a landscape to match her own – one that was bare, bleak, dark and beleaguered, as the wind swept in capricious blasts through the frost-blackened leaves and withered branches of the trees outside. From the room below, from which she had been banished after she had refused so much as to touch the doll, came the familiar sounds: a never-ending disputatious wail of misery and unhappiness, punctuated by silences more deadly than the strife. Like a traveller in a foreign land, she observed the hell people create on the one hand, her own loneliness on the other. She was on a journey. She knew that now. A journey where feeling would matter less than looking. The purpose of the journey was to remind her what the underworld of life was like, so that she would never confuse it with its more reassuring surfaces. It was irrelevant if no one else understood this, provided she herself understood it and – one day – found a way of accepting it.

When they fetched her down, the soldier Bess was to marry had arrived – a blond giant of a man from New Zealand. She ate her dinner calmly and then, while the others adjourned to the parlour, she sat on her chair in the kitchen, her mind closed to further thoughts, and studied the wallpaper, engrossing herself so deeply that the periodic gusts of laughter from the parlour made no impression on her. So remote did she become that she jumped when she saw Bess and the soldier standing before her. Bess touched her on the shoulder.

'Come on, kid. I know what the old witch did. Dot told me.'

Only then, as Bess put an arm round her, did tears trickle down the child's cheeks.

'Here,' the soldier said, tilting her chin up as he produced a khaki handkerchief, 'have a good blow. Soldiers don't cry now, do they?'

And with each holding one of her hands, they led her into the parlour, ignored Sarah's protests, and placed her safely between the two of them on the sofa.

'Now then, Mother,' the soldier drawled in his slow way. 'How about another round of that game you seem to like so much. What do you call it now – Happy Families?'

BOOK 2

1944–52

The woods are lovely, dark and deep,
But I have promises to keep,
And miles to go before I sleep,
And miles to go before I sleep.

Robert Frost

PART 5

Cuckoo Time

'Stop wiggling your toes. You're supposed to be dead!'

'Why do I always have to be the body?' Meg asked.

' 'Cos you're a tich,' Dot replied.

Swathed in bandages and with both arms and legs in splints, Meg lay tied to an improvised stretcher made by Dot and her friend Vinny from two broom handles and an old coat belonging to Miss Cuthbert of the St John Ambulance Association.

'Now,' Miss Cuthbert called, clapping her hands together, 'I want two girls to stand on one side of the stretcher and two on the other. When I blow the whistle take up your positions facing the body. Do please try to remember the drill. You, Josephine and Marjorie Perkins, must turn left. Dorothy and Lavinia, right.'

'No, no,' she cried. 'If you walk off like that the stretcher will come apart and the body fall to the ground. Let's try again. Good! Now – knees bend. Grasp the stretcher handle, lift . . . and run!'

'Gently,' Miss Cuthbert shouted, as the four girls galloped down the hall to the cheers of other would-be stretcher bearers seated on the floor. Halfway down they met a barricade composed of chairs piled one upon the other. 'Lift, don't throw the stretcher over!' But Miss Cuthbert's words were lost in the roar that went up from the children, and the body was hurled across.

Dot, grinning triumphantly, bent down to unstrap a shaken Meg.

'Just you wait,' the child muttered, 'till you're the casualty!'

Meg, at seven, liked important-sounding words. She discovered 'casualty' after Sarah Dawkins unexpectedly agreed to let the two girls attend First Aid Classes in St Swithin's Parish Hall. Each Saturday afternoon, Dot and Meg shot up the hill, racing to be the first that week to fasten to the Parish Hall door the banner that was their unit's rallying cry:

DEATH IS NOT TO BE ASSUMED BECAUSE SIGNS OF LIFE ARE ABSENT.

'It's St Valentine's Day on Monday,' Dot observed inconsequentially. 'I wonder who my true love will be.'

Inside the hall the children loudly exercised their choice between being 'wounded' or 'rescued', a 'casualty' or a 'bearer'; and spent most of their time bandaging and tying each other up (to the envy of the boys whom Miss Cuthbert kept hanging about outside because she said they were too rowdy to be admitted to her classes). They learnt the difference between reef and granny knots and practised doing 'pick-a-back' for carrying the 'wounded' about.

When there were no boys outside, it meant they had gone to the quarry. If that was the case, that was where Dot wanted to be. As soon as First Aid was over, she scurried along Quarry Road, dragging Meg with her as a protection against wagging tongues.

'That's a rifle he's got there!' Like a pack of hounds the boys drew together and edged cautiously forward in the direction of a newly erected barbed-wire fence, half hoping to take the guard by surprise, half hoping he would challenge them – just as if they were the enemy. Inside the fence, men were moving about with pickaxes and shovels, piling rubble and soil into a bomb crater. The guard wore khaki but the men were clad in navy blue. Stamped across their backs were the bright yellow letters POW. When the boys got bored, they grew restless. Still hoping to catch the soldier's eye, they whispered furtively among themselves. One boy stooped to pick up a stone. Others followed suit and, egging each other on, hurled the stones into the crater.

' 'Ere, Mister,' one of them called, kicking the fence with his boot. 'Want any 'elp with this lot then?'

The soldier's glance was brief, disdainful.

'Why don't yer shoot the bastards?' jeered another, while the rest dissolved into nervous laughter. 'Nah! 'E's yeller!'

This last sally sent them all prancing about, sputtering derisively with imaginary guns: bup, bup, bup . . . bup, bup, bup . . .

The soldier turned, his right hand gesturing in the direction of his weapon. The boys' eyes widened in a mixture of horror, uncertainty – and pure delight. 'Ga'arn, yer cheeky devils!' he shouted, as they fled, tumbling noisily into each other.

Seeing the girls approach the fence, one of the boys yelled over his shoulder: 'Watch it, Dot. Yer don't want 'im fer yer Valentine!'

The soldier slung his rifle back and fumbled in his jacket pocket for a cigarette. Standing just beyond the barbed wire, Dot pretended to smooth Meg's hair. 'Sister is she?' he asked conversationally, giving Dot an appraising eye.

'Not really.' Dot flashed him her Rita Hayworth smile and sidled closer. 'She just lives with me.' Now Dot affected a tragic face like Veronica Lake, or was it Joan Crawford? 'She hasn't any parents . . . comes from one of those places . . . you know . . .' Dot put her hand to her mouth and whispered loudly from behind it, 'An orphanage.'

' 'Ow long she bin there?'

'Getting on for three years. Mind you, she's not stupid – well, not really. She can read and write.' Meg felt the soldier's eyes on her and hung her head. 'Now then,' Dot said briskly, prodding the child in the back. 'Enough of that. I've told you before, it's no use feeling sorry for yourself.'

Meg's scowl deepened. She hated Dot when she played the 'little mother' game.

'Poor little sod,' she heard the soldier say. 'What about you then? Evacuee, are yer?'

'Who, me?' Dot was shocked. 'Whatever gave you that idea! I've been here six years – ever since my mother died.'

'What about yer Dad?'

'He's a pilot – flies a Spitfire.'

'I see.' The soldier winked at Meg. 'So yer look after 'er then.'

'Well, you could say that. I mean . . . if I didn't, who would? I blame them.' Dot jerked her head in the direction of the men working below.

The soldier carefully stubbed his cigarette out with the toe of his boot. 'I dunno,' he said at last. 'They're not such a bad lot. Glad to be 'ere, if yer ask me. There's good and bad everywhere and Jerry's no exception. My job is to see they don't run off: that's all.'

'You're not saying you like them!'

'Nah! But 'oo else 'ave I got to talk to in this dump? I'm a Londoner. What's there to do 'ere? It's like trying to roll out the barrel all on your ownsome!'

Dot laughed. 'I'd love to see London. I was born there.'

'Is that right . . .?'

Sensing that Dot and the soldier had forgotten about her, Meg started to inch quietly away. Then she bolted.

Circling the top of the quarry, Meg pushed aside a gorse bush concealing a track that led to a hollow inside the quarry. One quick wriggle and she was under the barbed wire and clambering down the track. Across the hollow stretched a second fence: a rusting coil of wire cutting her off from the bank where the celandines grew. Beyond the bank lay the bomb crater. When Meg was picking flowers or hunting for shrapnel, she went under this fence too. Today, she stayed on the quarry side, her arms wrapped round her legs, her head resting contentedly on her knees.

When she next looked up, she found herself staring through the wire into the bluest eyes she had ever seen. Momentarily she thought of Kathy. But these weren't Kathy's eyes. Kathy's eyes were midnight blue. These, to Meg, seemed as bright as forget-me-nots sprinkled with dew and they belonged to a man – a man who was spreadeagled among the celandines.

Blinking rapidly, Meg scrambled away from the barbed wire and dived under the quarry fence. The man, seeing her move, smiled hesitantly, and then closed his eyes. From the safety of some bushes, Meg peeped out at him. Who was he? What was he doing in the hollow? No one other than herself ever came there. She chewed indecisively on her thumb.

*

A week before Lady Day – 25 March – and two days after her fourteenth birthday, Dot left school to go out to work. The weather was still see-sawing back and forth between bitter frost and sparkling sunshine. Out in the lanes, wind-ruffled and shivery, the spiky-branching blackthorn was dusted with snowflakes as well as early spring clusters of white star flowers. Free from the older girl's custodial presence, Meg temporarily forgot about the hollow. Instead, she raced back to school to play hopscotch, leap-frog, skipping and ball games with her new friend, Josie Perkins. Around her the world was beginning to glisten and throb with life. As the March winds blew, they sent her running helter-skelter all over the place looking for yet one more thing to explore.

'What do you do, you little moggy?' Sarah cried, cuffing her on the back of the head. 'Dance your way to school? This is the second time this year Cissie's had to buy blakeys to put on the toes of your shoes!'

But nothing could dampen Meg's high spirits as she saw the new world emerging around her: bare twigs in the hedgerows dappled with shoots, piercingly green; silver-tipped pussy willow; catkins shimmering with gold. She had never wit-nessed the arrival of spring before. Now, as the days passed, she scampered about finding violets, primroses and paper-thin windflowers – all thrusting their way through mounds of dead leaves; and watched the birds chasing each other from bush to bush, piping and whistling and rippling with sound that soared and dipped, and soared again.

'When's cuckoo time?' she asked her friend Char'ty, when the trees were bursting into leaf and the bracken had started to unfurl.

'When the weather starts 'otting up,' Char'ty replied.

'It's hot now.'

'Ah! But where's the caterpillars?' Meg frowned. 'Stands to reason the cuckoo woan come till 't'as summat t'eat.'

Meg looked thoughtful. 'What's a caterpillar?' She turned her head away as she spoke.

Char'ty's face remained impassive. ' 'Airy worms with 'un-dreds of legs on 'em.'

'Ugh!' Meg grimaced.

'An artful bird, the cuckoo,' Char'ty went on. 'The ma lays its eggs in t'other bird's nest; when the young'un is 'atched, it pushes t'other birds out afore they kin fly.'

'Why?' Meg wanted to know, thinking of the nest she had found in the fork of a tree. It was made of leaves and moss and was lined with scraps of wool. At the bottom lay six grey-blue eggs spotted with brown. Char'ty said it was a linnet's nest.

' 'Cos they get 'ungry – like you.'

'I'm not a cuckoo!'

'Bird o' passage – that's the cuckoo: when the oak and the ash do bear their leaves, the cuckoo comes wi' the April breeze . . . when the rain clouds gather in July, 'tis then the cuckoo makes ready to fly.'

'Rain clouds,' Char'ty continued. 'They'll be leaving the woods for the fields . . . Ready to fly.' Seeing Meg's anxious face, Char'ty smiled, adding: ' 'Course, yer could be a robin, 'cept robins get a mite too fond of 'umans.'

'By the way,' she remarked, as they made their way into Back Lane, 'caterpillars turn into butterflies.'

'No they don't,' Meg retorted. 'I know what a butterfly is. How can a worm be a butterfly!' She stopped. 'What about the legs – what happens to them?' she asked uncertainly.

'Can't say as I know. P'rhaps it's magic. There's a lot o' magic in these parts.'

At the first possible opportunity, Meg set off in quest of a caterpillar. Char'ty said they lived under leaves. Finding none in the wood, or in the hedgerows, Meg made for the hollow, only to hesitate as she approached it. What if the stranger were there? She crept timidly forward. The hollow, to her great disappointment, was empty. But when she wandered in the direction of the quarry entrance, she saw the stranger standing in a group of men, a little distance from the guard. When he caught sight of her, peering through the fence, he winked and rubbed the side of his nose with his forefinger. Delighted with this secret sign of recognition, she impulsively copied it – and then ran away.

When the next day he appeared in the hollow, Meg pretended not to see him, concentrating instead on the daisy-chain she was making. Now and then she peeped – to see if he was noticing her – but each time his eyes were shut. Gazing at the bright blue sky, flecked with puffs of thin white cloud, she played dreamily with the chain; swinging it from side to side, slipping it over her head, looping it in coils round her wrists. Soon her eyelids began to droop when, floating in the air, there came a song, lilting and soft – hovering, then settling, over the jagged wire separating the child from the man.

He's singing in his sleep, she marvelled. And using made-up words, just like I do sometimes. She slipped away, unwilling to disturb another soul who like herself had a private language and sought solace in being alone. Halfway up the track she stopped and, on impulse, turned back. Mr POW (for that, she decided, must be the stranger's name) was awake. Approaching the fence, she removed the daisy chain from her neck and pushed it through the wire. Mister POW hesitated, as if uncertain what to do. Then, crouching down, he picked it up and started to swing it loosely in his hands. Meg, who was following all his movements with her eyes, nodded shyly and turned to go.

'*Danke schön, gnadiges Fräulein,*' Mister POW said gravely, still using his made-up words. '*Was ist ihr Name?*'

Meg shook her head sadly. What was it Miss Wilkinson had said? 'Any girl found speaking to a prisoner of war will be reported to me and severely punished. It will be regarded as an act of gross disobedience.'

She withdrew quickly, but not before she had bestowed on him her sweetest smile – and received his, in return.

*

'None of you know what work is,' Sarah grumbled as she stood at the scullery sink filling a pail of water. 'Well, don't just stand there, you stupid dolt! Get on with the blackleading.'

Now that Dot was working, it was left to Meg to help Sarah with the household chores during the school holidays. With Sarah the routines of life never changed. Each morning she got up at half past six. After emptying her chamber pot, she cleaned out the kitchen range and laid a new fire. Next she set about preparing breakfast for Cissie and herself. By seven o'clock, it was Dot and Meg's turn to rise. Scrambling into her clothes, Meg's first task was to fetch bread from the bakery in Netherfield Road. After breakfast, Meg and Dot washed the dishes (as well as themselves) in a small enamel dish-bowl, and then returned to their rooms to make their beds. While Dot carried in the coal and swept the kitchen floor, Meg dusted the chairs and polished the scullery tap.

The scullery was down some steps leading off the kitchen. Inside there was a table, a chair and a cracked mirror, a gas-fired copper, a wringer and a gas stove which Sarah rarely used (except when there was no coal and the kitchen range was out of action). With gas supplies short, she found the stove unreliable as well as expensive, and would throw a tantrum whenever a penny was needed for the meter under the stairs. The scullery also contained the pantry where perishable foods could be stored. On the floor stood a tall brown bottle which, when empty, Meg took to the local corn chandler's; there, with the aid of a long metal funnel, the proprietor filled it with a pint of malt vinegar from a wooden cask. Next to the vinegar bottle stood a silver-topped siphon of soda water, some Eno's fruit salts and a quantity of pre-war elderberry wine bottled in heavy stone jars. The jars were much given to exploding spontaneously (invariably in the middle of the night), causing great alarm to the household, while the soot that fell down the scullery chimney created more mess than if a bomb had fallen outside. Milk and fats were kept in earthenware coolers which never really worked: the milk turned sour and the margarine melted into a sticky puddle. Then there was the sink, shallow and made of stone, only a few inches deep and nearly as old as Sarah. Chipped and cracked, it stood on high brick pillars and was surmounted by a single, massive brass tap, the importance of which was acknowledged by the polishing it received daily. The tap, for Sarah, was a symbol of control, the only supply of water in the house. No one else was allowed to turn the tap on or off – only to clean it.

Sarah, who liked her home to be spotless, kept Meg busy in the holidays from seven in the morning until two in the afternoon. Monday, being washday, Sarah boiled, rinsed and starched the laundry, calling on the child to help carry water and turn the heavy handle on the wringer. While Sarah pegged the washing out, Meg had to blacklead the range, shine the brass fender and fire tongs, whiten the kitchen hearth, polish the kitchen floor and help Sarah clear up generally in the scullery – remembering always to give a special clean to the scullery tap. On Tuesdays there were the bedrooms to clean ... and the scullery tap. Wednesdays, Meg scoured the gas stove (even if Sarah hadn't used it), scrubbed the scullery table till the wood turned white, and washed and polished the brick floor ... and the scullery tap. Thursdays, there was the parlour to dust, the doorsteps to be whitened, the stair-rods to polish as well as the front door knocker, the lid of the copper ... and the scullery tap. Fridays were easier. All Meg had to do (apart from the scullery tap) was clean out the lavatory, sweep the passageway between the front and back gates, and 'birch' the brick yard outside the back door with a stiff broom and bucket. If there were an hour or so to spare, she was expected to clear all outside paths and passages of snow (if it were winter) and of weeds at all other times. Occasionally, if Sarah thought Meg had worked exceptionally well, Cissie might be permitted to give her a farthing, which – unlike her pocket money – Meg was allowed to spend as she chose.

After the midday meal had been cleared away, Sarah changed her corsets, shoes and frock, brushed and combed her hair and, assured that all was in order (including the child sitting silently on her chair near the window), she called a temporary truce with life. She laid her head on the kitchen table and slept and snored till nearly tea-time.

'You can fetch the darning now,' Sarah announced, when she woke up. 'The trouble with society,' she said, as she threaded a needle, 'is its riff-raff. Bone idle, the lot of you! In my day everyone knew their place, and woe betide you if you forgot. Now we were in trade. You should have seen my mother – quiet as a lamb. I doubt she raised her voice or hand to a living soul. My father, Mr Dobbs, was a different kettle of fish. Handsome enough, with his black silky whiskers. We lived in Limehouse then, close to the Isle of Dogs. You never saw the river, even though you could smell it. No, to see it, you had to go down to Shadwell, or through the Rotherhithe tunnel to Southwark. Round us, there were nothing but high walls and gates with ships' masts towering above . . .

'Mr Dobbs was a fishmonger. Every morning, at four o'clock, he'd take the cart down to Billingsgate. The worst mistake he made was when he tried the fish market at Shadwell. Everyone knew it never worked. You sold fish by hawking it about or from a proper shop – not from a stall, as he tried. Mind you, he knew his way around. He'd served his apprenticeship and he was a journeyman when he married Mother, back in '68. Grandfather Dobbs, Father's father, was a waterman – ferried people from one side of the river to the other, or carried goods to and from the ships. But the business was dying, once they had improved the docks and started building better bridges. So he decided his sons must do something different. He put Mr Dobbs into fish. Paid a premium, he did, to have him taken in, which wasn't easy in those days. No, the fish should have worked as, of course, it did at first. But with nothing but Paddies to buy it, what can you expect? A feckless lot, if ever I saw one! It was the Paddies, never two brass farthings to rub together, who pulled Father down!'

Sarah sighed.

'D'you know what Mr Dobbs used to say?' she asked. ' "I'll not have my children walking about like beggars. It's a fur muff she shall have on Sundays."

'And I did. A real beaver one. How he loved to swing me up in the air and call me his little lady – me, in my red flannel petticoats and Dolly Varden hat and my hair streaming down to my waist. I was the youngest you see – the youngest girl, that is.

'Another thing Mr Dobbs was strict about was he could read and write, you see, though Mother couldn't. Well, it was like that when she was small. A lot of people couldn't read in the 1850s. But for all that we were respectable. No board school for us. Monday morning, she'd give each of us a silver threepenny bit – that's what it cost to attend the Church School. When you're respectable, you always pay to go to school. Once you let anyone in for nothing, look what you get.'

She gave Meg a disapproving look.

'It would do your lot good to have had our headmistress. "The Governess", we called her. If she stopped to speak to you, you had to curtsey when you answered and address her as "Madam". But what a tartar she was!' Sarah threw her head back and shook with laughter. 'The stupid ones were made to wear a dunce's cap and stand with their faces to the wall. If you misbehaved, you'd get the cane, or she'd hang a board round your neck for the rest of the day. It only happened to me once, after I dropped and broke my slate. When Father found out, he gave me the strap, even though Mother tried to stop him. I never forgave him for that. It was the drink you see . . . That's why I signed the pledge, and made Mr Dawkins do the same. An animal he was – when he was in the drink. It wasn't so bad while Mother was alive. He was afraid of her – of the way she stood up to him. But when . . .'

Sarah wiped what looked like a tear from her eye.

'Nothing went right after that,' she muttered. 'I was twelve when I left; that would be 1888. I had passed what they called the Proficiency Test, so I got my Labour Certificate early. That meant I could go out to work. I didn't want to, but with his drinking we needed the money. I went to a furrier in Spitalfields to begin with. They were Jews – friends of Mr Dobbs. Ate a lot of fish as I recall. They gav⁀ me half-a-crown a week and full board and lodging. It's hard, leaving home when you're only twelve, and the work was hard, too. But they were good people – treated me like a daughter, even though I wasn't one of them.

'Of course, we'd moved to Southwark by then. I used to go home on Sundays – if that's what you could call it. He'd set up a fish-curing business – haddocks and the like – just off Tabard Street, close to Borough High Street. It was near there that Little Dorrit lived, so Boz (Charles Dickens) said. Mother loved Boz. She used to ask me to read her something from Boz when she was ill. It was living in Tabard Street that finished her off – living in a slum full of smoke and filth. It was his fault – all his fault. I told him so to his face, even when he brought the strap out. He killed her. They said it was bronchial pneumonia. I say she was too afraid to tell him how ill she was. She was only forty when she died, and she never complained . . .'

Meg shifted uneasily on her chair. She was nervous when Sarah talked about Mr Dobbs, for Sarah's moods could shift dramatically. If she didn't start shouting, she might hit out at someone – Meg, for example.

'No one knows how hard it was,' Sarah said bitterly. ' "I'm not looking after him any more." That's what I told my sister when I asked her to take me in.

' "Well, don't think you can stay with us for long," said she.

' "I'll fend for myself then," said I.

' "What, and starve?' said she.

' "I'll see you all dead, first," said I.'

Sarah licked the end of her thread and tied a knot. 'And I did. They've all gone. I outlived the lot of them. What did I do? What did I say to this family of mine? Rot you, I said. I can look after myself and you needn't worry: I'll kill myself before I come to any of you again for help.'

Meg glanced anxiously at the clock during these sessions, to see how much longer it would be till Cissie and Dot returned from work. Sarah, meanwhile, was rummaging in the cupboard next to the kitchen range. 'I know it's here somewhere,' Meg heard her say as Sarah pulled at the lid of a heavy black box.

'Here we are!' she declared, unfolding a piece of torn and yellowing paper.

Rent 2s

Clothing 1s

Stove oil and candles 4d

Food 3s

Savings 6d

Soap, starch, condiments, blacking 2d

Total 7s

'Seven shillings – that's what I had to live on for a week in 1890.'

To Meg, who had only the occasional farthing to spend, it sounded like a very large sum of money.

'Guts – that's what it takes! That's the trouble with you lot: you haven't any. Nothing but whining and moaning, instead of getting off your backsides and doing something. None of you could have done what I did. D'you know what they'd say in the 1890s? Any girl trying to support herself on less than nine shillings a week would end up on the streets. Well, I proved them wrong! I had to give up the fur business on account of the dust settling on my chest, but the family I worked for found me a cheap room just off Petticoat Lane with another Jewish family. It was cheap because I did jobs for them on Saturdays – that's the Jewish Sunday, what they call the Sabbath. Strict Jews won't do anything on the Sabbath, not even light a fire or answer the door. Some people might think it funny – me working for Jews; but when you're a girl and only fourteen, they're the best people to be with. They look after their girls. You'd never find a Jewish girl on the streets – never!

'The room was unfurnished, of course, and all I had to start with was a mattress on the floor. I scrounged some packing cases from the market, used one as a table, one as a chair, and one for my paraffin stove. That's what I cooked on, and used to keep me warm. Sometimes, I was so cold I'd line my jacket with newspaper, and spread it between the blankets on the bed. That's when I was trimming umbrellas.

'The first few months were the worst – when I was fourteen. Trimming umbrellas is seasonal work and sometimes there wasn't much left over for food. I'd try to have at least one decent meal a day, for I daren't risk falling ill. Even with a fever, I never took to my bed or that would have been the end of me. So, one good meal, with bread and dripping or black treacle the rest of the time. The trouble was that everything was all right provided I earned that seven shillings. If I didn't, it meant the Mission.'

Meg glanced at the clock again. Mention of 'the Mission' was even worse than Mr Dobbs for sending up Sarah's blood pressure, with all its predictable consequences.

'Canting hypocrites,' Sarah stormed. 'What did they know about life? All I needed was three shillings a week . . . a pound of meat pieces for fourpence; half a pound of dripping at tuppence ha'penny; onions a penny; potherbs tuppence; split peas a ha'penny . . . For eightpence I could make a stew on top of the stove – that lasted four meals . . . Bread was ninepence a week, tea fourpence, a tin of milk fivepence ha'penny, potatoes tuppence ha'penny . . .' She stopped. 'How much is that?'

'Two and sixpence ha'penny, I think,' Meg volunteered nervously.

'So there'd be fivepence ha'penny left . . . a bit of bacon, perhaps, with an egg and a tomato . . . I could do haddock and potatoes for tuppence . . . Fridays were worst. I didn't get paid till Saturday, and then perhaps there wasn't much work – no work, no food. That meant the Mission: soup and bread. Have you thought, they said, of going into service? The cheek of it! Me – the daughter of a fishmonger! It's all right for some, I told them. But others have a position to keep up. My mother would have turned in her grave at the thought of one of her daughters becoming a common skivvy . . .'

'Well,' she snapped. 'And what are you staring at? Get outside and weed the path!'

Thankful to escape, Meg worked diligently at her task, digging out the roots of grass that snaked beneath the crazy paving with a bent table fork. It would be school soon, she was thinking. Only a few more days, and she would see Mr POW. Tugging at the grass, something caught her eye, and her fingers closed over a small object gleaming in the sunlight.

Surreptitiously she scooped it up and slipped it down one of her socks. Upstairs, she set about cleaning it, first with a kirby grip, and then with her tongue – licking away the more stubborn dirt. The object was a brooch, shaped in the form of a letter 'M'. Delighted with her find, Meg tiptoed out of bed to retrieve a pencil stub and a scrap of paper. She was going to write a letter – one she had been thinking about for a very long time . . .

33 Pricklers Hill,
Witheringham,
April 14th 1944.

Dear Mother
How are you? I am very well.
I wonder if you remember me.
I am your dorter Margaret
Chandler. I live with Mrs Dawkins.
I am in Standard 4. My teachers
name is Miss Harper. I am
nearly eight. I want to come
home.
Yours Truly,
Margaret Chandler,
P.S. I hope you like the present.
The M stands for Mother.

'Liar!' Sarah screamed, as she thrashed the child. 'You stole it. I know you did. You're a thief – a nasty little thief. I'll have you locked up!'

No punishment was too great for Meg's crime.

'I'll not have a thief in my house. I never have, and I never shall. You gave me that brooch,' Sarah declared, turning to Cissie. 'When she admits the truth, then I'll reconsider the matter. Found it, indeed . . .'

Ten days had passed since Sarah found the matchbox in which Meg had hidden the brooch and letter; ten days – and still no one was allowed to speak to the child, including next-door neighbours, all of whom had been told of her wickedness. When she was not at school or in bed, she sat on the back doorstep. If it rained, she was permitted to sit in the lavatory, as it was outside. She entered the house only at meal-times, when she ate alone in the scullery, and when she went to bed. As she crept through the kitchen on her way upstairs, Sarah ordered Cissie and Dot to move away as if the child were in some way infectious. 'When Satan's around, you can't be too careful,' she heard Sarah say.

Meg was defiant – at first. But as the days passed, she started to feel isolated and afraid. Against her ribs she felt her heart lying heavy as a stone. When she ate, her throat ached so painfully she could barely swallow, and the food tasted like sawdust. At night she cried herself to sleep. During the day the tears trickled silently down her cheeks in a flow she could not stem.

When the weeping ceased, the child no longer felt anything. Barely touching her food, she now refused to eat at all.

'That's enough,' Cissie announced.

'I'll say when it's enough,' Sarah retorted.

'Not this time . . .' Cissie approached the child, who was sitting with her head on the scullery table. 'All right, Meg, it's over now.'

Cissie brought her into the kitchen. 'I think,' she said, 'it's time you told Mother you're sorry.' Meg concentrated on the feel of Cissie's warm hand.

'It's the truth I want,' Sarah flung at her daughter.

'Can you say you're sorry for behaving badly?' Cissie asked gently. Meg shook her head. 'Will you say it for me?' Meg looked up and tried to speak, but what came out was inaudible – even to the child. 'Well, that will have to do. Come and sit down, and let that be an end to it all.'

Across the room Meg felt the old woman's beady eyes on her. 'Your mother's dead,' she remarked conversationally.

Meg turned her head towards the window.

*

Cissie was round-shouldered and dumpy and grew whiskers on her chin. She had dyed black hair – dyed because Sarah firmly believed that if Cissie's employer so much as saw one thread of silver in her daughter's hair, he would sack her. Not immediately, for there was a wartime shortage of labour to fill civilian jobs, but he might be tempted to do so after the war, when the girls in uniform were 'demobbed'. It might not matter then that Cissie had always worked for the same employer (a retail firm of chemists that ran its own book club – Lacey's Circulating Library). When Cissie started work there in 1914 as a fourteen-year-old straight from school, she earned five shillings a week. Thirty years later, having worked her way up to become an assistant in the library section, her weekly wage was £2.

Lacey's catered for fastidious gentlewomen who would rather pay than use the public library. They knew their patronage would ensure the entire library stock was devoted to light romance (for which they had a passion – always provided the book had a happy ending and virtue was seen to triumph). Membership of Lacey's also guaranteed that the book you borrowed had previously been read (or at least handled) by someone as well-bred and, above all, as clean as yourself. Books borrowed from Lacey's never carried the label that was stuck into public library books at this time:

> The Public Health Act, 1936, provides that no person suffering from an infectious or contagious disease shall borrow or use any book from the Library, nor shall any person having a book from the Library permit the same to be used by anyone suffering from an infectious or contagious disease. In cases where an infectious or contagious disease has broken out in a Borrower's house after books have been borrowed, the books must NOT be returned to the Library, but be delivered by hand to the MEDICAL OFFICER OF HEALTH.

Sarah, as a widow, was financially dependent on Cissie. Not yet seventy, Sarah did not qualify for a State pension at that time and her husband, a self-employed man, had not thought to contribute to one of the private pension schemes. Mr Dawkins' death in 1936 clearly took the family by surprise.

When he died, he left Sarah virtually unprovided for. A little money came from the sale of his business, and then there were the savings Sarah had secretly built up from her housekeeping money (but these she was always determined to keep intact).

All the time, Sarah feared the loss of Cissie's weekly wage. Were it to vanish, she and Cissie would have immediately dropped from manageable poverty to absolute penury. Until she thought of taking in children, it was their sole means of support. She did her utmost to allay her anxiety by encouraging Cissie to look old-fashioned. The image of the staid 'maiden daughter' would, Sarah decided, reassure the gentlewomen at Lacey's; they shared Sarah's own conservatism – a conservatism which meant that Sarah disliked anything that could be termed 'modern'. As she, Sarah, had never cut her hair (neither had Sarah's mother – whose hair, it seemed, was once so long that it reached her knees), she saw no reason why Cissie's hair should be cut either. Occasionally Cissie was permitted a change in style, but for a number of years even this had been denied her. So though Cissie's hair was regularly dyed, she still wore it in two neat plaits wound round her ears in what was a decidedly dated fashion known as 'ear-phones'. This gave away her age far more obviously than a few grey hairs.

Cissie lived a life that was even more circumscribed than Meg's or Dot's. Cissie had to sleep with Sarah and she was not allowed to go anywhere (other than to work) without her mother. Meg never saw her go for a walk on her own, not even a stroll in the garden. True, she didn't have to ask permission to stand up, sit down, go to the lavatory or leave the room, as the two girls had to. But Sarah always wanted to know *why* Cissie wanted to leave the room. Occasionally, when the weather was fine, Cissie took Sarah out on her afternoon off from work. Sarah would lock the doors of the house and tell Dot (who had the same half-day) to meet Meg from school, and not to return to Prickler's Hill before six o'clock. She then handed over enough money to buy the two girls a bun and a cup of tea.

'Don't – she'll see you!'

'It's all right. I'll only take one. Just make sure you keep a proper look-out . . .'

Dot and Meg were sitting alone in a tea shop. Near them, on the windowsill, stood a display jar filled with Fry's chocolate cream bars. As Dot slid out of her chair and dived in the direction of the jar, Meg closed her eyes and tried not to faint.

'Will you be wanting anything else?' the waitress asked.

'No thank you, Miss,' Dot replied pertly, a chocolate bar safely concealed in her coat sleeve.

Outside, Meg fought down the desire to run. 'How could you?' she stormed, once the two of them were safely round the corner and into Iron Mill Lane. 'Suppose she'd seen you? We'd have got locked away. I don't ever want to come out with you again!'

'Oh, shut up! Why d'you have to spoil everything? I only wanted to see if I could – that's all.'

Meg was trembling at the thought of ending up in a dungeon with all her hair cut off. When she calmed down, she realized that Dot wasn't with her. Turning round, she saw Dot standing in the middle of the pavement with an angry expression on her face. She was looking down at the package.

'Folded cardboard,' Dot snorted. 'Can you beat it, I pinched a dummy. How's that for luck? And don't say it serves me right or I'll thump you!'

They walked on in silence towards the 'wreck', where the swings, as usual, were all locked up. It had started to rain.

'Were none of them real?' Meg ventured at last, as they entered the grottoes. Dot ignored her.

The grottoes (or 'dripping wells' as they were sometimes called) were artificial caves created from the overhang of an outcrop of stone which had narrow wooden seats inside. In front was a boating lake. Above the grottoes lay the everyday world of the railway goods depot and its coal yards. Their contribution was an all-pervading smell of coal dust and the intermittent clangour from the shunting yards – the banging of trucks against each other and the high-pitched screech of their flanged wheels on the rails. Inside the grottoes themselves the effect was one of suffocation – the lack of oxygen adding to the psychological fear of being shut away, underground.

'Dot, I don't like it here. Can we go?'

Dot looked at her accusingly. 'You didn't go to First Aid last Saturday.' Meg pulled a face. 'She'll find out, you know.'

'Not unless someone tells her.'

'How d'you know I won't?'

'Because,' Meg answered matter-of-factly. (When they were both supposed to be in church on Sunday morning, Dot went off to meet a boy. Who was she to start telling tales?)

Dot laughed. 'Here,' she said, pulling out a tattered copy of *Picture Show*, 'have you seen this picture of Betty Grable? Isn't she lovely!' Meg examined the picture critically – the blonde hair, wide smile, bare shoulders and spiky eyelashes. 'D'you think I look like her?' Dot asked eagerly.

'We-ell . . . your hair's as thick, though it's a different colour, and your teeth are straight, and when you put boot polish on your eyes they look a bit like that.'

'Hang on a tick,' said Dot, rummaging in her bag for a mirror. 'Vinny gave me this. It's one of her Mum's. See what a difference it makes.'

Dot dipped a finger into what was left of a tube of lipstick and carefully applied a little of the colour to her lips. Next she dabbed some cream on her face and covered it with dark powder. From a tin of vaseline she took some jelly and smeared it over her eyebrows till they looked wet and greasy. 'How's that?'

Meg nodded. 'Yes, it's good, 'cept you've turned orange. And you'll be in awful trouble if she catches you with all that on. She'll call you a . . .' Meg struggled to recall the word.

'Strumpet?' Dot remarked dryly.

'That's it. What's it mean?'

'How should I know? You're supposed to be the clever one.'

Meg waited for inspiration. 'I know it's something to do with powder and paint, and people who put them on their faces . . .'

'Like Aunt Cissie? She wears talcum powder on her face on Sundays. But I don't think anyone would call her a strumpet. She always looks as if she's just come out of the Ark!'

'But she wasn't in the Flood!'

Dot groaned and returned to gazing at her reflection in the mirror. 'P'rhaps I'll be a film star one day,' she sighed. 'If only I could go to the pictures more often. It isn't fair the way she takes all my money. Out of fifteen shillings a week all I get back is a shilling pocket money – the stingy old cow!'

'What are they like?' Meg asked, as they made their way back to Prickler's Hill.

'What?'

'The pictures.'

'Haven't you ever been?'

Meg shook her head. 'Once I think. I can't remember properly.'

Dot stood still. 'If I tell you something, d'you promise not to tell?'

'As if I ever do!'

'She'd kill me if she found out. Sometimes when she thinks I'm at night school on Mondays, Vinny and I go down to the flea-pit in Iron Mill Lane. You can get in for ninepence. The films are a bit sissy – Buster Keaton and all that, but it's good for a laugh.'

Meg's eyes widened in admiration. Then she thought of something. 'Who told on me – about First Aid?'

'Who d'you think?'

'Beryl Saunders?' Dot nodded. 'How d'you know?'

'I got it from Vinny. You needn't worry. Vinny sorted her out.'

'Thanks,' Meg muttered.

'What'll you do?'

'Ink . . .' Meg said thoughtfully. 'I'm ink monitor at school next week.' She and Josie Perkins would be responsible for adding water to the ink powder and pouring the mixture into the inkwells with the aid of a funnel and jug.

'You'll catch it. You'll have her Mum after you as well as Miss Harper.'

'Not if I make it look like an accident. Josie can always jog my arm, can't she? Just as Beryl Saunders is sitting down I'll aim for her face.'

*

'Don't bring that stuff in here,' Sarah shouted, pushing Meg out of the door. 'Take it back to the wood this instant. You'll put a curse on us all, you silly little fool. Don't you know may's unlucky?'

'Is it?' Meg asked Char'ty disconsolately, still clutching the bunch of white hawthorn blossoms she had picked earlier.

'So some folk say. It ain't never made sense to me neither. The 'awthorn stands for good 'ope. Wot made yer pick it?'

'It's Holy Thursday.' Char'ty looked nonplussed. 'You know – Ascension day – the day Jesus sails up to Heaven on a white cloud. Well . . . there it was – everywhere.'

'Wot?'

'The blossom. Just like clouds, I thought, clouds that have come down to earth. That's how Jesus sailed up – I think – in a sort of white mist.' Meg's voice trailed away. 'Actually, it was Josie's idea to pick it – Josie Perkins. She's invited me to her birthday party, and I thought . . .'

'Yer thought,' Char'ty said, finishing the sentence for Meg, 'that if yer brought 'er a present, t'ole witch'd let yer go.'

Meg nodded. 'I'm not allowed out to tea, or to have anyone back.'

Char'ty lay back, gazing up at the young oak leaves. 'When's your'n?'

'My birthday? May 31st. I think.'

'Why doan yer ask Dot? She's bound t'know.'

'Yes – but she'd just laugh, and tell everyone . . .' Meg stood up to go.

' 'Ere,' Char'ty called after her. 'Ah've jist thought o' summat t'cheer yer up. It'll be Midsummer's Eve next month. P'rhaps Ma Dawkins'll take off – shoot up in the sky like . . . wot d'ya call it . . . Ascension? Mebbe she wouldn't 'ave the 'awthorn 'cos it's wot she rides on, on 'er broomstick. 'Cept she's a bit 'eavy!'

'You mean she'd fall off?' Meg started to giggle.

'Ta, ta!' Char'ty called.

Meg was still giggling when she emerged from Nokes Wood.

'You sound happy,' a voice called from behind a privet hedge. It was Mr Loveday. Straightening up, he removed his panama hat and mopped his brow with a handkerchief. 'Phew!' he announced, 'it's warm today.'

Meg smiled shyly. Mr Loveday was standing in a field of flowers – marigolds, columbines, irises and stocks. She stared at them. Normally Mr Loveday grew vegetables on his allotment.

'You should be at school,' he scolded.

'Not today. It's a half-holiday.'

'It'll be Whitsun soon. I suppose you're going to tell me you have another holiday then.'

'Yes – two days.'

Mr Loveday shook his head, but he was smiling. 'What's that I see in your hand?' he asked, looking at the may. Meg gasped. She had forgotten all about it. 'Here,' the old man said, 'give it to me. I don't suppose Mrs Dawkins will be wanting it.' Meg looked crestfallen. 'You mustn't mind,' he went on. 'Lots of folk are superstitious. It's beautiful stuff, but I'm not sure I'd have it in my house. You can't go against custom – not in these parts. I'll tell you what, why not give her these instead?' He held out a bunch of sweet-smelling stocks. 'She must have been wondering where you'd got to,' he said, 'so you've been helping me, haven't you?'

Meg ran off, waving her thanks. Nathan Loveday watched the child disappear down the lane. Nothing but skin and bone, he told himself. Bend her in half and she'd snap like a twig. Or would she? She had more colour in her cheeks these days, and the way she skipped and danced along . . . well, she must be all right. He knew why she had picked the hawthorn. The elder groves would be out soon; and the roses. A pity when the blossoms had to fall. Then they'd look less like earth-bound clouds and more like falling snow.

Meg went to bed in the middle of the afternoon – or so it seemed to her as she lay shielding her eyes from the rays of a sun still blazing at seven o'clock in the evening. Dot, in her room next door, was setting her hair in metal curlers – something Meg would have hated to sleep in. It was bad enough when Sarah wound Meg's hair in rags. It was all right for Beryl Saunders to look like Shirley Temple – it didn't do for Meg. She didn't mind plaits. But ringlets! She sat up and, flinging back the bedclothes, practised some somersaults.

'Now then,' Dot called, as the bed creaked loudly, 'what are you up to in there?'

Meg pulled a face and lay still.

It hadn't been too bad, she decided. Not as bad as the first time they gave her the doll – at Christmas. Almost a week had passed since they tried it again, on her birthday. It was the same doll, and once more she had refused to touch it. There had been other presents to console her; a whipping top from Dot complete with thong for spinning it round, some transfers from Josie, and Char'ty had promised her string for a cat's cradle. Down in the hollow Meg was making a nest, weaving the grass and twigs together, getting it ready for its first layer of mud. Mister POW hadn't known it was her birthday, because he had started making the animals weeks before. The first one was a little wooden horse – carved, as she now knew from watching him do it, with a penknife. When he pushed the horse through the barbed wire she was afraid to touch it at first. But when he turned his back, she grabbed it. After all, there was no one she might show it to and it was dangerous to carry it around with her, so she buried it under some leaves. Now she had a whole family of animals: horse, pig, dog, cat, and it was time to make them a proper home. They would be safe in the nest she was building.

Tomorrow she would take Mister POW a posy. The blue-bells had faded, but she could make it with silverweed, forget-me-nots, buttercups and daisies, binding the stems with plaited grass and wrapping them in moss to keep the posy moist. It was a pity she had eaten all her sweets. Last week she gave him a wine-gum, saved from the ration Sarah doled out on Sundays. It was a bit grubby and sticky, but then it had been in her mouth first. She couldn't hide it in her sock until Sarah turned her back. By the time she licked it clean it had shrunk, so to make it look like a proper sweet she wrapped it in a beech leaf and tied the ends with grass.

Clapping her hands together to get his attention, she threw the sweet as high as she could, over the fence.

'*Danke schön*,' he called, looking puzzled. She pointed to her mouth. '*Ja, ja*,' he said in his made-up language. '*Sehr gut!*' Then he added, speaking slowly: 'Very good . . .'

It was dark when the child woke up – or nearly so. Summer nights in early June were never more dark than a deep, deep twilight. With her face turned to the wall she listened, straining her ears for the sound which had woken her up. Perhaps she was mistaken. She rolled over, folding her arms under her neck, and stared at the sky. No moon or starshine tonight. They were there – the moon and the stars, but hidden behind rain-laden clouds looming heavy and grey above the tree-tops in the Wood. She listened drowsily to the house – to its barely perceptible beat, a bit like a slow minim: ta, aa, aa, aa. She clapped her hands together silently, the way Miss Harper taught everyone to do it. All of a sudden she jerked upright, holding her breath. There it was – the sound again. There! She pushed back the bedclothes and padded noiselessly to the window, curling up on the old tin trunk, her toes tucked into the hem of her nightgown. Faintly at first, now creeping nearer. She stuffed her fist in her mouth to stop herself trembling. The vibration grew so strong that the house started to shake; and now the room was filled with a deafening roar.

'What's happening?' Dot called in a frightened voice.

Meg pressed her face against the windowpanes.

'Come away, Meg. Do you hear? Come away this instant!' It was Cissie, standing in the doorway flashing her torch.

'It's not a raid.' Cissie tugged at her arm. 'Let's move downstairs. I doubt if anyone's going to sleep any more tonight.'

Everyone was late for school on the morning of Tuesday, 6 June when the BBC announced that the Allied landings in

Normandy had taken place during the night. Some children did not turn up at all. At Assembly they sang:

> When a knight won his spurs, in the stories of old,
> He was gentle and brave, he was gallant and bold.
>
> And let me set free with the sword of my youth,
> From the castle of darkness the power of the truth . . .

'It's the end of the war,' Beryl Saunders declared (for once Miss Harper was letting the children talk quietly instead of doing Scripture). Meg, who was yawning as Beryl spoke, misheard her and thought Beryl had said 'It's the end of the world.'

'What d'you think, Meg?' Josie asked.

'No, I don't think so,' Meg answered vaguely. 'Otherwise we wouldn't be here, would we?'

'Quite right, Margaret,' Miss Harper interrupted cheerfully. 'We'd all be out celebrating. What's the matter, you look surprised?'

PART 6

The Great Adventure

When the engine of the pilotless aircraft stops and the light at the end of the machine is seen to go out it may mean that explosion will follow, perhaps in five to fifteen seconds.

Ministry of Home Security
16 June, 1944

'If you're out in the street, go flat on your face when the engine starts coughing,' were Sarah's instructions to Meg. 'Then get back here.'

'Psst!' Josie went to Meg in class. 'Something's going on.' She glanced swiftly about her to see where Miss Harper was. 'A strange man came to our house last night, and my Mum was crying. I thought it was about Dad – him being in the Army. But it wasn't. When she came into the kitchen she grabbed hold of me and said she wasn't ever going to let me go – no matter what they did.'

'What did she mean . . . let you go?' whispered Meg.

'It's some sort of secret. I'm not supposed to tell.'

Meg stared anxiously at her friend. Before she could speak again, the Vicar arrived. Over his long black cassock he had donned the white surplice he normally wore only in church; stranger still, when the classes congregated in Miss Wilkinson's room, they were joined by the Infants. The Vicar looked solemn. So did the teachers.

'Close your eyes,' the Vicar commanded. 'Let us imagine that each of us is a ship going on a journey.'

Eighty pairs of eyes opened wide.

'When we are on a journey like that, what would we do to make sure that nothing happens to the ships?'

Eighty pairs of eyes opened even wider.

'It is perfectly possible, you see, to be sailing along without colliding or getting in the way of others and yet to have something wrong with the ship itself such as . . . a hole in the hull. What would we do then?'

Out of the corner of her eye Meg saw one of the big girls place a finger to her temple, and gently screw it back and forth.

'Ah!' the Vicar exclaimed, pointing to the girl, 'I think we have someone here who understands.'

'Who, me, Sir?'

'Come along. There's no need to be shy.'

'Her brother's a sailor,' someone called from the back.

'What would he do, Madge?' others chorused.

'Jump overboard!'

The children began to giggle. Even Miss Wilkinson seemed to have difficulty suppressing a smile. The Vicar looked puzzled. 'It's only the stupid ones who stay with a sinking ship, Sir,' the girl explained. 'If you do that, or so my brother says, you'll end up with Davy Jones at the bottom of the sea.'

'Ah! Of course!' the Vicar murmured, 'the hole – how silly of me.' There was a pause while he stood lost in thought, Bible in hand and eyes fixed on the ceiling. He took a deep breath and tried again. 'It may be that the convoy, and our particular ship, isn't sailing in the right direction. Suppose our destination is . . . New York, and we are heading for . . . Calcutta. If that is the case, then the whole purpose of the journey has been missed. We shall never reach New York, shall we?'

It was the children's turn to look puzzled, while Miss Wilkinson moved uneasily on her chair.

'You do see, don't you, that the question we must ask ourselves is where are we going? Are we going to the right place? If not, if we are on the wrong course, wouldn't it be better to heave to and change?'

'Perhaps, Vicar,' Miss Wilkinson whispered hurriedly, with a nod to Miss Harper seated at the piano, 'we should now sing our closing hymn.'

God is working His purpose out as year
  succeeds to year,
God is working his purpose out and the time
  is drawing near;
Nearer and nearer draws the time, the time
  that shall surely be,
When the earth shall be filled with the glory of
  God as the waters cover the sea.

Why if those bombers are 'ours', Meg asked herself, am I
sitting under the kitchen table? It was the second time that
night the siren had wailed the alert. The siren wailed in the
daytime too, but it was the waiting at night for the sound of
the 'all clear' that made her so tired. After she fell asleep
eating her dinner, even Sarah showed some concern. 'You'll
end up looking like an old woman,' she said.

Meg stared at her reflection in the bedroom mirror, searching for signs of wrinkles. Relieved to find none, she wished
nevertheless that the bones in her face didn't show so much,
nor the dark shadows under her eyes. Was she peculiar? She'd
heard people saying that she looked like an elf. Now Sarah
was talking about her being old. All she wanted was to be
normal.

The effects of the raids turned the ordered routines of Meg's
life topsy-turvy. Now, as each day dawned, she no longer
knew what it would bring. School, when she arrived, might
be shut; or if open, and she was late, no one seemed to notice.
Miss Harper might even decide to send everyone home – in
the middle of a lesson. Sometimes Meg went. Other times she
stayed to play with Josie. Also Sarah might keep her away
from school, sending her instead on an errand to Witheringham where it was rumoured that a greengrocer had just
received a consignment of tomatoes. More enjoyable were the
days when Meg played truant, spending the time with Josie,
who since her sister joined their mother in going out to work
had to do most of the daily shopping for food; which meant
hours of having to stand in queues

It was on one such occasion that Meg and Josie watched two

Spitfires approach 'the enemy's new weapon' – a doodlebug – just as its engine was starting to cut out. Tipping it gently with their wings, the Spitfires changed the doodlebug's flight direction away from the area of St Swithin's School. When it nose-dived and exploded, it was very near to the quarry. Only then did Meg remember to throw herself to the ground. But people often just stood and watched the doodlebugs – dark shadows that roared overhead with jets of flame shooting out of their tails. It became scary only when the spluttering sound of their engines faltered. Then it made a crack-crack sound. If it didn't hit you directly when it exploded, you could still be injured or killed by its blast.

Suddenly Meg remembered that she hadn't seen Mr POW for weeks – not since before Whitsun, when the doodlebug had exploded near the camp. She ran to the entrance of the quarry, but the place was deserted, except for the guard.

'You,' he called. 'What yer doin' 'ere? Clear off!'

A frightened Meg backed away from the fence. Where was Mr POW? Might he be in the hollow?

'I know something you don't know!' Meg spun round. It was Beryl Saunders. 'They're all locked up – the prisoners.'

'Why?'

'They're bastards – that's what my Mum says. It's them who've sent the flying bombs.'

'What d'you mean?'

'The doodlebugs! Ooh, you *are* stupid Margaret Chandler!'

'You're stupid, too. Fancy not knowing how to spell receive – i before e except after c!'

'That was yesterday,' Beryl protested. 'I forgot, that's all. Everyone forgets something sometimes.' She moved forward conspiratorially. 'My Mum says the Jerries have sent the doodlebugs to pay us back for the Invasion. They've locked the POWs up so that no one can speak to them – in case they give away secrets. Like they were spies!'

Meg felt herself flush. 'Where've they put them?' she asked, trying to hold her voice steady.

'How should I know? It was round about Whitsun. Over Toddington way the place was crawling with soldiers – thousands and thousands of them. And there were military police out, searching people's baskets and asking to see their identity cards. That was before D-Day, of course. They stopped Josie Perkins' Mum, did you know that?' Beryl eyed Meg suspiciously. 'Why d'you want to know where they've gone?'

'Me?' Meg feigned surprise. 'What makes you think I'm interested. I just wanted to see how clever you are. Since you seem to know so much, p'rhaps you're the spy they're all out looking for.' With that, she seized Beryl's skipping rope, whizzed it into a sideways loop, and proceeded to 'bump'.

'You're horrible you are! I'll tell my Mum about you . . . you Ole Tin Ribs Chandler!'

Meg flung the rope down and poked out her tongue:

> Tell-tale tit,
> Your tongue shall be slit,
> And all the dogs in the town,
> Shall have a little bit . . .

Beryl ran off defeated, but it was Meg who – deep inside – was crying, only no one could hear it except herself.

The hollow lay in ruins. The child crouched, breathless from running, and gazed stony-faced at the desolation. The trees stood bare, their branches reduced to jagged stumps. Dangling from the trunks were lengths of bark, stripped away like torn flesh. Strewn around were mounds of leaves. Stretching out a hand to touch them, the child withdrew it quickly when she uncovered a dead blackbird, half its feathers blasted away. There were other dead – thrushes, linnets, finches, a tiny shrew lying belly upward, its thin orange legs sticking in the air. The flowers, she whispered, where are the flowers? On the ground she glimpsed something white and, stooping, found a spray of elder, half covered with debris, its blossoms miraculously intact. At the foot of the tree she sat down and retched. The smell of the tree's wounds was overpowering. She wanted to run but found she could not move; she flattened herself against the tree, hugging its trunk to stop the trembling.

The sky lay leaden. Nothing stirred: no wind, no air, no birds, no butterflies, no rustling in the bushes . . . She cradled the elder spray in her arms, burying her face in the delicate tracery of the still fresh flowers. There was no sound – save that of the throbbing in her head and in the distance the retreating call of the cuckoo. Tomorrow, she told herself, is St Swithin's day – 15 July. How did the rhyme go? 'Rain, rain, go away, come again another day.' She must remember to recite it. Otherwise it would rain for forty days and nights, the same as the time Jesus spent living in the wilderness. Tomorrow was Saturday. If Monday were St Swithin's day, she would have been sent to church if, that is, school was open. It should be – on a Monday – but there was no telling any more. Some said school was closed because of the doodlebugs, others on account of everyone catching nits. She put her hand to her head, running it over the short remaining wisps. She was glad Mister POW wasn't there to see her with all her hair cut off. How cross Sarah was when the school nurse sent her home with a note and a bar of black, pungent-smelling soap. She'd expected a beating, but for once all Sarah did was scream. Now that she thought about it, Sarah hadn't really hit her for days. Sarah had even made her a new frock: midnight blue, with buttons like glittering stars.

Still she waited, watching the darkness at the edge of the hollow. Already the tall summer grasses were tangled and withered to winter straw. She scanned the sky anxiously. Would the birds come? She couldn't leave the hollow – and its memories – till they arrived. But what if Char'ty were wrong? After all, she had been wrong about Midsummer Eve. She had sat up all night waiting for Sarah to take off on a broomstick, whiling away the hours staring at the winking stars and watching the ragged clouds chase each other across the moon. Like now, she had looked out on a darkening world; except that then it was night. Now it was day – or was it? It didn't feel like day or night, for that matter. She didn't want to think about what it felt like . . . not yet.

The vigil lasted an eternity. Then they came. First a few followed by a stream: the wandering parties of rooks, starlings and sparrows – some flying in line, others breaking formation and wheeling in circles immediately overhead. The child struggled to her feet to watch the birds gather, ready to leave the woods and hollows in quest of new, more open territories. Some, like the cuckoo, were off to foreign lands.

She laid the elder spray across the barbed wire, and left.

THE GREAT ADVENTURE
EVACUATION WITHOUT TEARS

From a railway station one morning this week there departed one of the happiest trainloads of children that could be imagined – departed to a destination that must remain nameless. As they set off on this great adventure, these children – uprooted from their homes for a time – were too excited for tears. Where they were bound for they did not know. The entraining of the children was a tribute to the organisers of the evacuation . . . Education authorities, local authorities, the WVS, and railway authorities had co-operated so magnificently that there was never a hitch. Congregating at 7.30 a.m. at the station, the children had only to wait two hours for the first of the trains to reach them. By ten o'clock that night most of them had arrived safely at their destinations where they were taken to a church hall, fed and given a quick medical inspection.

Witheringham and District Gazette
21 July, 1944

When Cissie shook Meg awake on the morning of 18 July, the child was having a bad dream. Drenched in sweat, her throat swollen, her head aching painfully, she was trying to remember where she was.

'Six o'clock,' Cissie whispered. 'Time to get up.'

After breakfast (which Meg could not eat) Cissie took her to the railway station. Meg was carrying her gas-mask and a canvas haversack containing a change of clothing. By nine o'clock the station was thronged with schoolchildren – both from the town and from neighbouring villages. If some of the children had been told, before boarding a train, that they were being sent away because of enemy rocket attacks, others – like Meg – had not, and were very confused. Not that the explanation would have helped much, since neither the children, their parents, nor any of the adults supervising the evacuation knew where the children were going. Only the senior railway staff knew the destinations, and they were not allowed to tell.

Twelve hours after the train steamed out of Witheringham station, Meg arrived at her destination – it was Wales.

'It's a high fever she has. Call me again if she gets delirious . . .'

A damp flannel. Soft voice. Brown eyes. Dark wavy hair. 'Go to sleep, bach,' a woman said.

She is in a boat on a lake in the drill hall at St Anne's. Hundreds of children, trying to clamber aboard. Someone is rowing them across the water. The boat has a hole in its side. The boat is sinking . . .

'Can you hear me, bach?' Sing-song voice . . . someone holding her up, spooning liquid into her mouth. Cool, so cool – lapping it thirstily. 'What do they call you, Margaret Chandler?'

'Meg. My name is . . .'

Kathy. And if one green cottage should accidentally . . .

'It's all right, bach. It's only a train.'

Kill . . . Kill . . . Smother and choke, water trickling down her legs . . . Sheets of fire, black smoke, bright red sky. Is it Cherrytree? Is it the shelter? Sirens blaring, bells clanging, whistles blowing, children running everywhere – fighting, pushing, clawing, screaming down the metal staircase with the wooden treads . . .

'Quickly, Evan – I can't hold her!'

When the screaming ceased the child was no longer struggling. A man was holding her wrist. Nearby stood the woman with the sing-song voice.

'What happened?' the man asked.

'Just as the train was pulling into the station I found her trying to crawl down the stairs. When I picked her up, didn't she just go mad and fight me like a wild cat. Terrified she was, I can tell you that. I'm not even sure she knows where she is. Worries me, it does.'

'It could be the fever. That, or nightmares. We've several cases with these evacuees. She's past the crisis as far as the fever's concerned. It's rest she needs now, and plenty of it. She's very weak. The question is: do you think you can manage?'

'It's not what I bargained for — a sick child. But no, I couldn't turn her out. She's as good as gold most of the time, not a peep out of her. No fussing like. She hasn't asked me for so much as a glass of water. Never opens her mouth, to tell you the truth, except when her mind's wandering.'

'Well, keep her warm and give her plenty of fluids. She looks too frail to me, and if she isn't recognizing you by tomorrow, then I'll have to move her to hospital . . .'

'There's your haversack,' Sarah was saying, hanging the canvas bag over the child's shoulder. 'Your ration book's in your coat pocket; your identity card and clothing coupons are in the bag. Don't take your coat off. Don't take your gas-mask off. Now, be off with you! — Off with you! — Off with you! . . .'

'Would you like to see the train, bach?'

Meg's legs wobbled as, supported under the arms, she was led to the window. Through the glass she looked down — on a railway station.

'That's right,' the woman said, laughing at the child's bewilderment. 'It's on the platform we are. As soon as you're strong enough, we'll ask Mr Evans — that's my husband — to take you up into the signal box.'

The child pushed her face against the glass and stared, her eyes darting frantically in every direction as she searched for a tree . . . some flowers . . . a patch of grass. But the world before her seemed totally grey — leaden sky, dark slate roofs, dismal-looking buildings, grimy goods' waggons, metal rails, stone platforms, broken-down fences . . .

'We're GWR,' Mrs Evans explained. 'Great Western Railway. Only a small one, mind you: a two line track with junctions further up. Evan Evans is the stationmaster — issues the tickets and collects them as well as operating the signals.

Not that there's much traffic. Mainly freight. We're coal in these parts.'

She led the child back to bed, staying to tuck her in. 'It's a station house you're in, bach, in case you've been wondering. The house shakes when the goods' pass through. You'll soon learn to shout if you want to make yourself heard, though I always think it's best to speak only when it's quiet, if you understand my meaning. Otherwise you'll find it aggravating.'

Mrs Evans smiled at the child, a warm, enquiring smile. 'You'll be liking Wales, I'm thinking.'

'Now, Margaret Chandler, what happened to your haversack?' the billeting officer was asking. 'We've checked with the railway authorities and searched for it everywhere. No one's seen it. Did you, truthfully, have it with you on the train?'

The child kept her eyes fixed on the wall behind him.

Jones the Billet (as Mrs Evans called him) pressed his fingertips on the table impatiently. It was the second time he had called at the station. 'She's not deaf is she? If she doesn't talk, it could be she can't hear?'

'There's nothing wrong with her ears,' Mrs Evans replied tartly. 'And she can talk, but only to me – not to others, and never if she's aggravated. You'd best leave the questions to me, but mind your talk. She's already answering me in Welsh, the cheeky monkey!' She turned to the child.

'Megan, bach. Did someone take your haversack from you?'

The child nodded.

'When?'

Meg looked blank.

'Was it at the station in Witheringham?'

Meg nodded.

'When they took it away, did you see them put it on a trolley?'

Confused, the child shook her head and looked away.

'If it went on a trolley, you see, it would have gone in the guard's van,' Mrs Evans told the billeting officer. She turned to Meg again.

'Did you have it in the carriage with you?'

Meg shook her head decisively.

'What about in the hall?' Mr Jones butted in. 'Did you see it there?'

Meg rubbed her eyes. She did not want to remember the hall . . . the stumbling in the dark . . . tired, lost, afraid. The babel of voices . . . the strange faces . . . the crush on the train . . . the world flashing by . . . a world full of children . . . children she didn't know . . . the great silver fish dangling in the sky . . . pendulous . . . heavy. What someone called barrage balloons. Darkness . . . noise . . . everyone talking . . . what were they saying? Sometimes she seemed to understand. Other times, the words tripped and skipped like pebbles in a stream. She was tired and felt funny in the head. Then the grown-ups were there, choosing children to take away with them. Some of them looked at her, crouched on the floor. No one wanted her when they saw her hair. Then Mrs Evans came and read the label round her neck. Mrs Evans was nice . . . Mrs Evans was special . . . But even she laughed and called her 'a featherless chick'.

'Megan?'

Meg looked away.

'Are you upset, bach?' Mrs Evans asked, putting out a hand to stroke the child's head.

'If you ask me, Mr Jones, it must have been lost at this end. I'm thinking someone took it by mistake and then, perhaps, when they saw the clothing coupons, was tempted to keep it. Her clothes are good – their quality, I mean: new sandals, dress, hand-knitted vest. She obviously comes from a good home – folds everything neatly and what have you.'

'That's all very well, Mrs Evans, but she only has the clothes she arrived in. It's a cold enough summer but what about the winter? It's the devil's own job to get replacement coupons. Her identity card is no problem, yet I very much doubt they'll issue her any clothing coupons, which means trying to kit her out from anything we can find.'

'I'll not have her wearing boys' boots – I've told you that already. Ugly they are, and she's a pretty enough child now that her hair's grown a bit. I can manage a skirt and jumper, even some socks. But she needs a change of underclothes, some proper shoes, and night attire. Look at her dressed in one of Evan's shirts. Every time she gets out of bed she trips over the tail!'

Mr Jones stood up and looked down at Meg. 'Are you sure there's nothing wrong with her – mental like? Didn't she come from an orphanage originally?'

'There's no call for talk like that,' Mrs Evans reproved him sharply. 'Haven't I had the schoolmaster in? She wouldn't read aloud for him, of course; but she did the sums he set her quick as a flash, and a composition too. Very pleased he was, I'll have you know. Leave her be till school starts, that's what he told me. It's shock she's suffering from – nothing more.'

As the weeks passed, as no one pressed or made any demands on her, the child shut herself off in a world of sleep and silence, reducing her energy needs to no more than those required to wash herself and eat. Whatever other resources she might once have possessed were now gone; squandered in the months spent learning to adapt to the strange world she was pitchforked into when she left the orphanage, and the harsh life she endured with Sarah Dawkins. Now, in the absence of conflict, among people who were kind, it was as if she had lost the will to struggle further, slipping daily into greater depths of inertia and melancholy.

Outside the room in which she lay, the rain beat relentlessly against the windowpanes in sweeps of water that rattled and poured down the pipes and along the gutters. She turned from the gaunt high-ceilinged room, the black-streaked sky, the wind blowing continuously in all directions, and buried her head beneath the bedclothes. Why did she have to listen to this ceaseless moan, this lament for a world that was shrouded in tears?

'Was I a baby once?' she asked Mrs Evans, as they sat together at the kitchen table. Mrs Evans was making a pie. Meg was reading a letter.

'Of course you were. We all were – once upon a time.'

'Kathy's got a new mother,' Meg announced, frowning. 'And a new baby sister. Her granny's going to send for her soon. She's going to live with her.'

'That's nice,' Mrs Evans remarked, lifting the pastry on to her rolling pin in one deft movement before depositing it in a pie dish. 'You'll be going home too, one of these days – back to Witheringham. Just think of that.'

The child stared at the woman, watching her smile. 'That isn't *really* my home,' she tried, hopefully.

'It is now, bach . . . Seen my pastry cutter, have you?' Mrs Evans crossed the room as she spoke and began rummaging through a drawer in the kitchen dresser.

Meg looked down at the letter. 'How did Kathy know I was here?'

'Ah! Well it was to be a surprise. Kathleen Woods, you told me. Your best friend, you said. So what did I do but put my thinking cap on. She'll have been evacuated too, I told myself – and in all probability to Wales. So why not ask Jones the Billet to look out for her, to please our Megan here.'

'Meg.' The child spoke sharply.

'What's that, bach?'

'My name is Meg – not Megan.'

Mrs Evans laughed, and then stopped, when she saw Meg tear Kathy's letter into pieces and fling it in the fire.

'She's gone!' the child shouted, as Mrs Evans began to remonstrate with her. 'Don't you understand? They've all gone . . . I hate you! I hate you! Leave me alone!'

Later, Meg cried, her head in Mrs Evans' lap.

Every night they came – a long line of children dressed in grey . . . wisps of badly-cut hair. Some held hands, the tiny ones sucked their thumbs . . .

Meg was helping Mrs Evans feed the chickens with a mash made from bran and boiled potato peelings, when she saw Mrs Evans stoop down to touch something white.

'What is it?' she asked, waving the hungry birds away and hurrying forward. 'Let me see!'

'No, bach,' Mrs Evans' voice was sharp. But she spoke too late; Meg was already pulling at her hands. The chicken was still breathing, its neck a mass of raw flesh and half torn-out feathers.

In the kitchen she listened to the Evanses talking. In front of her lay a book full of numbered dots. When she drew lines between the dots, faces appeared – as if by magic. Megan, Mrs Evans' grown-up daughter, gave her the book. She liked Megan – her merry smile, her mop of dark frizzy hair. Now that Meg was better, the older girl often sat down and played dominoes with her after tea. And on one occasion, she brought Meg a piece of yellow satin ribbon from the shop where she worked.

'There we are, bach,' Megan said, tying it round the child's hair, 'aren't you a pretty girl then?' And Meg, radiant with pleasure, had smiled at herself in the mirror.

Yes, she liked Megan, but it was to Mrs Evans that Meg clung, following her about the house like a small shadow, worrying if she didn't know where Mrs Evans was; and then worrying about worrying if she couldn't find her immediately. Sometimes she tiptoed out of bed and stood for hours outside Mrs Evans' bedroom, just to listen to Mrs Evans breathing . . .

'I told you it was a weakling, right from the start,' Mr Evans was saying, as he shook open his evening newspaper. 'I'm only surprised it lasted as long as it did. They don't like them weak, you see.'

'But fancy them pecking it to death,' Mrs Evans sounded distressed. 'I've not seen that before. Cruel I call it.'

'To you, maybe – but not to them. Survival of the fittest, that's the rule for most species and chickens are no exception.'

Meg was standing in the dark by the bedroom window. Outside, a rooster crowed . . . then another. In the distance she could hear the clump, clump of boots – the miners on their way to the pit. Why was Kathy going home – back to her own family – when she, Meg, couldn't even stay with Mrs Evans? If Kathy belonged, why didn't she? Who was there left to belong to? Not Sarah Dawkins! Who then? . . . Herself? . . . Perhaps it had only ever been herself.

She climbed back into bed and wrapped her arms tightly round her body. 'I mustn't be weak,' she whispered aloud, rocking herself back and forth and struggling not to cry. She hugged herself tighter – so tight she could feel the bones hard against her fingers. It was, she realized, as if she were feeling – for the first time – the very things that held her together.

'Now, bach, why won't you eat your dinner?'

Meg sat and scowled at her plate. 'What is it?' she asked tersely.

'Chicken,' said Mrs Evans.

'Rabbit,' said Megan, entering the kitchen.

The two women looked at each other. 'Oh, Mam,' Megan shook her head, 'haven't you just put your foot in it!'

Out in the scullery, Meg was helping the older girl with the dishes. 'Would I lie to you, now?' Megan asked her reproachfully. 'Of course it was rabbit. Mam just got confused, that's all.'

'Prove it!'

'However can I when all that's left is a pile of bones?'

'You can show me the chicken – the one that was wounded.'

'I can't do that, bach. It wouldn't be right – it's passed on you see. Dead, if you'll pardon the expression.'

Meg turned her back.

'Mind you,' Megan went on slowly, 'I was getting ready to bury it.'

'When?'

'Tonight – but first I must find it a coffin.'

'What's that?'

'A sort of box. When someone dies, it isn't respectful to bury them without first laying them out in a coffin. I could bring one home from work, I was thinking, but we'll also need some flowers.'

'Flowers!' Meg echoed. 'There aren't any!'

'Leave it to me,' Megan whispered. 'I'll borrow that bunch of paper violets from Mam's second-best hat, and there's the corn dolly my Aunty Joyce gave me when I was little.'

The funeral took place in the chicken run. Megan dug a hole while Meg watched. The coffin, tied with string, lay on the ground. Crouching down, Meg started fiddling with the string.

'What are you doing?' Megan panted, as she attacked the beaten down earth with a coal shovel.

'I wanted to look at it, before it's buried . . .'

'You mustn't do that, bach. It's gone to heaven, you see. Prancing around in a full coat of feathers it is. We might offend it if we take a peep at it now. Right – I think that's deep enough. Ready are you?'

Meg nodded. They placed the coffin carefully in the hole. Looking to see what Megan did next, Meg sprinkled some dirt over it and then, placing her hands together, bowed her head. 'What are we doing?' she whispered.

'Saying a prayer.'

'What prayer?'

'Can't rightly say, bach. Anything you like, I reckon.'

Meg thought for a moment. 'Can I say it out loud?'

'If you like.'

'For what we have received, may the Lord make us truly thankful.'

'Megan,' she asked, 'what's the matter?'

Megan was choking and, with tears in her eyes, was frenziedly piling earth over the coffin.

It was slippery on the mountain. Each time she neared the top, she slithered back again. To get any sort of foothold, she had to jab the toes of her boots as hard as she could into the crumbly earth – earth the like of which she had never seen before; black, and as cindery as embers in a dead fire. In the biting wind, her eyes blinded with grit and her mouth full of dust, she pushed on to the next slope – to where there was grass; to where, from that distance, she might find a tree. But where in this grey land was the sun? She would give anything, just to catch a glimpse of an orange-streaked sky.

'Just look at you, bach!' Mrs Evans exclaimed. 'Where have you been? You've had us all worrying and here you are looking as if you've been down the pit. It's six o'clock, and you out there in the dark. It was to the police I was going.'

Meg said nothing.

'Is it on the mountain you've been?' Megan asked, as she undressed the child before putting her in the tin bath in front of the kitchen fire.

'It's not a mountain,' Mrs Evans scolded, 'it's the tip. I wish you'd never taken her there, that I do. She's not been at school again today, so Mrs Price's girl told me.'

'Now, bach,' Megan said, 'you've got to go to school. If you don't you'll have Mam in trouble.'

Still Meg refused to yield.

'Is it the boots you're upset about? Have the others been laughing at you?' Mrs Evans asked from the doorway.

Meg squeezed the water out of the flannel and scrubbed at her face.

'More likely the fighting,' Megan said, looking up at her mother. 'Mrs Thomas said there was trouble last week – our kids ganging up on one side of the playground, the evacuees on the other. A real war, she said. The teachers can't handle it – too overcrowded, they say. There's been talk that it won't be long now before the evacuees all go home.'

She turned to Meg. 'Am I right?'

Meg looked away.

'I'll tell you what, bach. Why don't you and I strike a bargain like. If you go to school from now on, I'll have a big surprise waiting for you when you get back tomorrow.'

Meg opened her mouth to speak.

'First the promise,' Megan warned.

Meg nodded her head vigorously. 'What is it?' she whispered.

'Hallowe'en!'

While Meg ate her tea Megan and Mrs Evans chattered

about what happens on the night of 31 October – the night before Allhallows or what, in Witheringham, they knew as All Saints' Day.

'Will there be lots of ghosts visiting?' Meg asked.

'Now, that I can't say,' Megan explained. 'They're not bad ghosts, you understand. Just the souls of the departed returning to be friendly like. Mam will make some little tarts, and we'll leave a few out to make the ghosts feel at home.'

'I've seen them already,' Meg volunteered, in a rush of confidence. 'They visit me at night when I'm in bed.'

'Is that so,' Megan responded, with a quick look at her mother. 'Kindly are they?'

'Oh, yes. Very kindly. Well . . . *now* they are.'

'That's all right then. Allhallows Day, you see, is the start of winter. Mam here will tell you that when she was a little girl they used to light bonfires the night before, on Hallowe'en, and everyone danced round them, waiting for the witches and fairies to appear.'

'Do you believe in fairies?' Meg asked. 'I don't.'

Megan laughed.

'What about witches?'

Megan laughed again.

'You shouldn't laugh,' Meg told her severely. 'There *are* witches. I know one – a real, live one. 'Course, I haven't actually seen her on a broomstick. She's too heavy, you see. Broomsticks are made of hawthorn wood. Did you know that?'

'Elder.' Mrs Evans spoke suddenly. 'Witches always ride on the wood of the elder tree. They'll never burn it – that's how you discover whether someone's a witch or not. Offer them some for their fire. If they refuse it, then you know. Mind you, not all witches are bad. Most are very good. My granny used to reckon her mother was a witch – a good one, of course . . .'

As Megan tucked her up in bed, Meg was shivering with excitement. 'Megan,' she coaxed, 'please tell me the surprise now.'

'Tomorrow! After we've had our tea, you and I will be setting off.'

'On a journey?'

'Wait and see!'

When Meg returned from school next day, she found Mrs Evans seated at the kitchen table scooping out the centres of what looked like two enormous turnips. 'I think that'll do,' said Mrs Evans, as she scrutinized her handiwork. 'All we need now are two holes for the eyes . . . one for the nose . . . a big, wide one for the mouth . . . and two at the top to hold the string. Now for the candles – and the mangelwurzels are lanterns!'

As soon as it was dark, Mrs Evans gave the signal and the two girls, who had wrapped scarves round their faces to disguise themselves, opened the front door. 'I've tied a stick to the string, so the candle won't burn your fingers,' Megan whispered while Meg gazed in awe at the lantern that she was now holding aloft – at the grinning face she saw. 'There's a train held up near the signals,' Megan went on, 'so we can have some fun with the passengers.'

Meg followed the older girl out of the house to the edge of one platform and clambering down, hopped across the railway lines to the platform opposite.

'Thank goodness Da didn't see us,' Megan giggled, as the two of them crept past the tiny booking office where Mr Evans was talking on the telephone. 'He'd have a fit, if he knew what we were up to. Anyone would think trains were sacred! Fanatic he is – about trains – I mean.'

Beyond the booking office it was dark, with no lights now visible other than the flickering glimmer from the lanterns. Approaching the train, they heard voices and the sound of doors and windows being opened and shut. Meg clutched Megan's hand tightly.

'Jesus!' She heard someone say, in a smothered voice, 'I don't believe it. Hey, boys, get a look at this!'

'I'll be damned! I do believe . . . it's trick or treat?'

'Hallowe'en! For Crissakes – it's Hallowe'en!'

The word was bawled from one end of the train to the other. In the hullabaloo, Meg found herself being lifted into one of the carriages, which was full of strange soldiers.

'They're GIs, bach,' Megan shouted gleefully.

The child, clinging desperately to her lantern, was being passed from soldier to soldier down the corridor.

'Aw, c'mon buddy, give her to me!'

'You're scaring the little lady.'

'Like some gum, honey?'

'Naw! It's candy she likes, isn't it, doll!'

Meg was enraged. She had ended up on a soldier's lap and someone had taken her lantern. She was angry, too, that Megan took no notice of her predicament. Megan was enjoying herself. 'That's right,' Megan was saying, 'we live in the station house. My father's the stationmaster.'

'And the little lady's your baby sister?'

'No – an evacuee. She came here away from the rockets, the V-1s.'

'Poor little doll. Have some candy,' the soldier crooned. (Meg's pockets were full of candy by this time, but she accepted more.) 'Are you away from your Mommy then?'

Meg stared at the soldier disdainfully.

'C'mon now – you can tell me.' He clutched her tightly as Meg again tried to wriggle free.

'You mustn't mind if she doesn't talk. She'll never speak to strangers. She's an orphan you see.'

At this piece of news, the soldier's head dropped. First he groaned and then he started to cry. Grown-ups don't cry, Meg told herself fiercely. Grown-ups never cry.

Just when she thought she would not be able to contain her embarrassment a moment longer, Mr Evans appeared. She held out her arms to him. 'Come on,' he called good-naturedly. 'You'll have to hand her over. It's long past her bedtime and your driver's ready to take you on. Half an hour from now and you'll be safely in barracks.'

As Mr Evans put her down, Meg tugged at his hand and whispered in his ear. 'Who's got her lantern?' he asked.

'Here,' shouted the soldier on whose lap Meg had been sitting. 'I got it back for her. Tell her I'll come and see her on Sunday . . .'

And on Sunday he did. He came to dinner. He came to dinner every Sunday, after that.

'Oh, come on, Meg. Say something to him – for my sake!' Megan sounded cross, but Meg refused to yield.

'Now then, Megan,' Mrs Evans reproached her, 'leave the child be.' She turned to the soldier, whose name was Joe. 'She's shy, and not given to talking much anyway. You mustn't take it personally. It was weeks before she'd even talk to us. So sit down and make yourself comfortable.'

'I haven't upset her, have I? I thought she'd like the teddy bear – I really did. I thought . . . well, I thought maybe I could make it up to her, seeing as she hasn't a Mommy or Daddy. I mean to say, kids like to get presents, don't they? It hurts that she won't even touch it . . .'

Meg caught Mr Evans' eye and could have sworn she saw him wink. It wasn't that she didn't like Joe – just that he made her nervous; so nervous, in fact, she dreaded his visits. Nice though he was, she didn't want to marry him. After all, that's what Mr Evans told her: it was on Hallowe'en you chose the person you were going to marry. Why otherwise would Joe visit her each Sunday? That explained why she wouldn't speak to him, why she wouldn't look at him, wouldn't even acknowledge his presence in the house, though sometimes, when she thought he wasn't looking, she would smile at him.

'Don't worry,' Mr Evans whispered, when the others were out of the room. 'Perhaps it's our Megan he's really after – pretty as a picture she looks in her new nylon stockings. No, I don't think you've anything to worry about, bach. I don't think it's you he's after whisking away.'

Meg breathed a huge sigh of relief. Still, just to be on the safe side, she would carry on as before. You never knew: a lot of girls were now marrying GIs.

'It makes you remember,' Mrs Evans said. 'Armistice Day, November the 11th, 1918. That was the first one, you see. We remember them today, the ones that died. Everything stops: trains, buses, the miners down the pit, the people in the street. No one does anything for two minutes – just to remember . . . There were a lot of boys from here: a lot of boys we lost.'

Mrs Evans wiped her eyes with the corner of her apron. Meg looked up at her in dismay, her own eyes filling with tears; this was the second grown-up she had seen crying, and it disturbed her profoundly. 'It's all right, bach,' Mrs Evans said, holding the child close. 'It was my brothers, you see. I lost three of them – and my father as well.'

But Meg was concentrating on the feel of Mrs Evans' hand stroking her head. 'What's the poppy for?' she asked, fingering the red paper flower that Mrs Evans had pinned to Meg's jumper that morning.

'The Fields of Flanders, bach. They were full of poppies.'

The woman and the child lapsed into silence as they sat, watching the clock. In the distance a chapel bell began to toll. They stood up. Meg, her eyes fixed on the clock, counted the strokes. On the eleventh, an eerie quiet pervaded the room. Outside, the station was still. Meg strained her ears for sounds from the village, but heard nothing. For two long minutes, it seemed as if the whole world had come to a halt.

'Remember to write, bach,' Mrs Evans was calling, as the train steamed out of the station – the train that was returning the child to Witheringham.

The moon was cresting the top of the trees. The sun, a ball of orange, perched low in a sky striped primrose, gold and violet.

'Yer look different,' Char'ty said, studying Meg's face. 'Not so skeered.'

Meg smiled, and poked the fire which Char'ty had lit at the top of Nokes Wood. The wood lay muffled, the trees etched with frost and icicles that tinkled when anything moved. How easy it would be, she was musing, to turn into a block of ice.

Char'ty continued to scrutinize her closely. Then she stood up. ' 'Ere!' she called, moving towards a thicket. 'Ah've summat to show yer.' She stooped and lifted away a mound of dead, frost-blackened leaves.

Meg, crouching down, peered at the tiny animal lying in a nest beneath the leaves. It looked like a dead mouse.

'It's not what yer think,' Char'ty said, cradling the little creature in her hands. ''T'ain't dead.'

'But . . . but it's stiff!'

' 'Course it is. It's 'ibernating, ain't it? 'Tis a dormouse that's gorn to sleep fer the winter.'

Meg stretched out a finger to touch it. 'Why?' she asked quietly.

'When times are bad, ain't it best to sleep? 'Course 't'ain't the same for 'umans – or not exactly.'

Meg said nothing. All her attention was riveted on the dormouse, as she watched Char'ty replace it gently in its nest and cover it up with leaves.

'They keep their 'eads down, yer see, and wait fer the thaw. But then – I doan 'ave to tell yer anythink abaht that, now do I?'

PART 7

There'll Always Be An England

VICTORY IN EUROPE

Buy Your Victory Decorations Here
Red, White and Blue Bunting only 1/3/4d a yard

V-E Day, 8 May 1945, dawned hot and sultry. From midday onwards the bells rang incessantly. Down in Netherfield Road they borrowed trestle tables from the Toc H Hall for a street party. Pennants fluttered limply. Union Jacks lay draped over tables and hung from the windows of neighbouring shops and houses. Children exchanged news of fathers overseas . . . presents they would get when mother's 'ship comes home' . . . the bonfire party they were going to that night. Someone wheeled a piano outside and people jumped up and down singing:

> Knees up Mother Brown,
> Knees up Mother Brown.
> Under the table you must go.
> Eeh-eye-eeh-eye-eeh-eye-oh.
> If I catch you bending,
> I'll saw your leg right off.
> Don't get the breeze up,
> Just get the knees up,
> Knees up Mother Brown.

Did 'Victory Party' mean the same as 'Birthday Party'? If it did, why were the bells ringing? Meg couldn't remember ever having heard bells ringing before – not church bells that went on and on. It was difficult trying to work it all out, and her thoughts returned to the book she had been reading the night before which lived in the bookcase on the chest of drawers at the foot of her bed, and had belonged to Mr Dawkins. Every night now, Meg raided the bookcase, taking care as she read to keep one ear permanently cocked for the sound of footfalls; the instant the stairs creaked, she thrust the incriminating volume under the mattress and feigned sleep. If Sarah caught her, she would get a thrashing.

These days Sarah used her bare hands. The heavy walking stick vanished early in 1945, after the beating to death of Dennis O'Neill who – as a child in the care of a local authority – had been boarded out with his brother, with a farmer in Shropshire. When the facts leading up to his death were discovered, the Borough Council responsible for Meg's maintenance immediately dispatched three of its councillors to Prickler's Hill, without waiting to inform Sarah or the LCC of their visit beforehand. Once inside the house, they explored all the rooms, examined Meg's clothing, and endeavoured to speak to Meg herself. Sarah, who maintained she did not know who they were and threatened to report them to the police for trespassing, planted Meg firmly behind her, as if she thought the child was about to be abducted.

'I do not,' she wrote afterwards to the LCC in great indignation, 'allow such people into my house. I am a respectable woman and they were not at all a nice kind of person. If this happens again, I shall have to give Margaret up and charge you for postage.'

Most of Mr Dawkins' books were written by early twentieth-century writers: Zane Gray, Rider Haggard, Captain Marryat, Baroness Orczy. Though Meg forgot their names, she always remembered the titles – *Riders of the Purple Sage, Convict 99* or her current favourite, *Retribution*. That retribution should feature in her thoughts on the very day the Germans officially surrendered to the Allies was pure coincidence. The story was about a vengeful countess who kidnapped her rival's son, spirited him off to a castle in Bohemia and locked him in a cage. There he lived like an animal with no one remembering even to trim his nails. This fact interested Meg greatly, since Sarah also forgot; and as the child did not possess any scissors of her own, nor had access to anyone else's, she regularly bit or ripped off the ends (both from finger and toenails) with her teeth – a double-jointed activity that called for considerable patience and skill.

Meg peered round, hoping to catch a glimpse of Char'ty, but none of the Wagstaffs were there. Perhaps they didn't like parties or, more probably, knew their neighbours wouldn't welcome their presence. No one, as far as Meg knew, liked gypsies. Beryl Saunders said they kidnapped children – just like the jealous countess. But Meg knew this was untrue. As for eating hedgehogs . . .

'You don't do you?' she had asked Char'ty one day.

'Me Ma don't, but me gran likes 'em. She cooks 'em in clay.'

'Ugh!' Meg pulled a face and then remembered something else. 'What about babies?'

'Gawd!' Char'ty yelped. 'You'rm not asking if Ah've 'ad me teeth into them are yer? 'Oo's bin telling yer tales like that?'

Meg hastened to reassure her friend that of course she didn't think Char'ty did any such thing. 'Anyway,' Char'ty went on, once she felt mollified, 'they'd be a sight too skinny for us – it's pigs we like, as yer well know.'

Taking another look round – with food on her mind – Meg caught sight of an awesome pile of fishpaste sandwiches standing on the table. As the grown-ups launched into a wheezy rendering of 'Roll out the barrel, we'll have a barrel of fun', she thrust a hand out but caught a warning look from Sarah, and dropped her hand disappointedly into her lap. Why, she wondered – and not for the first time – did Sarah always insist that denying yourself food when you were hungry was a way of proving you were 'better' than others? If this was supposed to be a party then she preferred the sort they gave at Sunday School. At least Sarah didn't get invited. Meg even received a present, which was more than she was getting today. She was given it at Sunday School for reciting by heart the opening verses of St John's Gospel. The significance of the text – 'In the beginning was the Word, and the Word was with God, and the Word was God' – only made sense when she saw her reward: a somewhat battered copy of a book entitled *Christy's Old Organ*. She was so pleased to own a book of her own at last, she did not in the least mind what the story was about; nor that it contained a moral about which she had doubts. This was that the hero's reward for dutifully accepting his lot in this life (dire poverty and suffering) would be found in the next and that therefore the sooner he reached 'Home Sweet Home' in the sky, the better for him.

What Meg read by this time mattered less than how much. She was addicted to any written material she could lay her eyes on. She regularly dipped into the Bible, since it was the one book Sarah allowed to remain in the child's room on the occasions she removed all the others. As a result, twice during her childhood Meg read the Bible from cover to cover, including all the bits that bored her, such as Leviticus and the Book of Kings. Then there was the browsing she did at school, the illicit night reading under the bedclothes or by moonlight, and the scanning of the backs of schoolmates' comics, while their owners read the fronts. Another regular source of reading material was the newspaper – but never new or neatly folded. She mainly read the sheets she laid on the scullery floor when she cleaned it, and the truncated stories on the squares of paper Sarah cut and skewered on a meat hook which hung on the inside of the lavatory door.

It was from newspapers in these various forms, and in particular from the local *Witheringham and District Gazette*, that Meg heard of the General Election of 1945. Plastered across the pages of the *Gazette* was the Town Council's Victory Slogan: ALL OUR PAST PROCLAIMS OUR FUTURE, followed by pronouncements or pledges from the three prospective parliamentary candidates for the area about how they would deal with that same future, if elected.

Conservative Candidate	*We must prevent nationalisation, make a super drive for houses, remove controls as soon as possible and see that the farmer gets a square deal. Some controls will have to continue for a*

	while, like rationing and building. You can't have people putting up tennis courts and the like. But we don't like Nosey Parkers or the Gestapo. As for the Russians, they are our friends. The only people they like are the Conservatives because Joe Stalin can talk to the Skipper.
Liberal Candidate	*The Conservatives are the party of appeasement, the Socialists of unbridled dogmatism.*
Labour Candidate	*We must make sure the interests of the people are safeguarded, and we must not forget our Russian Allies. It is cruel of Mr Churchill to ask for more babies when there are not enough houses for them to live in.*

When the election was fought, no one in Witheringham doubted that the outcome would be a Conservative victory.

Editor	*This corner of England has always been regarded as a Conservative stronghold, and if Mr Churchill's supporters poll as well as they did at the last General Election there should be no alteration in the present parliamentary representation.*

Nor was the Editor wrong – not, that is, where Witheringham was concerned. Nothing of importance had changed there for at least a hundred years; and visitors to the town left convinced that the town's true motto was *Nil Mutandum* rather than *Nil Desperandum*. In most parts of the land the Socialists swept to power with a landslide victory that was greeted with euphoria or prophesies of cataclysmic doom, depending on which party was supported.

One of Meg's first conscious encounters with a Witheringham resident was in the person of Miss Temple. Just who Miss Temple really was the child never knew. She simply summoned Meg to tea every other Thursday, after school. At first Meg thought she was one of the Vicar's ladies. More probably she was connected in some voluntary capacity with the Witheringham Boarding-out Committee: boarded-out children were officially termed 'children who have no known relatives or worthy friends'. This was still the era of 'the Visitor' and the concept of 'duty' was taken seriously in Witheringham, particularly by its ladies.

Unquestionably, the tradition to which Miss Temple could claim to belong was respectable (in all senses of the word), and who could say it was not deeply concerned with the welfare of paupers, from Mrs Kimmins, founder of the *Guild of the Brave Poor Things* and Miss Kirby, one-time Secretary of the *National Association for the Feeble-Minded*. It needed the practical common sense of a William Cobbett (1762-1835) to put the problem into everyday economic perspective. To the question 'What is a Pauper?', rare man that he was, he gave answer: 'Only a Very Poor Man'.

Miss Temple's preoccupation was with souls. While Meg was accustomed to having to say grace both before she ate and after, with Miss Temple it took a different form. First Meg would be asked to join her in kneeling, placing her hands together and bowing her head. Then, lifting one hand, Miss Temple placed it on Meg's head and in ringing tones declaimed Psalm 51, with all its implications of fallen women; and concluding with 'Then shalt thou be pleased with the sacrifice of righteousness, with the burnt offerings and oblations: then shall they offer young bullocks upon thine altar.' To make her address more directly pertinent Miss Temple passed on to her own improvised prayer: 'Lord! Lord! O Lord! I beseech Thee to hear me. Have mercy upon this Thy lost soul. Who is but a little child. But a child who has nonetheless erred – not as a sheep but a lamb. And a lamb which is gone astray . . .'

Dreary though it was, Meg put up with the performance simply because she assumed she had to. She enjoyed the tea and she liked studying Miss Temple's collection of religious texts, all embroidered in coloured silks with messages such as: 'Nothing in my hand I bring, simply to Thy Cross I cling.' These were framed and, with prints of the Holy Land, hung on Miss Temple's drawing-room walls. Fortunately for Meg, the tea parties lapsed after two years.

There must have been many cases of religious mania in Witheringham. With its heavily laden evangelical traditions it boasted no less than forty churches and chapels. Of these about ten were the parish churches of the town and therefore Church of England. Their rites and practices ranged from the occasional 'High and Crazy' to the more frequent 'Broad and Hazy' or 'Low and Lazy'. The remaining thirty or so establishments were 'Nonconformist'. Unlike the parish churches, they relied less on the organ and more on the harmonium to raise the spirits of their congregations, except where stricter conviction (or parsimony) dictated unaccompanied song. The Iron Mill Lane district sported names such as: Hope Gospel Hall; Mission of the Good Shepherd; Ark of the East Witheringham Brotherhood. Zemaraim Place, and other fashionable areas, catered for more esoteric sects: The Christian Scientists; Selina Countess of Huntingdon's Connexion (she who believed the rich needed evangelizing as much as the poor); The Plymouth Brethren; as well as less extreme forms of Methodist, Baptist and Quaker practice. For doctrinal completeness there was also a Catholic Church – St Aloysius in the London Road; while the town's handful of Theosophists were reduced to renting a small room close to the Colonnade.

Perhaps because Prickler's Hill lay on the fringes of Witheringham and really belonged to Clayhurst, there were only two such places of worship in the immediate neighbourhood. The Bethesda Chapel – known locally as 'the Tin Hut' – stood in Netherfield Road, shaking of a Sabbath Eve to the sound of tambourines and to cries of 'Hosannah', 'Hallelujah' and 'Glory Be'. St Swithin's, the parish church for Clayhurst, was half a mile up the hill in the opposite direction, and there Miss Skinner's rendering of "Rock of Ages" was not calculated to inspire confidence in the passer-by. Sarah, who was 'Church' (but never went), despised those who were 'Chapel', and would have nothing to do with them or even any buildings which happened to be nearby. When it came to choosing a school for the children who boarded with her, she rejected the nearest because it stood opposite the Chapel – though it was in no way connected. Instead, the children were sent to St Swithin's a mile away.

All this concern for Meg's spiritual welfare on the part of others had ironic consequences. When she was due to be confirmed in the Anglican faith, the Vicar thought it advisable to enquire whether or not she had been baptised. It seemed she had – but as a Roman Catholic. Further investigation revealed that, according to the LCC, Meg's religion was recorded both as C of E and Baptist. All very confusing, particularly since the Baptists only practise adult baptism anyway and the actual baptism was stated to have taken place a month before Meg was born! Nevertheless the Vicar deemed it wise to baptise her again. While such attention made Meg feel important, her more practical streak worried about how St Peter would react to such baptismal excesses – always assuming she managed to reach the pearly gates.

> I love thee Lord Jesus
> I ask thee to stay
> Close by me for ever
> . . . And love me . . . I pray . . .

'Surely,' Meg implored, 'if he loves other children, he must love me . . . mustn't he?' God, to whom she addressed her question, made no reply. In the picture which hung on her classroom wall, Jesus sat surrounded by children as small as herself, his long wavy hair shining brightly beneath a golden halo. 'When I go to Heaven,' she informed God, 'I shall sit as close to his left foot as possible. That way, no one will be able to push in front of me.'

She used to talk to God in bed. If she was cheerful, she chattered about what she had been doing at school, or related some (though by no means all) of her conversations with Char'ty. When she was miserable, she unloaded all the burdens of the day, her head buried in a pillow to stifle the tears. Sometimes she admonished him indignantly. Why had she been born, when no one cared if she lived or died? Why was Sarah cruel, Cissie silent, Dot cross, Beryl Saunders unkind to Janey Pratt who couldn't read or write? Why did Jesus have to die? And why did the Vicar keep saying Jesus had died for her, when she hadn't asked him to? Why didn't you save him? she asked God angrily. I would have – if I had been God. 'We must ask God's forgiveness because we are sinners,' the Vicar was always saying. Why? she demanded. What is it that I'm supposed to have done?

The Vicar was forever talking about sin. Meg found sin boring. Even Sarah disliked reading about it in the *Parish Magazine*. Perhaps that was why Sarah never went to church, though she made Meg go to the Children's Service on Sunday morning and to St Swithin's Sunday School in the afternoon. Sometimes Meg visited other Sunday Schools, once she discovered that provided she went Sarah didn't really mind where. This gave Meg the opportunity to explore the town, as well as increasing the number of Christmas parties she got invited to and the prizes she won. By 1946 she possessed two more books: *Talks with Aunt Kate* and *Doubting Thomasina*. At the Baptists' she attended Bible classes and sat examinations run by the Scripture Union. The Covenanters went in for recitation and liked giving free teas. Elsewhere they let her bang their tambourines. She even learnt to play the triangle and one girl taught her chopsticks on the harmonium.

If it rained she had to spend Sundays indoors. Sarah, who had not set foot in a church since Cissie was christened, nonetheless had conventional scruples about how the Sabbath should be observed. The adult members of the household (and this included Dot, now that she had left school) were allowed to read, knit or embroider (but never to darn) after 2 p.m. But Meg – as a child – had to sit on her chair by the window, her hands neatly folded in her lap, forbidden on pain of punishment to move or speak.

'Who knows,' Sarah would say virtuously, 'God might just take it into His head to pity you and make you good. There's not much of a chance, but we all live in hope.'

The tedium of such days was terrible and because Meg could not even blow her nose without first asking Sarah for permission she developed an irritating habit of twisting it from side to side. For two years she endured many miserable

Sundays like this till Cissie eventually took pity on her.

'Here,' she said one wet Sunday, fishing in her apron pocket, 'why don't you read your New Testament?' Adding, as Sarah looked up in alarm, 'You don't have to worry. They gave it to her at Sunday School.'

There was a pause as Sarah pursed her lips and stared suspiciously, first at her daughter and then at the child; but when she made no move to snatch the offering away, Meg opened it and soon appeared to be deep in reading. Not that Meg was reading. She was counting – the word 'straightway'. The last time she read St Mark's Gospel, she found that the number of times the word appeared came to forty-one. She was certain, however, that the correct total was forty-two. To make doubly sure, she would go through the Gospel twice and, if necessary, a third and fourth time.

Sarah's only other religious practices were: not serving meat on Fridays and insisting that all members of the household observe Lent. According to Sarah, the English word 'Lent' originally referred to the lengthening of the days which accompany the onset of Spring. At school, Meg was told it meant discipline and penance, and commemorated the time Jesus spent fasting in the wilderness. Lent began on Ash Wednesday, so called – she was frequently reminded – because ashes are the symbol of penitence and purification.

To compensate for being a sinner, Meg, like everyone else during Lent, was supposed to make a 'sacrifice'. This meant 'giving something up' – such as food, fibs and fairy stories.

'It's got to be something you really like,' Beryl Saunders told her in a voice full of self-importance. 'I'm giving up custard. What about you?'

'I'll tell you tomorrow,' Meg answered warily. Self-imposed punishment was something new, and she was none too sure she liked the sound of it.

She need not have worried since Sarah solved the problem for her. Meg's days were to be shortened. 'You'll go to bed ten minutes early,' Sarah decreed, 'and go without sweets on Sundays.'

Sarah's own 'sacrifice' for Lent took a different form. She gave up playing 'Sorry' with her friend, Amelia Truscott. At

171

half past three every other Tuesday afternoon, Amelia would come to tea. For the next three hours she sat quietly in Sarah's kitchen. Sarah did all the talking; Amelia merely cleared her throat. When Cissie returned from work and the tea things were cleared away, the three ladies settled down to enjoy their game; except during Lent, that is, when Sarah's monologue lasted until Amelia left, at half past seven in the evening.

The game of 'Sorry' consists of a board (similar to that used in 'Snakes and Ladders'), several differently coloured sets of pawns, and a pack of cards bearing instructions to 'start', 'move forward' or 'go back'. Each player chooses a set of pawns (Sarah always preferred red) and in turn takes a card. The aim of the game is to see who can get her pawns 'home' first. This entails capturing any belonging to other people that happen to be standing in the way, and shouting 'Sorry!' on arrival. Sarah usually won – chiefly because neither Amelia nor Cissie would challenge her when she cheated. Sarah and Amelia had been playing 'Sorry' ever since Mr Truscott, Amelia's husband, bought the Dawkins' mineral-water manufacturing business after Sarah's husband died. Not that Sarah ever allowed the word 'bought' to describe the transaction that took place between herself and Arthur Truscott.

'Daylight robbery – that's what it was,' she would declare after Amelia left. 'He should be ashamed of himself, taking advantage of a widow. He did the same to his wife, more fool her. Fancy running after a man half your age.' Sarah tossed her head contemptuously. 'Well it serves her right. Anyone with an ounce of common sense can see what he is – nothing but a devil, with his fancy women – *and* he drinks!'

Meg, who only ever saw Mr Truscott on Christmas Eve, when he stopped at the house to present Sarah with two complimentary siphons of soda water and some blackcurrant cordial, examined him carefully on the next occasion to see if he had horns. But Mr Truscott, a cheerful red-faced man, always kept his hat on when he entered the kitchen. Certainly he looked younger than Amelia, who was shy and elderly and, like Cissie and Miss Temple, had a moustache under her nose as well as whiskers on her chin.

The Truscotts lived in a large detached house at the top of Back Lane. Or rather, Amelia lived there, with her maid Edith. Mr Truscott only 'visited'. Like me, thought Meg, as she trudged up the lane, bearing a note from Sarah. Past the allotments and beyond Nokes Wood, the lane petered out into waste land. In the distance Meg caught sight of prisoners of war, digging foundation trenches in the wet, sticky clay for the new housing estate that would one day be built there. Shyly acknowledging the prisoners when they waved to her (no longer a forbidden action), she turned left into Shoebury Lane in the direction of the London Road leading to Toddington. Amelia's house, "Mon Repos", stood remote and aloof at the end of a cul-de-sac called Prospect Close.

'Ah!' said Edith, examining her closely when she opened the door in response to Meg's knock. 'You had better stay there.'

'Oh!' said Amelia, after reading Sarah's note. 'You had better come in.'

'Sit,' Edith sniffed, 'and mind you don't touch anything.'

The two women looked at each other – and then disappeared.

When it was time for Meg to leave, Edith handed her a scone. 'You had better not eat it in the street.'

Meg stood on the doorstep and hurried to consume the offering.

When Meg was older, Sarah sometimes sent her to Prospect Close in the school holidays, and it was then the two women attempted to teach her to sew.

'You'll have to unpick it,' Edith told her for the fourth week in succession, after examining her hem-stitching. 'The stitches aren't supposed to show through. If you would only hurry up and get it right, you could do something more interesting.' (Such as chain stitch . . . open chain stitch . . . double chain stitch . . .)

'Of course, he married her for her money,' Sarah told the child one winter afternoon. 'Well, there's no fool like an old fool. The way Truscott runs the business he's lucky not to get prosecuted. I know the tricks some of them get up to. Mr Dawkins never did such things. Methylated spirits in the oil – I ask you! Adultery, that's what it is. Father's cordials contained pure essences. He never went in for thinning. Lovely names they had . . .'

Sarah's voice softened as she began to recite:

'Anisette cordial, pepper punch, one we called winter cheer, polo tonic, cascadel, raisin wine – that was a good seller. And the colours . . . Father made such beautiful colours. Cochineal's the best – made from the crushed bodies of dried insects. Sometimes the raspberry cordial came out a bright crimson. There was no raspberry in it, of course . . .' She heaved a sigh. 'No,' she went on, oblivious to her admission, 'one of these days Arthur Truscott will come a cropper with his adultery, if he isn't careful – specially with his ginger beer. It happens, you know!'

Meg sat glued to her chair. She had listened to this tale many times, but still found it fascinating.

'Light the candle!' Sarah ordered, stooping to retrieve her handbag. Rummaging through it, she drew out an envelope from which she extracted a much-folded newspaper clipping. Pushing her spectacles further down her nose, she raised the candlestick aloft and began to intone:

' "It may be said that there is something attractive to snails in the taste of ginger beer but whether that be so or not a certain member of the species somehow found itself inside a ginger-beer bottle. It did not know it, but it caused a material departure in the view of the law of negligence almost amounting to a revolution affecting not only Scotland and England but the whole British Empire where His Majesty's Courts of Law function. The action of this particular snail introducing itself into a bottle of ginger beer in Paisley led to a litigation in the Scottish Courts which finally reached the House of Lords and which has determined the question of the liability of a manufacturer to a member of the public with whom he had no contact. The case is Donague v. Stevenson (1932 A.C. 562). The action was raised by a Mrs Donague against an Aerated Water Manufacturer in Paisley named David Stevenson. The lady was a shop assistant. The case alleged that she went into a Café in

Paisley with a friend who purchased for her a bottle of ginger beer, some of which the shopkeeper poured into a tumbler; Mrs Donague drank some of the contents of the tumbler and her friend was then proceeding to pour out the remainder into the tumbler when the snail in a state of decomposition floated out of the bottle. Mrs Donague averred that as a result of the nauseating sight of the snail in such circumstances she suffered shock . . ."

'You see!' Sarah said triumphantly. 'I've warned Amelia, time and again, to be careful. She should check the premises to make sure they're clean and free from any crawlies – that's what I used to do. Every Friday I was down there. Not a bottle or a siphon left the place without me polishing its cap. Mind you, it would be hard to get a snail into a siphon of soda water.'

Meg also knew about soda water; this was another of Sarah's favourite subjects.

'It isn't real, like the sort you find in natural springs,' Sarah was fond of explaining. 'Soda water's nothing more than tap water injected with "bicarb" and gas. When we started the business, Mr Dawkins told me all about it – thinking I'd understand on account of me being a wages clerk at a Vinegar Works when we met. Mephitic Julep, that's what he said they used to call it. "What's that?" I asked. "Poisonous Juice." I nearly died.

'So I said to him: "Are you asking me to poison people? Whatever do you take me for?" '

Sarah looked suitably horrified, while Meg nodded her head in anxious agreement. ' "It's true," he said. "But don't worry, Mother. You'd need an awful lot of carbon dioxide gas to do that. We'll only put enough in to give people a bit of a fizz." '

Meg thought of the soda water Mr Truscott gave them, standing on the pantry floor next to the vinegar bottle. Whenever she was sick Sarah made her drink some.

'After that, of course,' Sarah continued, 'I wouldn't ever let Cissie drink a drop. Mind you, Mr Dawkins always took a glass last thing at night.'

But he's dead, Meg thought in alarm, on hearing this story for the first time.

'And so do I,' Sarah added, much to the child's relief.

Apart from Amelia and the milkman, the only other visitors to the house were Cissie's insurance man (once a week), the landlord and the grocer (once a fortnight), Miss Braddock (quarterly), and – once a year – Cissie's old school friend, Muriel Hackett.

Some considered Muriel (or 'Hack' as she was known) a forbidding figure of a woman – six feet tall, with grey shingled hair and steel-rimmed spectacles. But in Meg's eyes Hack was always transfigured the moment she smiled. Wry and wolfish, her smile was full of intelligence and humour. According to Sarah, Hack's parents gave a sigh of relief when their daughter left home; seeing no matrimonial future for someone so unfeminine in appearance, they preferred now not to see her at all. It was a view Sarah shared, particularly after Hack invited Cissie – when Cissie reached thirty – to share a flat with her in London. Cissie, it seemed, refused outright; but Sarah was so shocked by the proposal that she threatened to lock her daughter in her room and to throw away the key. After Mr Dawkins died Sarah took drastic measures to 'contain' her daughter. As Sarah saw it, she and Cissie were on the brink of starvation. Since immediate economies would have to be made in every area, including social activity, she instructed Cissie to sever contact with her friends. Normally Cissie obeyed her mother without question, but on this occasion she refused; she had only ever been allowed one friend anyway – the importunate Hack. Reluctantly, Sarah agreed to reconsider the matter and eventually consented to the two friends meeting for tea: once a year on the first Saturday in July.

If Cissie dreamed of having a life of her own, such hopes had been dashed long ago. Although she had been an attractive girl (photographs showed her as slim and golden-haired), neither of her parents had any intention of letting her marry. Her father, when pressed (as he was by one suitor), said he considered young men unreliable. He favoured an older man for his daughter, fully aware that these were hard to find, most of them having died in the First World War. Sarah voiced her objections more bluntly. Cissie had a good home. Why think of marrying and setting up one of her own when she knew perfectly well – because Sarah said so – that all men, irrespective of age, were little better than beasts? In any case, it was her duty, as an only daughter, to stay at home and look after her parents. Not to do so was unnatural. It was 'bad' for parents and child alike. If Cissie went off she might get up to all sorts of undesirable things. Furthermore, Hack's offer was unrealistic. How could Cissie seriously consider financial independence when she was too poorly paid to support her mother and herself?

Cissie's difficulties were not just financial. From birth, Sarah had tied her daughter to herself as tightly as a spider binds a fly. She had brainwashed Cissie into believing that she would never survive in the rough and tumble of the world beyond her mother's protection. Caught in this web of domination Cissie's only defence was to develop personality traits which were directly opposite to those of her mother. The resulting contrast between the two women was startling, even to so young an observer as Meg. Cissie matched harshness with resignation, turbulence with inertia, aggression with appeasement. She coped with domination by offering absolute submission. She passed through life like a sleepwalker, apparently unaware of what was going on around her, including all avoidable chores and responsibilities. She neither helped lay nor clear the table, wash or dry the dishes, shop, cook, launder, iron, work in the garden, or clean the house. The only chore Meg ever saw her do was making the bed she shared with Sarah. When Sarah solved their financial problems by taking children as lodgers, Cissie simply carried on as usual, but with the added advantage that the children proved very effective lightning rods for deflecting Sarah's bad temper away from herself.

In opting to live her life the way she did, Cissie forfeited all powers of decision, of individual expression and of independent action. When she moved, it was like a run-down clockwork doll — stiff and slow. If Sarah questioned her, she answered in monosyllables in a flat, cracked voice. Since she never attempted to make conversation, it was difficult to know if she actually thought about anything. Yet Cissie, Meg was sure, knew more than anyone what Sarah was like — her drive for power, her frustrated hopes, her need to be always right, her deep insecurity. But the time was to come when Meg would wonder if it was not Cissie's submission to her mother which actually fuelled Sarah's tyranny.

PART 8

•••

Bread and Candles

If the material conditions of life in wartime Britain were poor, they were to seem as nothing compared with the years of austerity that followed. Early in 1946 there was a world shortage of food. Back came the grey bread of wartime (except that it was now rationed). The housing situation, due to bomb damage and population movements, was critical. Fuel was in desperately short supply. The winter of 1946-7, the worst for fifty years, deepened the misery. For three months the country was paralysed by snow, with ice drifts fourteen feet deep in places. Roads were blocked, transport immobilized. Sheep and cattle died in their thousands. Acres of winter corn and vegetables were ruined. More than two million people were temporarily unemployed.

As the candles were lit in Witheringham, the army pulled out of the town and its barracks were taken over by homeless families. Complaints about food ('what we eat now is little better than cattle food'), the paper shortage ('if we have another war, there won't be any paper coffins, just a lot of dust'), how residents treated visitors to the town ('people would think we didn't like them'), were met by threats to imprison anyone caught wasting electricity. With beer short, the Mayor expressed concern for 'the future of the world'. The Protestant Truth Society launched a campaign to 'save the town's youth' and called for the closure of cinemas on Sundays. The Witheringham Housewives League deplored the effect of 'communist propaganda on young people, who are little better than sheep'. The young people retaliated by calling the residents 'lethargic and stagnant'. A councillor 'trying to see things from both sides' said that 'all the residents really care about is whether the rates go up or down'. Warnings were given that frost and famine would shortly be followed by floods, since 'water has always been a problem in Witheringham' and 'some tenants in the newly-erected prefabs are turning into amphibians'. The Town Council announced its new postwar motto: 'Free and Unhampered Competition' and promptly raised the water rates by two shillings.

Meg's own memory of the winter of 1947 was one of elemental savagery: black, frost-bitten potatoes cooked without salt, soggy and vile-tasting; chilblains on fingers and toes – cracked and festering; foraging for wood in the snow; crouching against snow banks, eyes wounded with cold; shadowing the coal-man up hill and down – darting to catch his droppings; endlessly slipping, sliding, falling.

When Cissie fell on the ice and smashed her teeth, a dentist extracted the stumps. Normally if a member of the household complained of a wobbly tooth Sarah took a thread, tied one end to the tooth and the other round a doorknob – and slammed the door hard (which may explain why Sarah herself was toothless). But after what happened to Cissie, Meg was not prepared to lose a single tooth through any external agency. Two toothless members of the household were quite enough, she decided.

Cissie's second mishap was equally dramatic, fulfilling what Sarah had prophesied for years: she got the sack. If Sarah was shocked, so was Meg.

'The reason you're being told,' Sarah informed Meg, 'is because I don't want it coming to you from some scandalmonger outside. The man's been after her for years, ever since he got taken on as manager. Too old-fashioned, he called her – not fast enough more like it. I know his sort!' Sarah tossed her head defiantly at Cissie. 'What your father would say, if he were here now, I just don't know. It's enough to make him turn in his grave.'

Sarah's reference to death clearly upset her. Throwing her apron over her face she flung herself in her chair and began to rock back and forth groaning loudly.

'It's no use, Mother.' Cissie's voice was matter-of-fact. 'What's done is done – and that's an end to it.'

'What do you mean?' Sarah thrust her apron down and sat up angrily. 'He set a trap for you, didn't he?'

'I just don't want any trouble.'

'Well what do you think this is, if it isn't trouble?' Sarah demanded hotly. 'You, I suppose, will simply sit there and tell me I have nothing to worry about. Jobs you'll say are two a penny. And all you have to do is go out and get one. Is that it?'

'I can always try. That's what you spend all your time telling me, isn't it?'

Meg sat agog. She had never heard Cissie answer her mother back before. She had never even heard her say so much.

'Hah!' Sarah snorted. 'And what about the little matter of your reference. Have you thought of that? How is it in all these years I still haven't managed to din an ounce of common sense into that thick head of yours? What do you think it's like out there? Tell me that!'

'It's where I've been for thirty years. I think I know something about it,' Cissie said quietly.

Sarah made a menacing gesture with her fist. For an appalled moment Meg thought Sarah was going to hit her own daughter. Instead, she seized a loaf of bread, pressed it to her chest, and began sawing at it with a knife. 'Five shillings! Can you believe it? You got the sack for taking five shillings . . .'

Meg's jaw dropped in amazement.

'I was accused of taking five shillings,' Cissie corrected her mother. 'That's not the same as doing it.'

As Cissie spoke Meg stole a glance at the woman's face. Then she returned to her dinner – two slices of bread and dripping, washed down with a cup of hot Oxo. She so admired this change in Cissie, pleased that for once Cissie was mustering the courage to speak up. Then Meg choked, and so violently that Cissie had to get up and bang her on the back. But it wasn't the bread that caused the seizure, it was the effort Meg was making to stop herself from bursting into laughter. It had come to her in a flash. This was no alleged theft. Of course Cissie had done it. She had probably been doing it for years. Cissie wasn't dazed or distressed: she was relieved. Cissie knew it . . . Sarah knew it . . . and now she knew it!

But the matter was very serious. Although by Spring 1947 there were plenty of jobs vacant, Cissie's problem was that she had been sacked on the spot without a reference. Wherever she applied for work she was going to have to admit this. To have no reference meant only one thing: you had been dismissed for some serious misdemeanour. Once Sarah was over the first shock she rallied magnificently. Calling for paper and pen she drafted a letter. This she proposed sending to several of the gentlewomen who patronized Cissie's employer, Lacey's. Concealing nothing (and emphasizing the iniquity of the charge which, because it besmirched her name, had been levelled as much at her as her daughter), she asked if they would act as referees for Cissie. All the ladies replied in the affirmative; and two of them went so far as to cancel their subscriptions to the Lending Library, so distressed they were at what Lacey's had done to their 'dear Miss Dawkins'.

For six months Cissie was unemployed. Sarah visibly shrank under the strain and the atmosphere in the house was unusually subdued. Dot, by this time an attractive seventeen-year-old, had the wit to exploit the situation to her own advantage. Sensing that Cissie's misadventure was serving to undermine Sarah's authority, Dot went out of her way to snub Cissie (taking her cue from Sarah herself), and was blatantly disobedient. Night after night she went out, despite Sarah's attempts to stop her. One night Sarah locked the high gate leading to the back door. Not till Dot was reduced to hysterics, as she banged on the front door and pleaded with Sarah through the letter-box to be let in, did Sarah relent – and only after Dot promised to behave herself in future. 'Otherwise,' Sarah warned her, 'I'll see you get put away.'

For Meg's part, the affection she felt for Cissie deepened as her compassion was aroused. It was painful to watch another being treated as the pariah. True, Cissie wasn't banished to the scullery to eat her meals alone, but for weeks Sarah would only speak to her daughter through Dot or Meg.

Cissie was the scapegoat?
Cissie was the thief?
But whoever lived in Sarah's house
Was bound to come to grief!

Ultimately the crisis was financial. It finally highlighted something which must have gnawed at Sarah for years: the declining value of Cissie's contribution to the household's income. With a weekly wage of £2 7s 6d in 1947, Cissie had been grossly underpaid for years. From this wage, Sarah allowed her to keep half-a-crown a week as pocket money. She then allocated £1 for her and Cissie's clothes, 8 shillings went on rent, 1 shilling on Cissie's insurance, 6d each on their respective burial clubs, and 10 shillings were put aside as Sarah's own savings. This left a balance of 5 shillings. When added to Dot's earnings of £1 and the 13s 6d she received for Meg's board and lodging, Sarah was left with a weekly income to cover household expenditure for four people of £1 18s 6d.

What kind of unemployment benefit (if any) Cissie received during this time, Meg did not know. The very idea that she might have to dip into her savings gave Sarah palpitations. On several occasions the child had to hurry to fetch her a glass of brandy to brace her against such an appalling anticipation. Why, Sarah asked them all, one dark and gloomy afternoon as Cissie sat unravelling a worn-out cardigan, was it always a member of her own family who brought her to the brink of destitution? First her father, Mr Dobbs, dissipated her inheritance (for which crime she had refused to visit him when he was dying in the workhouse or even to attend his funeral). Next, the savings she so painstakingly accrued over the years before her marriage went down the drain – when a shop that she had leased as a young bride failed. (This time her husband, the landlord and her customers were blamed.) Mr Dawkins died (he should have known better), leaving her with little more than what she herself had had the good sense to put aside without his knowledge. Now all her remaining savings – including what she had put away after caring for other people's cast-off children – were under threat, because Cissie had let her down. Not to mention Dot and Meg, who were 'eating her out of house and home'. Nobody cared.

Everything she did turned to dust. The sooner they sent her to the workhouse the better. She wished she were dead.

Sarah's brooding, tantrums and threats to commit suicide lasted six months – long enough for Meg to learn never to admit to poverty outside the house, such was its terrible shame and disgrace. It was a lesson that stood her in good stead for shortly afterwards her life (as much as Cissie's) was about to undergo a major change. Early in 1946, Miss Wilkinson had sat her down one day and told her that she was to take an examination. She was to write a composition, do some sums, answer some written questions, and fill in several sheets of paper covered with symbols. At no time might she put up her hand or speak. With a stopwatch at the ready, the head-mistress gave the signal to start. Around her, lessons continued as before. Subsequently, Meg was told that she had won what Miss Wilkinson called a 'scholarship'. When nothing further happened, Meg forgot about it, since she had no idea what it was. And when, some weeks later, an alderman from Witheringham's Town Council presented her with two books (for coming top of St Swithin's), she assumed this was it. Not till the following year did she learn that she had been given a place at Witheringham Grammar School, starting in the autumn term of 1947.

While Cissie looked for work, Sarah was writing to the London County Council. Miss Braddock no longer kept an eye on Prickler's Hill. Miss Gosling was now Meg's 'Visitor'. A friendly, more relaxed woman, Miss Gosling called at the house every month and even approached Meg in the street in an effort to speak to the child alone. But Meg remained as reticent with Miss Gosling as she had with Miss Braddock. Undaunted, Miss Gosling set about cultivating Cissie. Perhaps what Miss Gosling (who was middle-aged) hoped, was that Cissie – at forty-seven – could be persuaded to play a more 'positive' role in Meg's life, and Meg could then have something more resembling 'normal' home life. But all Miss Gosling succeeded in doing was to get Cissie to cut her long hair and adopt a more up-to-date style.

In the matter of Meg's school uniform, Miss Gosling joined forces with Sarah to wage a memorable battle to secure a clothing grant from the Borough Council responsible for Meg's maintenance. Fittings took place, the clothes were ordered, everything was ready – except the cash: £8 7s 10d. The Borough Council responded to the news of the scholarship with a cautious mixture of pride and suspicion. Into what unplumbed depths, it seemed to be asking, was this duckling of theirs straying now? Back and forth the letters flew. Correspondence from the Borough Council always opened nervously. 'I most humbly beg to acknowledge . . . Adverting to your telephonic communication of the 1st ultimo . . . I take pleasure in forwarding herewith . . .' The LCC was much more self-assured: 'Are you aware that . . . Attached please find . . . Will you please attend immediately to . . .'

Aware of Sarah's readiness to complain, the Borough Council also knew that she never missed an opportunity to extract more money from them. In the matter of the school uniform they refused to grant a penny of the money requested until Sarah had agreed to produce bona fide bills for the money required – a week before term at the grammar school started. So enraged was Sarah that thereafter she adamantly refused to spend any of Meg's clothing allowance (3s 6d weekly) on school clothes. If two years later, when Meg suddenly began to grow, she turned up at school looking like a scarecrow in clothes that were far too small for her, that, Sarah said, was the Council's fault – not hers.

'What d'you mean – your tunic's too long?' Sarah was emptying the contents of Meg's satchel on to the kitchen table when she spoke. 'Of course it's long. If you think a girl from this house is going to show her bottom every time she bends over, you've another think coming.'

She adjusted her spectacles on the end of her nose and laboriously leafed through Meg's pile of new exercise books, scowling suspiciously at their many blank pages.

'There's an inspection on Monday,' Meg told her. 'Everyone's tunic has to be three inches above the knee when they're standing up, and not touching the floor when they kneel down. It's the same with hair. Miss Giddings says if we wear it loose, it mustn't touch our shoulders. Otherwise it's to go into bunches or plaits. She's threatened to cut any girl's hair which isn't right.'

Sarah's eyes narrowed. Meg hurried on. 'It's the rules, you see. There are so many: no running in the corridor or on the stairs; no eating in the street wearing school uniform; no walking about with your hat off or your blazer unbuttoned. Then there's homework . . .' Meg gestured dispiritedly in the direction of her satchel. 'If you don't hand it in on time, you have to report yourself to your form mistress, and she might send you to Miss Underwood, the headmistress.'

'What are you babbling about?' Sarah demanded. 'When I agreed to let you go to the Grammar, no one told me I'd have books littering my table every evening. It isn't right! As for rules – the only person who makes rules in this house is me. So you can tell Miss Underwood from me: she can put that in her pipe and smoke it. Educating girls is all wrong, and as for educating them above their station, that's downright criminal. French indeed! You'll have Boney after you. A girl's place is in the home – not gallivanting around and filling her head with nonsense. Brain fever – that's what you'll end up with, you mark my words!'

Meg, seated on her chair, stared out of the window. She wasn't even sure she cared all that much. After the first week at the new school, she was bewildered; she longed for nothing more than to be allowed to return to the leisurely world of St Swithin's. The grammar school was so big – with its many classrooms, corridors, playing fields and pupils; its regimented timetables and rules governing dress and behaviour. Worst of all were the bells. One rang every forty minutes to mark the end of a lesson, followed two minutes later by another announcing the start of the next. In that two minutes, she had to scurry along with hundreds of other girls, all dressed like herself in navy blue serge tunics and white blouses, to find the right corridor, leading to the right classroom for the right lesson, bearing the right books.

The only person who made it all bearable was Miss Fairchild, her form mistress. With her warm smile and soft voice, Miss Fairchild was one of the nicest people Meg had ever met. The teacher had a special way of looking straight at you and, even when you said nothing, seemed to understand what you were feeling. It was what she looked forward to each day she went to school – to seeing her form mistress. But how would Miss Fairchild react if Meg didn't do her homework? Didn't produce the penny a week all pupils were supposed to contribute to 'Voluntary Service'? Although Meg now had 3d a week pocket-money, Sarah took a penny of it for 'Savings', Cissie a penny for 'Christmas and Birthdays'. The remaining penny Meg wanted to keep for herself. Then there were the needles and wool she was supposed to take on Fridays, to knit into squares someone else made into blankets. Weren't they for the lonely sailors who spent their time watching flying fish jumping about in the Pacific Ocean? Or were they for the people living in the jungle, in the hospital where the doctor with the white whiskers played the organ? What had Miss Fairchild said to her? 'I don't want you to worry, Meg, if there's anything you can't bring. All you have to do is to tell me. Will you do that?' Meg doubted it, but somehow believed Miss Fairchild would still understand. She turned from the window and caught Cissie's eye. Surprisingly, Cissie winked, then leant forward to study her knitting pattern.

'Of course we can't have her breaking any rules. After all, Mother, who knows better than you when it comes to rules?' Sarah sniffed. 'There's always that extra half-a-crown to consider,' Cissie continued placidly. 'It seems a shame to have to send it back, after all the hard work you put into getting Meg her uniform. But you know what Miss Gosling said: the maintenance only goes up from 13s 6d to 16s for girls who are in secondary education. If they throw her out of the Grammar for not doing her homework, you'll have to give it back, won't you?'

Sarah looked horrified. 'They wouldn't do that. That money's mine!'

'Of course it is – and quite right too. But she'll have to do the homework.' Sarah looked disconcerted, while Cissie turned to Meg. 'How much are you supposed to do?'

'An hour and a half each evening. The amount goes up every year, till it's about three hours a night.'

'What about weekends? I don't think we can agree to you doing it then.'

'I should think not,' Sarah butted in. 'This is a Christian household.'

Meg flashed Cissie a grateful smile. With the problem of homework almost resolved, she was sure she would manage somehow or other. She knew Sarah would always take advantage of her (and of anyone else), once she knew where they were vulnerable. And there were many occasions subsequently when Sarah, for no apparent reason, confiscated the child's books. To guard against this, Meg speeded up her powers of concentration. Anything that had to be learnt by heart she could do in the street on her way to school. Writing and sums might be done in the school lavatories at break or, if pressed, by moonlight in bed.

Before long, and helped by Miss Fairchild's presence, Meg swooped like a hungry seagull to devour every morsel of knowledge that came her way – or almost. It took one look at a dissected frog pinned up in a specimen case outside the science room to kill stone dead any budding interest in biology she might have had. Geography fared badly too. Not having encountered an atlas before, she could not make head or tail of maps, and she possessed no coloured pencils for doing map work. Similarly, the lack of a set of instruments put a blight on her introduction to geometry – though it was also her inability to understand, in the case of Pythagoras, how the square on the hypotenuse could be equal to the sum of the squares on the other two sides, when all she ever saw looked like a windmill. There were other children at the school who were just as poorly equipped when it came to material belongings. An ingrained sense of shame, however, coupled with a fear of ridicule, prevented her from admitting the fact. She preferred to be thought careless, even lazy, rather than ask if she might borrow equipment – unless it were a hockey stick or tennis racquet: only a handful of girls owned things like these. But handicaps of this sort made little difference to Meg's performance in the subjects which really interested her, nor did they affect the friendships she quickly formed with fellow pupils. In one particular respect Meg even had advantages. Since she belonged nowhere (or so she felt), she experienced none of the strain some of her friends underwent in adapting to the attitudes which dominated the school. She felt neither absorbed by them nor rejected. She accepted what she liked, discarded or ignored anything which did not appeal to her (such as the petty snobbery some girls displayed when they discovered a prefect's father was – say – a bus conductor). If the school had faults, they lay more in the pressure which resulted from the emphasis placed on academic achievement.

'Stop being silly. I won't ask you again.' Sarah spoke sharply. 'Give me that packet now!'

Cissie continued to knit, leaning forward to consult her pattern . . . slip one, knit one, pass slipped stitch over. 'I told you when I started that I wasn't going to hand over my wages any more,' she said, not looking up. 'When you understand that, I'll give you your money and – a surprise as well.'

'Give me the wages! I don't want a surprise,' Sarah exclaimed.

'No!'

Dot (who also had to hand over her pay packet unopened) sat watching the proceedings like a hawk, while Meg tried to conjugate the French verb for 'to have': 'j'ai, tu as, il a, elle a . . .' (if she's lucky, the child thought).

'Well, you can get out for a start,' Sarah snapped at Dot, who was all ears.

'I'll stay, if you don't mind,' was the unexpectedly pert reply. 'Go on, Aunt Cissie. If you're going to keep your money, then I shall keep mine.'

Sarah raised her arm as if to strike the girl.

'Don't you touch me, you old . . .' Dot flung at her.

'Go on,' Sarah's voice was dangerously quiet, 'say it.' But Dot, sensing that she had gone too far, subsided, her cheeks scarlet. 'I think,' Sarah continued, 'Miss Gosling should know a little about your doings. You've got a shade too big for your boots just lately. One word from me – and she'll have you put away. And don't think I shan't be able to prove it, either.

It'll be my word against yours.' Dot shrugged her shoulders insolently.

'Stop it, the pair of you. This isn't something to fight about.' Cissie, laughing good-humouredly, reached for her bag.

She had just completed her first week in a new job. This was for a timber merchant. The job was easy; the hours were good; she was her own mistress in a little shop with a cosy room at the back of a store stacked with wood samples; she had Saturday afternoons free; her employer was kind (when she told him about being dismissed from Lacey's, he brushed the matter aside); she had privacy for the first time in her life; she could sit down, instead of being on her feet all day; she could make herself a cup of tea when she felt like it; she was free to knit or read. And – she was paid more than double the wages she had received at Lacey's. Cissie had good reason to be happy: what had seemed a tragedy six months ago had proved to be a blessing.

'Now,' she announced, standing up. 'None of you are to interrupt. Here's the money I used to pay you.' She laid out £1 5s od on the table in front of Sarah. 'And here's the money for your clothes.' Cissie added a further 10s.

'Where's yours?' Sarah wanted to know. 'You know I always buy yours. You don't know how to buy clothes – rubbish, that's what you'll get.'

'I'll have to learn, won't I,' Cissie told her. 'After I've put my clothing money aside, that will leave me with two pounds and fifteen shillings. The fifteen shillings is mine.' Sarah stared at her daughter in astonishment. 'I think that's fair, after all these years, don't you?'

Sarah had the grace to look uncomfortable, while Dot's mouth dropped open.

'From the two pounds left, you can have one – to do exactly what you like with. And I'll keep the other. Now,' Cissie said, smiling in her usual self-effacing way, 'for the surprises.'

To Dot she handed a bottle of scent (Woolworth's "California Poppy"). For Meg there was the wooden pencil-box with the sliding lid that she had been hankering after for months. Sarah got a new teapot.

'Humph!' Sarah growled, prodding the pot with her finger. 'If that's how you're going to spend your money, you'll not get far. Anyway, what exactly are you going to do with that other £1?'

'Well, I thought we might start by enjoying ourselves more, now that I have Saturday afternoons off. We could go shopping and then to the pictures. You can pay for tea out of your pound, and I'll buy the tickets out of mine.'

From then on, at two o'clock each Saturday afternoon (in fair weather or foul), Meg was bundled out of the house and given strict instructions not to return before 8 p.m. Such unexpected freedom delighted her at first (as well as the 6d Cissie gave her to buy her tea). Some afternoons she spent with friends, but only with those who did not mind the fact that she never returned the invitation; and she was careful not to go too often. In spring or summertime, she usually made for the Graze, since she no longer frequented her old haunts, the meadows and woods around Clayhurst. She found the Graze beautiful with its springy turf and wide, open spaces. Sometimes she lay in the grass watching cricket, or she went rock-climbing; or she explored a new wood, stopping to gather wild flowers to take to school on Monday mornings. Then she returned to the house dusty and tired, but always refreshed. Winter was different. If she sat too long in the public library, the librarian would look at her suspiciously. In any case, it closed at half past five. Bored with trailing aimlessly around the town, she would make for the 'wreck' where, shivering with cold, she sat on a seat in the shelter until it was time for her to return to the house.

Occasionally she explored the Colonnade, browsing for hours in second-hand bookshops; or she visited the stamp shop. Here too, she could lose the odd hour or two, without interruption or pressure to buy. Sometimes she made a purchase, but not without prudently deliberating the matter first. One day, while agonizing about which of two stamps to buy, she was startled when someone leant over her shoulder and said: 'I should have that one, if I were you.' She looked up to see an old, bespectacled man gazing down at her.

'Why?' she asked cautiously.

'It isn't as common as the other, but it depends on what you're after. Colonials, is it?'

Thereafter, when they encountered one another in the stamp shop, he always smiled and nodded and made a passing remark such as: 'Well, I suppose it's just as well to go for colonials. Nearly done, you know. Always felt it was a mistake – but there you are . . .'

One day, when she was climbing Naboth's Walk, she noticed the old man some distance in front of her, walking very slowly. Every few yards he stopped, as if to get his breath. Then he staggered and, thrusting out a hand in an effort to stop himself falling, dropped his bundle of newspapers and books on to the pavement. Meg hurried forward.

'How kind,' she heard him say, as she bent to retrieve his belongings.

'Are you all right?' she stammered, noticing his pallor.

'Nothing to worry about. Just getting old, but do you think you could be very kind and carry that stuff indoors for me. I live just here,' he said, gesturing towards a gate. 'My house-keeper's there.'

Meg found herself in a large, airy room. It was lined with books and had windows at both ends which stretched from floor to ceiling. There were books everywhere – on the table, on chairs, even on the floor.

'Are these all yours?' Meg blurted out.

'Mine . . . others' . . . does it matter?' The old man lowered himself wearily into an armchair that also looked as if it were about to collapse. 'Take a look round, if you like. I'll ask Mrs Pritchard to make some tea.'

Meg stared at the bookshelves. Here was a collection the like of which she would not come across again in a private house – not, that is, for many years. 'Have you read them all?' she asked, her curiosity overcoming her shyness.

'If I have it hasn't helped me much.' The housekeeper came in with a tray of tea. 'I hope you've a second cup there. My young visitor is a novitiate in the art of philately and needs some refreshment just as much as I do.'

Mrs Pritchard smiled and gestured to Meg to sit down. 'Here,' the old man called, sweeping a chair clear of a pile of books, 'try this one; and while you're about it you can have a look at some stamps.'

Before long, Meg was spending every Saturday afternoon like this. At three o'clock sharp, she appeared on the old man's doorstep. Sometimes she accompanied him to the stamp shop where, to her surprise, he might exchange several stamps for just one. Other days, when it was too wet or cold for him to venture out, the two of them sat in silence, reading or poring over his stamp collection. When she first started visiting him, he had questioned her about her family, but her face must have told him all that he needed to know, for the subject was discreetly dropped and never referred to again.

One day, after she had been tidying a pile of albums, he beckoned her to fetch him one – a large Stanley Gibbon, bound in hard covers with sheets of tissue paper laid between the pages. 'You can have that,' he told her gruffly. 'Mind you take care of it. You'll be hard put to find another as good. No stamps in it, of course. You'll have to do that bit yourself.'

Meg held the album to her gingerly, quite at a loss to know what to say – even how to thank him. Later, she laid it carefully on a shelf, leaving it there when she put her hat and coat on to leave.

'Don't you want to take it with you?' the old man asked in surprise.

Meg shook her head, frowning awkwardly.

There was a silence in which he seemed to be debating something with himself. 'All right,' he said at last. 'It can stay here . . . if that's what you want.'

The following week, the old man greeted her with another surprise. Handing her a magnifying glass, he let fall on to the table a pile of heavily-franked stamps. 'I want you to examine these under the glass. If you look carefully, you'll see that each stamp bears a letter of the alphabet as well as a set of numbers. Your job is to group them by letter and then put them in numerical order. Do you know what they are?' he asked. She shook her head. 'Penny reds – two hundred of 'em. After you've classified them, they can go in your album: they're yours.'

Sometimes, as they sat together, he encouraged her to tell him about school and showed great forbearance when she chattered childishly about the various pranks she and her friends got up to.

'What's your favourite lesson?' he asked one day.

'Poetry,' she replied without hesitation.

'Ah!' He threw his head back and examined her over the top of his glasses. 'And to what poet are you particularly partial?'

The phrase intrigued her. She tried to think. 'It depends,' she replied at last. 'Sometimes it's Byron . . . or it might be Yeats. Then I like Masefield.'

'Not bad, not bad, could be worse . . .'

In unison they began to chant:

> The Assyrian came down like the wolf on the fold
> And his cohorts were gleaming as purple and gold;
> And the sheen of their spears was like stars on the sea,
> When the blue wave rolls nightly on deep Galilee . . .

He swivelled in his chair, stretching out a hand to take a book from a shelf. The page he opened had a marker in it. It was clearly a familiar passage he now read aloud:

> Now is the time for stripping the spirit bare,
> Time for the burning of days ended and done,
> Idle solace of things that have gone before:
> Rootless hope and fruitless desire are there;
> Let them go to the fire with never a look behind.
> The world that was ours is a world that is ours no more.

'Binyon, Laurence – but you should read Auden.'

He sank into a reverie. The child felt, rather than heard, his thoughts travelling backwards. 'And Swift,' he murmured. 'We mustn't forget our Jonathan. Not, as Dryden was wont to say, a poet as such. But he spoke the truth for all that. There was a man who knew what the human race was really capable of . . .'

He turned to Meg. 'So it's a poet you want to be.'

She shook her head.

'Why not? You write the stuff, don't you?'

'Yes . . . No . . . Oh you wouldn't understand!' Suddenly she was in tears.

'Let me try,' the old man said quietly, listening to the muffled voice that was trying to explain what it felt like to be twelve years old, in 1948, when you have only just discovered that war does stop, only to start again.

Sitting in class one sunny afternoon a few weeks earlier, Meg had been reading an anthology called 'Poems of Today' – a rather inaccurate title, since most of the contents had been composed either by poets who were dead or who, if living, must have been exceedingly old. But the past – when it bore no relation to her own – possessed a life of such vitality and wonderment, and she flew to it as swiftly as a bird might dart for its nest. With her head full of magic gleaned from story and history books, from legends and myths, this remote past was a sanctuary of pleasure and peace. It was where, for her, poetry belonged.

It never occurred to Meg to see any connection between the poems she was asked to compose for homework (a request many of her classmates greeted with groans) and the idea that, somewhere in the world, people might choose to write poetry rather than do anything else. The fact that she enjoyed doing poetry homework she kept to herself for fear others would think her peculiar. Recitation was a different matter. Everyone enjoyed that (even if they disliked learning chunks of verse by heart). But the impact poetry made on her at this stage was wrapped up more with sound and rhythm than with what the poet was trying to say.

From choice, she would have sat for hours listening contentedly to someone reciting ballads, or a poem such as Walter de la Mare's 'The Listeners'. Most of all she hoped Miss Thurkle, her English teacher, would ask her, Meg Chandler, to recite something. Then she might agonize between Long-fellow's 'The Song of Hiawatha' (of which she knew long passages by heart), or Tennyson's 'The Lady of Shalott'. Usually she opted for the latter because she knew the dramatic effects she practised might amuse her classmates. Her favourite style of delivery was a monotone, designed to enhance the poem's natural rhythm, and she recited it at breakneck speed till she reached the lines everyone (other than Miss Thurkle) was waiting to hear:

> She left the web, she left the loom,
> She made three paces thro' the room,
> She saw the water-lily bloom,
> She saw the helmet and the plume

(Pause, lower voice to whisper, adopt funereal speed)

> She . . . looked . . . down . . . to . . . Cam . . . elot.

(Long pause, raise voice, gradually increase pitch to scream)

> Out flew the web and floated wide;
> The mirror crack'd from side to side;

(Loudest scream possible)

> 'The curse is come upon me' cried

(End with matter-of-fact tone)

> The Lady of Shalott.

'I am not sure,' Miss Thurkle announced finally, 'that the time hasn't come to give Tennyson a rest.' And Meg, who found Longfellow's charms were also beginning to wane, turned to other favourites.

More recently, the class had been 'studying' the English war poets. Half-listening as a classmate recited from Rupert Brooke – the rest of the class were supposed to be following in their books – Meg was rifling through the book in search of something more interesting. Time and again, she returned to a particular poem – one which attracted, but at the same time unnerved her. It possessed what she could only have described as a special 'sound' – and one she recognized instantly. Yet the poem made her uneasy, even irritated her, because she could not play with it in any way; nor did she know how to give it the attention it so obviously deserved. More disturbing, it seemed to be saying something she knew already . . . something she was refusing to accept. She turned to others by the same poet. They were equally fluent, equally condensed. Even when exposed to the perfunctory treatment she was giving them, they communicated an extraordinary sense of completeness. She was, quite simply, reading very good poetry: so good, in fact, that she could not imagine ever being able to do the same. Saddened by such an early recognition of her lack of talent, she turned with relief to another page, to read Siegfried Sassoon's poem *Everyone Sang*. At first reading, it seemed so joyful:

> Everyone suddenly burst out singing;
> And I was filled with such delight
> As prisoned birds must find in freedom,
> Winging wildly across the white
> Orchards and dark-green fields; on – on – and out of sight.
>
> Everyone's voice was suddenly lifted;
> And beauty came like the setting sun:
> My heart was shaken with tears; and horror
> Drifted away . . . O, but Everyone
> Was a bird; and the song was wordless; the singing
>
> will never be done.

Suddenly, it happened. She was flying apart, as if someone had just punched her very hard. *Why had they all burst out singing? . . . Because they had thought the war was over!* Struggling to her feet, she began to shout. She could see eyes staring at her – shocked but curious. She had to tell them, didn't she? She had to make them understand what had just crashed through to her own consciousness . . .

At that moment the bell began to ring, announcing the end of the lesson. When the classroom was empty, Meg stood at Miss Thurkle's desk gripping the edge in an effort to steady herself.

'What is it, Meg?' Miss Thurkle was regarding her with concern.

'I'm sorry,' Meg began, only to stop as she felt the tightness in her throat and chest worsening. She felt the stammer, which had been bad when she was younger, beginning to rise, and automatically took a deep breath, slapping her hand rhythmically against her leg, as Miss Fairchild had taught her to do. Concentrate, she told herself. Concentrate – count – breathe. Gradually the irregularity of her breathing ceased, and she tried again. 'There's something I don't understand. Is it true there have been two wars? The first one . . . it's in the book . . .'

The anthology lay before them. Miss Thurkle, disconcerted by the child's expression, picked it up and began leafing through it.

'There!' Meg jabbed the page with her finger.

'Wilfrid Owen?'

'Read it,' Meg urged huskily.

Anthem for Doomed Youth

What passing-bells for these who die as cattle?
  Only the monstrous anger of the guns.
  Only the stuttering rifles' rapid rattle
Can patter out their hasty orisons.
No mockeries for them; nor prayers or bells,
  Nor any voice of mourning save the choirs –
The shrill demented choirs of wailing shells;
  And bugles calling for them from sad shires.

What candles may be held to speed them all?
  Not in the hands of boys, but in their eyes
Shall shine the holy glimmers of good-byes.
  The pallor of girls' brows shall be their pall;
Their flowers the tenderness of patient minds,
And each slow dusk a drawing-down of blinds.

There was a long silence before the child spoke again, the tears trickling down her cheeks. Miss Thurkle turned her head away from both the poem and the child's face, as if to seek some reassurance in the trees beyond the window. 'That was the first one, wasn't it?'

Miss Thurkle inclined her head.

'Then . . .' Meg stopped. The tears were streaming so fast she could not see. She was trapped in a bubble, empty of sound, other than the persistent buzzing going on in her ears.

The woman and the child waited as if there were, and always had been, all the time in the world.

'I didn't know, you see . . .' A whisper, a sigh.

'What?' Miss Thurkle's voice was remote.

'The first one . . . I didn't know there was a first one. I

should have, but I didn't. Then came the second. Only I didn't know it was the second. I thought war was always there. I didn't know that it started ... and ended ... and started again ... I didn't even know it was over – the second one, I mean ...'

Miss Thurkle kept her eyes fixed on the top of the desk, on the poem spread out before her.

'It finished,' the child's voice told her, 'in 1945. Didn't it?'

'Meg ...' Miss Thurkle's voice trailed away.

'That war has been over for three years and this,' Meg's tongue curled round the word, 'is what they call peace.'

It was very quiet in the room when Miss Thurkle finally stirred. Yet she could not look at the child's face without revealing her own expression. Meg saw it – saw the pity she did not want. Saw, too, the sadness; and beneath the sadness something else – helplessness. There was no need for further words and Meg, who had been stroking the edge of Miss Thurkle's desk to feel the reassuring pattern of the wood grain, turned abruptly and moved towards the door.

Across the room came Miss Thurkle's voice. 'He was a good poet, Meg. Remember that.'

'Yes,' the child replied. 'I know ... and he was killed – in the war.'

And then she ran. Ran to the playing fields where, for a while, she would not have to listen to – bells.

As she wept, the old man murmured to himself, 'How does the Binyon finish?

> Earth cares for her own ruins, naught for ours.
> Nothing is certain, only the certain spring.

You and I, child, know what we mean. For others, it's a game, foolish and sad. What is war but the charnel house created out of people's frustrated hopes and fears?'

She did not know his name, not even after he died and his housekeeper handed her the stamp album he had given her.

PART 9

◆◆◆

Knocking Down The Aspidistra

'I didn't say I would kill her – just that I wish she were dead.
Like if you were to drop a thunderbolt on her,' Meg suggested
hopefully. God, to whom she was addressing her remarks,
refused to be drawn. Instead, Dot, bearing a lighted candle,
suddenly appeared in the doorway between the two girls'
rooms.

'What is it?' Meg asked, sitting up in alarm.

'Ssh!' the older girl whispered. 'I've got to talk to you.
Come next door, and I'll shut the door to the stairs.'

'I'm leaving,' Dot announced, seating herself at the
dressing-table, while Meg curled herself up at the foot of
Dot's bed. 'But I'm going to need your help.'

'What are you talking about?'

'I'll show you.' Dot pulled back the bedcovers to reveal
three paper carrier-bags filled with clothes. 'If I try to get
through the kitchen with these, there'll be hell to pay. You
know what she's like. I wouldn't put it past her to call the
police and say I stole them. And I don't want to leave anything
behind.'

'But I can't smuggle them out!'

'I'm not asking you to. Just to unlock the front door when
you come up to make your bed after breakfast.'

'Why can't you do it yourself?'

'Because she'll be watching me like a hawk, specially
tomorrow – to see if I know.'

'Know what?'

'It's my birthday.'

'I know that.'

'All right, know-all. Which birthday?'

'Aren't you eighteen?'

'Exactly.'

'So?'

'So – I'm off!'

Meg shook her head in bewilderment. She wondered if Dot was having what Sarah called a 'brain-storm'. 'You all right?' she asked her carefully.

'Oh, you are stupid sometimes! I thought you knew: when you're eighteen you come out of care.'

Still Meg didn't understand. Dot took a deep breath and began patiently to explain. 'D'you remember when Bess, my sister, spent Christmas here? Back in 1943, just before she got married?' Meg nodded. 'Well, she explained it all to me – secretly, of course. What it means is that at eighteen you're free – that you can just walk out. As simple as that.'

Freedom! Even the thought of it made Meg bounce up and down excitedly on Dot's bed.

'Don't!' Dot mouthed at her. 'What was that?'

The two girls stared at each other in the flickering candle-light, their hearts thumping wildly. A gust of wind caught at the window frame, making it rattle.

Meg giggled nervously. Then she thought of something. 'Take me with you,' she begged. 'I won't be any trouble, I promise.'

'What, and get me had up for kidnapping? No thank you! Look,' Dot said more kindly, when she saw Meg's crestfallen expression, 'you mustn't be so scared of her. Learn to stand up to her, like I do.'

Meg thought of the war which had been raging between Sarah and Dot over the past few months. Day and night each hurled abuse at the other, until Sarah started punching and slapping Dot and pulling her round the room by her hair. Listening from her bed, Meg had lain trembling, her hands clamped tightly over her ears in an effort to smother the sounds, as well as to stop her own hysterical impulses to run screaming from the house.

'You didn't stand up to her when you were my age,' Meg told the older girl bitterly. 'You know you didn't. It's only this last year you've done that. You were thirteen when I first came here – a year older than I am now. Yet I remember you did nothing but run to her with tales. You'd do anything to save your own skin. You never cared who got punished, so long as it wasn't you. And like a fool, I used to cover up for you. So don't you talk to me about standing up to her.' She made as if to leave.

'I'm sorry, Meg. I truly am. You must help me this time. I can't do it without you,' Dot pleaded.

'Why should I believe you? All you want is to get me into trouble. If, as you say, you can just walk out, then why don't you do that? I thought you said that when your sister ran away, they cut off her hair and locked her up in prison.'

'Only because she borrowed money – to get away before she was eighteen. And anyway, it wasn't prison: it was the Land Army she went into. Of course I wouldn't risk it if I thought they could make me come back. But they can't. And some day, the same will be true for you – when you're my age. Don't you see? I'm just scared she'll find some way of fixing it so that I'll never be able to leave. That's why I want to slip away quietly – to be gone before she realizes what's happened.'

What Dot was saying made sense – at least to anyone who had ever lived with Sarah.

'You know,' Meg told her slowly, 'that when you've left for work in the mornings, she goes through all your things. She'll know at once that your clothes are missing. Suppose she sends someone after you?'

'I've thought of that. Mary Garrett says I can stay at her house till it's time to catch my train.'

'What about your job?'

'I packed it in days ago.'

'But you'll need a job, won't you – for money, I mean.'

'Don't worry, I'll soon get another.'

'What about Miss Gosling? Won't you have to tell her? Otherwise everyone will think you've been murdered or something. Dot, are you sure – about just going off? I thought people couldn't do that till they were twenty-one.'

'That's the joke. If *she* were my mother, then I'd have to wait till twenty-one. But when you're in care, no one in the world is responsible for you after the age of eighteen except yourself. Miss Gosling's not a bad old stick. I'll ring her up, once I'm safely away.'

'Will you tell . . . about *her*, I mean . . . what she's like?'

'I wondered about that – but I don't imagine she'd believe me, or you, for that matter. Do you? You have to live here to know what it's really like. It might even make trouble for me and quite honestly all I want is to get away. I don't care about anything else. It's different for you – you've got more than me.'

'What?' Meg asked in astonishment.

'Brains, for one thing, though no one would think so sometimes. Just you make sure you use them and you'll be all right. You do know she's nuts, don't you – just in case the day comes when you think it's you that's gone round the bend?'

Meg felt a lump in her throat. She was going to miss Dot, even though the two of them had never been particularly close. 'Dot,' she began hesitantly, 'can I ask you something? Have you ever wished that something would happen . . . well, that she were . . .' She stopped, too fearful to go on.

'Dead?' queried Dot calmly. 'Oh, Lord . . .'

'Sometimes,' Meg told her, 'I've come close to pushing her down the stairs. The only reason I haven't . . .'

'Is because she goes down them backwards, which means she'd see you do it. Don't I know!' Dot laughed. 'What other brainwaves have you had?' she asked, fiddling with the contents of her handbag.

'We-ell . . .' Meg said slowly. 'I did wonder about poisoning her with Gees' Linctus – you know, the cough medicine she keeps on the shelf under the stairs. I was going to pour it into the teapot when she wasn't looking, as the label says "it is dangerous to exceed the dose".'

Dot grinned broadly. 'You could tip the whole bottle down her throat and I bet she'd only hiccough!'

'I know,' Meg giggled. 'Then there's the smell – not to mention the taste.'

'Forget it,' Dot advised. 'The best thing you can do is stick it out.'

'I can't,' Meg declared passionately. 'Not for another six

203

years. It's all right for you. In a funny sort of way, you've always liked fighting. I don't – I hate it. Aunt Cissie's no use. She's always let you or me take the brunt. Now there'll only be me ... Something odd happened the other day. Molly Aldridge – who walks to school with me – well, she's an awful cry-baby, so of course the others gang up on her.'

'Oh, there's always one of them!' Dot shrugged her shoulders impatiently.

'It always seems to be *me* who has to pull Molly out of it. Well, just as I'd done that, I suddenly felt I couldn't stand her and started to hit her myself. It was awful!'

'You thumped her one – so what?' Dot told her. 'Haven't you learnt yet that there are always people who need to be taught a lesson? That's the one good thing I've learnt from *her*. Always hit first, whether they've asked for it or not. That way they'll know exactly where they stand with you.'

'Why? So that you can end up like *her*?'

'Better that than be soppy, like Aunt Cissie. It's very simple: fight and you stay on top.'

'I don't agree. I don't see how anything can give you the right to bully and hit other people. It's ... it's degrading.'

'Well,' Dot yawned, 'I'll tell you this. If I have kids, and they step out of line, they'll catch it. 'Cos I'll be the boss then!'

Meg eased herself off the bed. 'Where are you going?' she asked.

'Better you don't know,' was all Dot would say, gruffly, and she turned her head away.

The escape went off smoothly. The front-door key was heavier than Meg expected, and her hands were slippery with sweat as she turned it. She was out on an errand when Dot crept down the stairs to freedom. Six years, Meg thought, when Sarah gave vent to fury. What shall I do? Another six years.

Why shouldn't Sarah die? Sarah was old as well as horrible. After all, hadn't it just happened to Mr Shipley next door; and he must have been years younger than Sarah. Meg would even offer to keep vigil while it went on, as she was made to do for Mr Shipley. But why had Mr Shipley wanted her to be with him? She hardly knew the man. Certainly not well enough to sit for hours on a hard wooden chair at the foot of his bed. She was so nervous after two hours sitting like this, she developed a tic in her left eye. Perhaps, she thought, it's because I'm thirteen. Thirteen's unlucky, isn't it?

'Must I go?' she pleaded with Sarah.

'You'll do as you're told,' came the uncompromising retort. 'But he must be far gone to have asked for you. Well, it'll be his funeral.'

Sarah started to chuckle, thought better of it, and gave the fire an energetic prod. The coals spat, glowed briefly, and then died back. Watching the room rapidly darkening, Meg wished Sarah would light a candle. It would be another hour before Cissie returned from work and the light was switched on.

'I did it when I was young,' Sarah remarked. 'It's customary and neighbourly among decent folk.'

Outside the wind howled like a sorrowing dog.

On the third day Meg was sure Mr Shipley wanted to speak.

'Would you like some water?' She addressed him as if he were deaf, enunciating the words loudly and slowly. But all he did was to stare at her while his hand, fragile as a young bird's claw, plucked feebly at the bed sheet. When the rattling noise started she fled.

'Stay with him, Meg,' Mrs Shipley cried as the child rushed past her on the landing.

Downstairs Meg made herself a cup of Camp coffee and tried not to listen. When the sound stopped, Mrs Shipley appeared in the kitchen.

'Is he better now?' Meg asked politely.

The woman looked at her blankly, and sank into a chair. 'Yes,' she said quietly. 'I suppose you could say that. He's dead.'

Now she had to sleep with Mrs Shipley.

'Only for three nights,' Sarah announced. 'That should see him all right.'

*

. . . The Third day He rose again from the dead. He ascended into heaven. And sitteth on the right hand of God the Father Almighty; From thence He shall come to judge the quick and the dead. I believe in the Holy Ghost . . .

There were three of them at the funeral: Mrs Shipley, Mrs Shipley's sister and Meg.

'Mind you behave yourself,' Sarah warned her, giving a final tug to the black armband the child was wearing.

'How long will I have to keep it on?'

'Until I say so. It isn't as if he's family. I wore black for a year after my mother died. She had a lovely turn-out: six paid mourners, a coffin with brass handles, four black mares wearing plumes. I wanted to plait their tails, but they wouldn't let me.' Sarah brushed what looked like a tear from her eye.

When they come to the Grave, while the Corpse is made ready to be laid into the earth

. . . She was leaning back to avoid having to look down. Raw, yellow, slippery with mud, the sides of the pit were scantily covered with bits of old sacking. 'He'll get wet,' she thought. 'There's six inches of water down there . . .' One of the ropes slipped. It looked as if Mr Shipley would be descending head first. A gust of wind lashed her legs. As she bent down to wrap her raincoat round them more protectively her hat lifted abruptly from her head. First it sailed, next it hovered a moment, then it began a slow descent – into the grave. 'Help!' she croaked, and closed her eyes.

How silly, Meg reflected, as she sat at her bedroom window one clear spring day, some weeks before her fifteenth birthday. Why hadn't she seen it long ago? It was so obvious. How many days was it since Sarah and Cissie had spoken to her after she had collided in the middle of the night with the aspidistra, which for fifty years had stood like a sentinel on its table in the parlour? She had lost count – but it must be almost a fortnight. She was sorry it was dead . . . sorry it was so old – a wedding present to Sarah all those years ago . . . sorry she was in the parlour in the middle of the night, but what else could she do? She'd searched the kitchen for her satchel. It wasn't there, and she did remember seeing Sarah take something into the parlour. They were all cross with her – not just Sarah and Cissie. At school they were cross . . . cross with her work, which they were saying was scrappy, untidy, careless. Soon, if she didn't keep up with the home-work, she'd be sent to Miss Underwood. She wasn't afraid of Miss Underwood. It was just that, without raising her voice or scowling at you, Miss Underwood could make you feel you had let her, the school, and yourself – down. It didn't matter any more if she came top in a subject. No one said 'well done' – only that she hadn't done as well as in the last examination. What was it all for? If coming top didn't seem to mean anything to them, then what did? She was so tired – tired all the time lately. Tired of working hard; tired of living at Prickler's Hill; tired of school; tired of Sarah and Cissie; tired of herself. Was Sarah right, after all, when she said that people like Meg should have been put down at birth because they were a waste of people's time and money?

Wasn't that it? She was of no use to anyone. She had been nothing but trouble from the day she'd been born. Superfluous, that was the word she wanted. She was super-fluous, only she'd been too cowardly to face the fact before. All that nonsense about belonging to herself, when what she was didn't seem worth belonging to. It had been stupid to go on hoping that somehow, one day, she would find someone to belong to. Was that what she'd missed all these years? Was that why she was moved to tears when she saw people smiling at each other?

She yearned for love and there was no one who gave it to her. She was never touched – except to be hit. And to whom dare she show affection? No one. So, hadn't the time come for her to go? Why carry on any longer? Tonight – while they're asleep, she told herself – I'll gas myself.

With the decision taken to die, the tension fell away. Across the dell, where the allotments stood, Mr Loveday was at his digging. What was he planting this year; vegetables or flowers or, as last year, a mixture of the two? He's getting old, she thought, really too old to allow his privet hedge to become so straggly. Soon the yellowy-green shoots would be covered in cuckoo spit: the gobs of froth that looked like saliva. It was a long time since she had flicked at them or, for that matter, worn foxgloves as fingerstalls. Char'ty was married, or so she'd been told. Did she like it in Toddington, away from the woods, away from the oak trees? The primroses must be out and soon the bluebells would be thrusting their way through the rich, damp-smelling earth over in Grunter's Wood. The windflowers would be there already. How fragile they were; yet they survived – not like the trees, which had mostly disappeared. They were chopping them down in Nokes Wood, killing the trees she loved.

When the crisis passed, she wept, the tears soaking through to the ashes in her heart. But once more, it appeared, she was destined to live. And why not, she asked herself as she recovered. The game wasn't over; she still had a card to play. The time had come to use it. She would summon her *Ka*.

Meg first learnt about the existence of her *Ka* when she raided Mr Dawkins' bookcase to read Rider Haggard's novel *Morning Star*. The story was of Tua – an Egyptian princess who was born under mysterious circumstances thousands of years ago. But lurking in the background is Tua's wicked uncle, Abi, and his evil counsellors, Kaku the Astrologer and Merytra, Lady of the Footstool. They conspired to murder the Pharaoh, her father, and force Tua to marry Abi, thereby seizing the throne and power of Egypt for themselves. With the Pharaoh dead, Tua and her faithful nurse Asti are locked in a tower, until such time as Tua submits. Rather than do so, Tua goes on hunger strike and resolves to kill herself the next day, by throwing herself off the tower walls. While Tua sleeps, Asti (who is also something of a magician) summons Tua's immortal double, her *Ka*. The *Ka* arranges for the mortal Tua and Asti to be spirited off to the safety of the desert. From there they set out in quest of Ramses, Tua's true love, with whom she is eventually reunited. Meanwhile, the *Ka*, taking on Tua's physical form, marries Abi in Tua's stead. She leads Abi and his friends such a life of unmitigated misery that all they can hope for is death.

Meg considered very carefully how Tua had dealt with not

doing what others wanted her to do. It seemed to her that the trouble with the *Ka* was that once it was brought to life, it wouldn't be easy to control. She would have to be very careful, particularly about letting it appear in the flesh – since she knew from the story that the *Ka* was capable of wreaking the most terrible vengeance. All she wanted, she told herself, was that the *Ka* should be there, within her, and at all times. She knew that the *Ka* would like this, because it got moody if separated for too long from the body, which it regarded as 'home'. When Sarah was being especially awful, the *Ka*, rather than Meg, could deal with it.

Once this was agreed, life for Meg improved dramatically. So much so, that even Sarah noticed: how, for example, Meg now looked at her as if she, Sarah, did not exist. Disconcerted, she reported Meg's 'insolence' to Miss Gosling who, in turn, discussed it with Miss Underwood. From being a docile, seemingly amenable child, Meg was turning into 'a turbulent adolescent'. But now if Meg thought of dying, there had to be more concrete reasons – such as the blood she discovered on her legs one morning, blood that flowed from somewhere inside her. Certain that she was suffering from some fatal disease, she told no one till Sarah sensed what was happening.

'So you've started,' Sarah announced baldly.

'What?'

'Don't you use that tone of voice with me, my girl!'

'But I'm bleeding – bleeding to death!' Meg wailed.

'That's the price you pay for being what you are. You'll learn. It's not all the bed of roses you seem to think it is. Go upstairs with Cissie who'll give you a thingummy. You're to put one on in the morning and one at night, and woe betide you if I find anything on the sheets.'

And that, it seemed, was that. At no time did Meg's thoughts return to the biology lessons she had once had. Though she remembered about how birds and fish reproduce themselves, she could recall nothing about human beings. If the words sex and menstruation had been used, she hadn't understood. Nor did any of the girls she knew ever refer directly to such matters. As for boys, she had never thought about them; but then, she didn't know any. Here, Miss Gosling helped. One of the reasons Meg was getting difficult, she told Sarah, was that the girl had no opportunity outside school to mix with young people of her own age. Meg must be allowed to attend a mixed youth club. It took six months to wear down Sarah's opposition.

'I'll not have her running fast and loose,' she declared – 'It isn't decent for a young girl to be out on the streets after dark' – 'You'll forgive me for saying so, Miss Gosling, but seeing as you've never been married, I can't see as how you can possibly understand my objections' – 'She'll end up boy mad, you mark my words.'

But Miss Gosling had her way. How she persuaded Sarah to give in, Meg never knew. It wasn't as if Sarah was getting tired, even if at seventy-five she was getting very old. Sarah didn't even tire now that Meg was fighting her – Meg who had never dared answer back when Sarah attacked her was finding, with the aid of her *Ka*, the courage to do so. She went further – such as the time she pinned Sarah against the wall after the woman had slapped Meg's face a dozen or so times.

'If,' Meg told her quietly, 'you ever lay a finger on me again, I promise you faithfully I'll kill you.'

Sarah's response was to stagger to her chair, calling for brandy. But after that, though there were other punishments, Meg was never again physically assaulted while she lived at Prickler's Hill. And, in time, Meg's preoccupation with her *Ka* faded.

Cissie too was changing. Having cut her hair, at Miss Gosling's suggestion, she now refused to dye it. Within months it was grey. Her hands, which had always been soft and well cared for, became grimy and calloused. Her clothes were drab. She dressed carelessly. More round-shouldered than ever, she slouched badly in her chair. Worse, for Sarah – who was fastidious about such things – Cissie no longer bothered to polish her shoes or check that her handkerchief was clean. The more Sarah nagged her, the more stubborn Cissie became. The whiskers on her chin were multiplying rapidly and her voice, always flat and cracked, deepened alarmingly. She looked tired, worn out. She visited the doctor a lot – a fact which did not appear to worry Sarah. If Cissie was ill, neither woman discussed the matter in Meg's presence. At night Sarah criticized Cissie. During the day Cissie knitted furiously in an effort to earn extra cash. Sarah, who refused to accept (let alone admit) losing control over what she considered was 'hers', had never forgiven her daughter for daring to take control of her own finances. To punish Cissie, Sarah waged a relentless war on Cissie's purse – forever launching the pair of them on spending sprees. Contributing little from her own funds, she was forcing Cissie to spend at a level neither of them could afford. Sarah wanted the parlour repapered; the kitchen range removed to make room for a modern tile-backed grate; new bedroom curtains; a more stylish kitchen rug; a different stair carpet; a fur tippet; holidays by the seaside; coach trips to London . . . and the saucepans were wearing out. The bid Cissie had made for independence four years earlier simply resulted in her being expected by Sarah to take on a confusing array of responsibilities. She was now put in the position of being the head of the household – as if she were Sarah's husband and Meg's father.

Aware that something was seriously wrong, Meg took refuge in her studies but, like many adolescents of sixteen, was too absorbed in herself and her own problems to worry much about other people. If she pondered the change in Cissie, she did not understand it. Fond though Meg was of her, Cissie for the most part remained simply someone who was there: rather like a piece of Sarah's furniture. All Meg had ever been able to do was accept Cissie for what she was: a gentle, unaggressive person who had the misfortune to be born the child of a tyrant. She did sometimes wonder what Cissie would do, when the time came for her to face her mother on her own. Meg disliked fighting as much as Cissie – it left her trembling and sick; yet since Cissie was unable, or unwilling, to join battle with Sarah, the task was left to Meg – to fight Sarah, to keep on fighting her – even though it was a fight that could never be won. It was that or leave. But where would she go? Was it the same for Cissie? Did Cissie any longer have a choice?

Every day Meg and Sarah had a slanging match. Sarah was indomitable. It was Meg who tired. Yet Meg would not – could not – give in. Something in her was refusing ever again to yield to Sarah.

'What is it that you want?' Miss Gosling remonstrated with her, after Sarah had complained.

'Freedom.' Meg's voice was firm.

'What makes you think you understand it?' Miss Gosling asked with a smile that reduced Meg to cold fury. That she, of all people, should be challenged on so sacrosanct a matter – she who, with all her sixteen years, knew more about the subject than most people would ever know in their lives!

'Couldn't you write me a note saying I had to go to the doctor, or something?'

Meg was sitting in Cissie's shop drinking a cup of tea. It was eleven o'clock in the morning and she should have been at school; but when she played truant she often visited Cissie. It was the usual problem: the homework she should have done the night before. At first, Meg used to make for the 'wreck'; sitting on a wooden bench in one of the dripping well grottoes, she rattled through a translation from Virgil's *Aeneid*. With GCE O Level examinations looming ahead, the amount of Latin she had to do each week had reached a formidable length. She was afraid that if she didn't get it done, Miss Shaw – who taught Latin – might take some action. Only last week she had called Meg up to her desk.

'What time did you go to bed last night?' she asked Meg.

'Half past eight,' Meg answered truthfully.

'When did you do this work?'

'Last night.'

'At what time?'

'I can't remember.' Meg shifted uncomfortably. She liked Miss Shaw but was sure the teacher would know if she lied. But all Miss Shaw did was push Meg's exercise book across to her. Meg, glancing down, saw that her writing was all over the page; none of it followed the lines.

'There's nothing wrong with the work itself – just how it's

written. If someone were to ask me when this was done, I would say in the dark in the middle of the night.'

Meg flushed and said nothing.

'I think, don't you, that you'd better go to Sick Bay and catch up on some sleep.'

The headmistress was after her too. She was nice – they all were – but it didn't help.

'You're much too thin, child, and you look exhausted. If something's the matter, please tell me about it. My door is open at any time. All you have to do is knock.'

'Yes, Miss Underwood. Thank you, Miss Underwood.'

Now it was Cissie's turn. 'Of course I'll write the note,' she said, 'but it isn't the answer, is it? If you don't go to school you'll be in real trouble. Perhaps Mother's right, and all this homework is too much for you. I know you don't want to leave school in the summer, but have you thought what it would be like to be independent, earning your own money, with no more horrible books to worry about?'

Hardly a day passed while Meg was preparing for her GCE examinations when Sarah did not bring up the subject of Meg leaving school. Her teachers wanted her to stay on to take A Levels, the LCC and the Borough Council had agreed to the idea but Sarah and Cissie didn't. Caught between the two camps, Meg took a snap decision. If she was earning money, perhaps she would be able to get away. The thought of another two years with Sarah was intolerable.

Within weeks of the decision, with the examinations over, she was depressed. The idea of being shut away in an office, away from her books and her friends made her restless and unpredictable. The climax came one sultry August evening. The pressure in her head had built up to such a pitch she felt something snap. Pushing her chair back, she stood up. Sarah looked up in astonishment.

'Where do you think you're going?' she said, as Meg made for the door leading to the stairs.

'Out,' Meg called, racing up the stairs.

'Come back here this instant,' she heard Sarah shout. 'How

dare you stand up in my house without my permission!'

Upstairs, Meg was giggling to herself hysterically. You fool, she kept repeating. How, for nine years, could you have let a silly old woman control you to the point where you couldn't even stand up unless she said so. Pulling at the wardrobe, she scrabbled behind it to retrieve the five shillings she had been saving painstakingly over the years. It won't go far, she thought, jerking her arms into her coat, but I can catch a train to somewhere, anywhere . . .

Fighting Sarah off, she made for the back door, only to find it locked and the key gone. She ran to the front door – but that was barred, too.

'Let me out!' she screamed, banging on the parlour windows, while Sarah pulled at her hair. Pushing the old woman from her, she got herself up the stairs . . . into her room . . . out of the window . . .

Meg stirred sleepily. Someone was in her room. It was very dark. There was a girl sitting on a chair by her bed. 'Do I know you?' she asked, peering at the girl.

'I'm in a lower form. My mother knows Mrs Dawkins. We heard you were ill, so Mrs Dawkins asked me to call.'

'What for?'

'I don't really know.'

There was a silence. Then Meg spoke again. 'What's the matter with me?'

'Brain fever.'

'I didn't . . . I didn't . . .'

'No. They pulled you in.'

Meg tried sitting up. Her head was swimming, just as if she had fever . . . 'So why are you here?' she asked, for the sake of saying something.

'I don't really know – I said you'd rather see one of your own friends, but Mrs Dawkins said No.' Meg nodded. 'P'rhaps there's something I can do for you. My mother's sorry for you,' she added inconsequentially.

Meg let this go. She was trying to think, trying to remember . . . why she had tried to jump out of the window.

'There is something. What's the date?'

'September the 2nd.'

'How long have I been ill?'

'Three weeks, I think.'

'When does school start – what day?'

'Tuesday, the 9th, why?'

'If I write a letter, would you post it for me? I haven't the money for a stamp, but I'll pay you back very soon, I promise.' The girl looked at her uncertainly. 'It's all right. The letter is to Miss Underwood, but I don't want anyone to know about it.'

'Do you mean Mrs Dawkins?'

Meg nodded.

'Okay,' the girl said, with a grin.

When Sarah stormed up the stairs a few days later, Meg knew Miss Underwood had answered her letter and, more important, had agreed to take her back to school for a further two years.

'You deceitful beggar,' Sarah raged. 'Going behind my back, making me look a fool. I'll get you for this – if it's the last thing I do. Out of that bed this instant!'

Meg allowed herself to be dragged out of bed, but gave it no thought. Her mind was still preoccupied with the idea that perhaps Miss Gosling was right. Perhaps till she changed her mind about leaving school, she hadn't fully understood what freedom entailed. It wasn't simply that to exercise freedom there must be a choice. The greater the area of choice, the more chance she would have of attaining the freedom which she longed for – to be rid of the unrelenting domination of Sarah and of anyone like her. Never again would she permit anyone to tyrannize her – never again in her life.

From this time on, Meg changed. Having thought through her decision carefully, she felt as if an enormous burden was lifted from her shoulders. Yet the consequences were strange. The self-discipline she had taught herself as a small child seemed to evaporate entirely. Moody before the collapse, she now became irritable, argumentative and given to passionate, if not irrational, outbursts. She fought with Sarah, with her teachers . . . with anyone who upset her. The school accepted this behaviour without comment. Sarah continued to attack her at every opportunity.

'For the last time,' Cissie shouted, repeatedly banging her fist on the table, 'stop it, the pair of you. You've done nothing all day but row. I've had about as much as I can take. If you so much as open your mouth again, Meg, you'll go to your room. As for you,' Cissie turned to Sarah, 'you know perfectly well that I'm ill, yet you persist in trying my patience beyond what any human being can endure. I'm sick of the very sound of your voice. I keep this house going, do you hear me? If you don't like it, you know what you can do!' Grey-faced and shaking, Cissie sat down.

'I see,' Sarah said. 'So this is what it's come to. Right. Well, you'll live to rue the day you said that to me, my girl.'

A few minutes later the front door slammed.

'She's gone out,' Meg exclaimed in alarm. 'But she never goes out, not alone. What'll we do?'

'Leave her,' Cissie said wearily. 'She'll be back. After all, there's nowhere for her to go.' She winced suddenly.

'Are you really ill?' Meg asked.

'It's nothing. Be a good girl and run upstairs. My tablets are by the bed.'

When Sarah did not return, Cissie turned on the radio and Meg made tea. It was peaceful, sitting quietly with Cissie in the kitchen. It was the only time in the nine years during which Meg lived at Prickler's Hill that she and Cissie had been alone in the house together.

'Why can't it always be like this?'

Cissie smiled. 'That's like asking for the moon.'

'What'll you do? When she comes back, I mean.'

'I don't know. I expect she'll sulk a bit, but she'll get over it. I should have spoken up years ago, even when Father was alive. Not let things go on like this for so long. Now it's too late.'

'I don't mean to quarrel with her,' Meg said. 'It's she who starts it, every time.'

'I know.'

'I hate it – the quarrelling. I hate it as much as you do. But what can I do? She's got to have someone to pick on. And I can't give in to her, not any more – not like when I was younger. Do you understand?'

'I'm not blaming you, Meg,' Cissie said quietly. 'I can't stand the rows either. With Father it was different; it was like what she's been doing to me lately – nothing but nag, nag, nag . . .'

'Why d'you let her?'

Cissie laid her knitting down and leaned back, her head turned in the direction of her mother's empty chair. She sat like this for several minutes before she spoke again.

'Nothing he did ever satisfied her. We were well off once, back in the 20s. Others were worried about being able to earn a living, but we were lucky. The business was good. Father gave her everything she asked for. You'd have thought she'd be happy, wouldn't you? She never was. She always wanted more. And when she got it, she hankered after something else. She even wanted the best for me – I knew that. She never wanted me to go through what she'd had to when she was a girl. Yet all I ever wanted was for her to stop nagging Father.'

'Did you tell her that?'

Cissie shook her head. 'I couldn't. Children couldn't speak like that when I was young. I've never been like you. No, I took after Father. He was a quiet man. Now if he'd been able to stand up to her, perhaps things would have been different. He wasn't weak, or anything like that. Just different. Strict in his ways. Perhaps what she wanted was a man with more "go" in him.'

'Like Mr Dobbs?'

'Her father? Oh, no. I sometimes think it was because of him she's like she is. He let her down very badly, and he was violent. She had a terrible time when her mother died.'

'What I don't understand is, if her father hit her, why did she hit others? I would have thought it would make her hate that sort of thing. That's how I feel about violence. Did she ever hit you?'

'No. But then I always did what she wanted. It's different

for you. Your generation's got far more freedom than mine ever had.'

'But children should be treated as people.'

'You really believe that?'

'Yes.'

'It isn't as simple as that, Meg. Today, girls like you can go and earn the sort of money which gives you independence to live as you like, even to leave home if you want. That was never possible when I was young. The wages were so low, you just had to live at home.'

'Is that why you stayed – because you couldn't afford to leave?'

'I don't know. I had my chances to leave, I can't deny that. I suppose I just didn't take them. When I was young, children still had to obey their parents. What they said was law. Then, as time passed, I don't think I really thought about it. Of course, when Father died, it was out of the question. Not in the state she was in. I knew I wasn't earning enough at Lacey's, but when I tried to explain this to her, she didn't seem able to take it in. There'd been a lot of unemployment then, and I think she thought it would be safer if I stayed in the job I had, rather than try to get one that was better paid. But I made up my mind to try, and then she tried to kill herself. I came home one night to find the back door bolted. I had to break in through the scullery window. She was lying on the floor with her head in the gas oven. What could I do? She cried – just like a little girl. She was so frightened.'

'Of being poor?'

'Not just that.'

'What?'

'Of being abandoned,' Cissie replied simply.

'Why did she hit Dot and me?'

'I don't know . . . I don't think she knew herself. It was just her way. Perhaps of controlling things. Maybe because she was hit herself. They say that violence breeds violence. She was a rebel, you see. She wouldn't have survived if she hadn't been. And she saw it in you. She wanted to crush it.'

'Why?'

'It threatened her.'

'How? I was only a little girl.'

'Yes, but it wasn't that. She didn't feel that someone like you had any right to stand up for herself. She wanted the world to stay as it was – where everyone knew their place.'

'But why? I'm as good as anyone else!'

'I know that, Meg. But it frightened her, she felt threatened.'

'I don't understand. She's never given the impression of being afraid of anything.'

Cissie smiled. 'You may be sixteen, Meg, and feel grown up, but you've still a lot to learn. People aren't always how they seem. The strong are often very weak inside; and those that seem weak, may have the patience that makes them strong. It's different for you. You've got your life ahead of you. What has she to look forward to?'

'It's not my fault if she's had her life. She didn't have to spend it punishing others and making everyone miserable, did she?'

'No. But there's nothing in the world that will change her. She is what she is. And that's what we both have to accept.'

'I don't think I can.' Meg's voice was trembling as she spoke. 'Not any more.' Outside, the church bells began to peal for Evensong. She looked at Cissie and took a deep breath. 'Perhaps if I weren't here, it would be easier for everyone. It would be like it was ... before I or any of the others came here. There would be just you ... and her ... if you see what I mean. Just the two of you ... Like it should be. After all, she's your family. Wouldn't it be best if I rang Miss Gosling and asked her to find me somewhere else to live? I'm sure she'd say yes, if she thought you agreed. She knows I like you – and I know she likes you. What do you think?'

Cissie was silent, her eyes on her knitting. Meg, waiting nervously, wondered if Cissie understood what she had said.

'Perhaps you're right,' Cissie said eventually, in a voice that seemed to have travelled from some great distance.

'You're not cross?' Meg asked anxiously. She was relieved when Cissie smiled.

'Ring Miss Gosling tonight, on your way back from church. But don't come straight home. Wait till nine o'clock. Mother's sure to be back by then, and safely tucked up in bed. I'll leave the back door unlocked, so that you can get in.'

Meg looked at Cissie doubtfully. 'Are you sure it'll be all right – when she returns, I mean.' She paused. 'If I'm going to church, I should really leave now. The bell is tolling . . .'

Cissie took Meg's hand and patted it gently. Meg brushed the woman's cheek with a kiss.

'Bye!' Meg called, closing the door.

God be in my head
And in my understanding

God be in my eyes
And in my looking

God be in my mouth
And in my speaking

God be in my heart
And in my thinking

God be at my end
And at my departing

While Sarah was in bed and Meg in church, Cissie tried to kill herself. Meg, who found the body, ran for help from the neighbours.

'Barbiturates.' Mr Loveday held out the empty bottle of tablets for Mrs Shipley to see. 'I've called an ambulance.' He took his handkerchief from his pocket and wiped some grey foam from the corner of Cissie's mouth. 'How many d'you think she's taken?' He swivelled round to face Sarah.

Sarah stood in her nightgown, her three strands of hair twisted into a single plait. She stared at the man and clutched the plait tightly. 'What are you talking about?' she demanded. 'How many more times do I have to say it? It's her time of life, I tell you. Nothing more than her time of life.'

Sarah looked down at her daughter. Cissie lay on the floor, her head in her mother's low chair. Sarah towered over the inert form. 'Get up!' she ordered. 'I shan't tell you again.' She pulled at Cissie's arm. 'Get up this instant . . .'

Meg was shivering uncontrollably. 'She can't hear you,' Mrs Shipley said. She took off her cardigan and wrapped it round Meg's shoulders. 'What did you do when you came in, Mrs Dawkins? What did you say to your daughter?'

'Do? Say?' Sarah looked bewildered. 'How should I know. I went to bed, didn't I? I went to sleep.' Sarah sat down. Her shoulders had started to shake. 'I gave her what for – that's what I did. She had no right to speak to me the way she had. Her own mother.' Sarah turned to Meg. 'You tell them,' she said. 'You'd know, so you tell them. You'd know I didn't mean it . . . did I?' She put her hands to her face.

There was nothing Meg could do. She couldn't speak. She couldn't cry. Yes – she knew what Sarah had said: she could guess. How many times had Sarah used the same words to her: 'By the time I've finished with you, you'll wish you'd never been born . . . you'll wish you were dead . . .'

Poor Cissie . . . Poor Sarah.

Meg left the house on Prickler's Hill; the school took her as a boarder. Eighteen months later she won a place at university and left Witheringham for good. She did return, but only to visit Cissie at work. Cissie never referred to that night, when she almost died, so nothing was ever said. Nor did they ever speak of Sarah Dawkins.